SAGE was founded in 1965 by Sara Miller McCune to support the dissemination of usable knowledge by publishing innovative and high-quality research and teaching content. Today, we publish over 900 journals, including those of more than 400 learned societies, more than 800 new books per year, and a growing range of library products including archives, data, case studies, reports, and video. SAGE remains majority-owned by our founder, and after Sara's lifetime will become owned by a charitable trust that secures our continued independence.

Los Angeles | London | New Delhi | Singapore | Washington DC | Melbourne

Advance Praise

Exciting writing buttressed by new documentation and presentation makes this an essential book for general as well as scholarly readers. Punjab, militancy, political and judicial behaviour are expertly provided in a straight and provocative manner.

Paul Wallace, *Political Scientist and Professor Emeritus, University of Missouri*

This is a thoughtful compendium of misdemeanours of the Indian state suffered by civil society in the wake of more than a decade of militancy and supposedly justified by it. Juxtaposed to plentiful official propaganda, the book is a grim reminder of what has actually happened, and is a timely warning that we should continually check our defences. Dona Suri has brought a neatness and a conversational touch which in no way lessens the anger and sadness that you will feel.

J. P. S. Uberoi, *Formerly Professor of Sociology, Delhi School of Economics*

A superb sum up of our times written with wit and loving detachment.

Rajwinder Singh Bains, *Senior Advocate, Punjab and Haryana Court and veteran human rights activist*

THE LEGACY OF MILITANCY IN PUNJAB

THE LEGACY OF MILITANCY IN

Long Road to 'Normalcy'

INDERJIT SINGH JAIJEE
DONA SURI

Los Angeles | London | New Delhi
Singapore | Washington DC | Melbourne

Copyright © Inderjit Singh Jaijee and Dona Suri, 2020

All rights reserved. No part of this book may be reproduced or utilized in any form or by any means, electronic or mechanical, including photocopying, recording or by any information storage or retrieval system, without permission in writing from the publisher.

First published in 2020 by

SAGE Publications India Pvt Ltd
B1/I-1 Mohan Cooperative Industrial Area
Mathura Road, New Delhi 110 044, India
www.sagepub.in

SAGE Publications Inc
2455 Teller Road
Thousand Oaks, California 91320, USA

SAGE Publications Ltd
1 Oliver's Yard, 55 City Road
London EC1Y 1SP, United Kingdom

SAGE Publications Asia-Pacific Pte Ltd
18 Cross Street #10-10/11/12
China Square Central
Singapore 048423

Published by Vivek Mehra for SAGE Publications India Pvt Ltd. Typeset in 11/14.5pt Adobe Garamond Pro by Fidus Design Pvt Ltd, Chandigarh.

Library of Congress Cataloging-in-Publication Data Available

ISBN: 978-93-532-8713-9 (PB)

SAGE Team: Manisha Mathews, Ankit Verma and Rajinder Kaur

To those who suffered

Thank you for choosing a SAGE product!
If you have any comment, observation or feedback,
I would like to personally hear from you.

Please write to me at **contactceo@sagepub.in**

Vivek Mehra, Managing Director and CEO, SAGE India.

Bulk Sales

SAGE India offers special discounts
for purchase of books in bulk.
We also make available special imprints
and excerpts from our books on demand.

For orders and enquiries, write to us at

Marketing Department
SAGE Publications India Pvt Ltd
B1/I-1, Mohan Cooperative Industrial Area
Mathura Road, Post Bag 7
New Delhi 110044, India

E-mail us at **marketing@sagepub.in**

Subscribe to our mailing list
Write to **marketing@sagepub.in**

This book is also available as an e-book.

Contents

Preface xi
Acknowledgements xxi

1. Normalcy 1
   'Normal' in the Rear-view Mirror 1
   Political Lead-up to Turmoil 2
   Economic Lead-up to Turmoil 3
   Installed or Just Plain Stalled? 4
   The Science with No Formulas 5
   Standard Practice 6
   Old Blood, New Blood 13
   Failed Experiments: Broom and Gloom 15
   Lonely on the Left 15
   Bloc Busters 18
   Reincarnations 21
   Splinters and Fringes 22
   Try, Try Again? 24

2. Due Process: Punjab 43
   Freedom of Repression 44
   Big Stick: TADA and POTA 46
   Bigger Stick: UAPA 48
   Water under the Bridge? 49
   A Slap on the Wrist 51
   Death of a Sarpanch 52
   The Terminator 56

Contents

	Insider's Story	58
	It Only Looked Like Murder	60
	A Generation Later	63
	How to Make Money in Government Services	66
	Kulwinder Kid Case	68
	Lesson for Judges	69
	Justice for Siso	73
3.	Due Process: Delhi	79
	The Fallen Tree	79
	Undeniable	80
	Getting at the Truth: Justice Nanavati's Findings	81
	Judges Speak Out	85
	Tipped Off: An IAS Officer's Recollection	86
	Tell-Tale Claims	87
	Figures from Ahooja	88
	The Aftermath: Year by Year	89
	Haryana Post Script	99
	Looking the Other Way	101
	Template for Riots	102
	Riots can be Profitable	102
	Teaching Lessons	104
	Price of Indifference	105
4.	If You Can't Be Good	109
	The Law: Not so Majestic	111
	Worth More Dead than Alive	111
	Pay Dirt	114
	Easy Targets	115
	When the Cops Say It	116
	Feeding Frenzy	118
	End of the Golden Age: Nayagaon	120

	The Court Starts Digging	122
	The Real Dispute	124
	A Natural Death	126
	Concrete Jungle	126
	The Wind Starts to Change	127
	Long Road to 'Normalcy'	129
5.	On the Cultural Front	133
	Radical Chic	133
	If It's Cool in California	135
	Hypothetically Speaking	136
	The World Laughs with You	138
	The Right to be Different	138
	Hearts and Minds … and the X-Box	139
	Menace at the Movies	141
	70mm History	142
	View from the Box Office	144
	Arrested and Booked	148
	Slow March of Fiction	149
	Summing Up	152
6.	Khalistan Redux	155
	Ramrajya Meets Sher-e-Punjab	155
	Millennium Fiascos	157
	Post-Traumatic Shock	159
	Sikhophobia	160
	20-Year Comeback Trail	161
	What to Believe?	167
	Ballot-Proof	170
	Budget Cravings	171
	Turf Cravings?	172
	Power Cravings?	174

Contents

For Real Indians — 175
On the List and Off the List — 176

Epilogue — 185
Bibliography — 197
About the Authors — 213

Preface

Thirty-five years ago, one turned on the television or picked up the newspaper to find any number of 'talking heads' declaring that 'India is fighting a civil war in Punjab': This was a reasonable assertion since the army was deployed and hundreds of people had been arrested for 'waging war against the state'. As in any war zone, defeating the enemy eclipsed all other concerns. Those peacetime luxuries, rule of law and the processes of democracy, became inevitable sacrifices. And not to forget that wise saw from the days of World War I: 'When war comes, truth is the first casualty'.[1]

Then, at some hard-to-pinpoint moment in the mid-1990s, the 'talking heads' changed their tune and decided that 'normalcy is returning to Punjab'.

'Normalcy' is a comforting word; it conveys the idea that problems are solved and good times are back. But anyone who has lived through, or read about, post-war conditions anywhere in the world—Germany, Japan, Spain, Serbia, Ireland, Iraq, Nicaragua, anywhere—knows that the absence of gunfire is just that and nothing more.

If only the damage from violent conflict were confined to buildings, bridges and roads. Such things can be rebuilt in a matter of months. Unfortunately, violence changes many other things. Some things—lost loved ones or destroyed cultural treasures—can never be replaced. Others, for example, trust and an expectation of fair treatment under law, typically take a long time to regrow.

When Punjab's decade of violence wound down,
What was lost or damaged?

Preface

What was changed?

What was the new reality?

How did political parties, civil administration, the judiciary and the police respond?

How did the citizens of Punjab respond?

All of these were important questions but the one great question that subsumed them all was a question of preference:

Was it better to remember or better to forget?

No one response has been forthcoming, and many responses fit the definition of oxymoron: 'firmly ambiguous', turning this way and that depending on the situation.

For instance, numerous union government ministers[2] addressed rallies in Punjab in which, in one breath, they called upon the people of the state to put the past behind them, and in the very next breath mentioned that the Punjab was under a mountain of debt to the Centre—the cost of anti-terrorist operations. In 2011, the debt burden on Punjab stood at over ₹69,000 crore. Since the 1990s, the state has been paying annual interest of more than ₹5,000 crore in debt servicing.[3] The central government does not forget this debt, and time and again it has refused to let the state government forget it either.

Contradictory attitudes to the past ripple out in all directions, and Punjab perfectly illustrates the oft-quoted observation of Milan Kundera:

> People are always shouting they want to create a better future. It's not true. The future is an apathetic void of no interest to anyone. The past is full of life, eager to irritate us, provoke and insult us, tempt us to destroy or repaint it. The only reason people want to be masters of the future is to change the past.[4]

The past is particularly difficult to brush away when it involves defence of native land, home, tradition, way of life, etc.

Preface

One of the controversies roiling the United States at this moment concerns memorials to the Confederacy, the losing side in America's civil war (1861–1865). One of the chief reasons why the southern states seceded from the United States and formed their own government—the Confederacy—was a determination to preserve slavery. That is hardly a noble motive. The South surrendered 150 years ago, but the war has not exactly ended. To this day, many in the South still revere and romanticize their great-great-great-great-grandfathers who fell fighting the Union Army. In cities and towns throughout the American south, parks, intersections and college campuses are home to bronze generals on bronze horses, frozen in mid-charge.

But US demography has changed, and now there are just too many voters whose passions are roused by the memory that their cotton-picking great-great-great-great-grandfathers were bought and sold by those glorious-in-defeat Confederate heroes. These people want the statues removed and preferably melted down. Angry confrontations have broken out between people whose views of the past are very different. History comes in many flavours, and people have a tendency to prefer flavours they have grown up with. Over the past couple of years, strong action to remove these memorials has, in many cases, been met with equal and opposite action from those who want the memorials left alone.

Demographic trends tell us that the anti-memorialists will get their way in the near future but getting one's way is not at all the same thing as removing hostility. Thomas Hobbes of *Leviathan* fame put it nicely:

> He therefore that is slain is overcome, but not conquered: he that is taken and put into prison or chains is not conquered, though overcome; for he is still an enemy...[5]

Recollection of suffering, grief and a sense of loss become a part of the community's bedrock identity and an affirmation of faith that endures over centuries. Remembrance of martyrdom is central to religion and culture in Shia Iran. Neither do Catholics forget. When Mass is celebrated, among other prayers, the priest recites the names and grisly executions of the 12 apostles and another long list of martyrs. All of this commemorated Christian blood and gore was spilled in the 1st and 2nd centuries AD. Jews sit down to the Passover meal and hark back several thousand years, 'Remember that you were strangers in the land of Egypt (and after that it got worse)'. Commemoration is part of every-day Sikhism. Every act of worship ends with the recitation of the *Ardas*, a prayer that recalls the life and teachings of the Gurus and tells over the sacrifices of Sikh martyrs:

> *Jinaa singhaa singhneeyaa ne dharam het sees dithe, bund bund kuttai, khopriya luhayiya, charukriya te churhe, aariaa naal chiraae ge, gurdwaraiya di seva layee kurbaniya keethiya, dharam nehee haariye, sikhi kesaa suwaasaa naal nibaahee, tina dee kamaaee daa dhiyaan. Dhar ke bolo ji Wahe Guru.*

(Remember the service rendered by those brave Sikh men and women, who sacrificed their heads but did not surrender their religion; cut to pieces, scalped, broken on wheels and broken into pieces, cut by saws, flayed alive; who sacrificed themselves for the sake of the gurdwaras; who did not abandon their faith; who kept their religion and saved their long hair until their last breath; Utter Wahe Guru.)

On the other hand, individuals and government are strongly motivated to obliterate or twist the past when an accurate history constitutes an accusation or condemnation.

For example, to tell the story of Punjab's troubles, one has to go at least a decade before the attack on the holiest shrine of the Sikhs in Amritsar in June 1984. In 1975, the Allahabad High Court convicted Indira Gandhi of electoral malpractices, but instead of accepting the ruling of the court and resigning as prime minister, she declared the Emergency, gave herself dictatorial powers and smugly told her confidantes that 'not a dog barked'. Punjab's Sikh-centric regional party, the Akali Dal resolved to oppose the 'fascist tendency of the Congress' and on a daily basis sent groups of party workers to defy prohibitory orders and go to jail in consequence. Mrs Gandhi returned to power in January 1980, wounded, ruthless and vengeful. Over four intrigue-filled years, tension between Mrs Gandhi and the Akali Dal built up. From June 5 to June 8, 1984 the army carried out Mrs Gandhi's order to pound the Darbar Sahib until Sant Jarnail Singh Bhindranwale and his followers were wiped out. For the weeks after that, any Sikh man was likely to be arrested. All it took was somebody deciding that he looked suspicious. And then came Mrs Gandhi's assassination on 31 October 1984, and the organized massacre of Sikhs in Delhi and elsewhere that followed.

Over the next decade, the rule of law was forgotten, human rights were forgotten, humanity itself was forgotten. The situation could begin to change only after a United Front coalition took over at the Centre. Those old enough to remember would know that Punjab's first peaceful Assembly election after 1980 was held when a Janata Dal politician (and a Punjabi) was prime minister. That was Inder Kumar Gujral. His tenure was very short (from April 1997 to March 1998), but he headed the central government long enough to ensure a fair Assembly election in Punjab in February 1997.

The events of this period are very much alive in the memories of people who lived through it all, people aged 50 or older. Even those born years afterward or who were too young at the time to understand or remember have soaked up the stories of their elders. Many examples from all over the world show us that many individuals are sensitive to painful histories, even though they may be generations removed from the actual events.

Bluestar and its aftermath are still too fresh to be forgotten. Controversially, in recent years, some Sikh congregations in Canada have proposed that names of Bluestar martyrs be added to the *Ardas*. So far, the idea has been ignored by Sikh institutions in India.

Preface

Trance, a 2013 English-language film, revolves around a criminal gang's attempt to force their amnesiac victim to remember the location of a costly painting. The film itself, like most thrillers, might have evaporated from memory, but for one epigrammatic line of dialogue: 'To be angry is to be a victim; I have moved on'. That line sums up the attitude of many people in today's Punjab. The requirements of studies, job, family are pressing and immediate; time spent brooding over bygones gets you nothing. Rather, it steals away time available for the business of getting on, getting by and getting rich. People have better things to do.

But one cannot reconcile with the past if the past is forgotten, or deliberately erased.

Is forgetting possible anyway? Plenty of Punjabis who personally experienced the events of the 1980s and 1990s are still alive. Do they have a choice when it comes to remembering or forgetting? What can they do but remember the past and deal with it in one way or another? For that matter, a dwindling number of Punjabis who personally experienced the events of the Partition are still alive and carry painful memories. We occasionally shed a tear for the suffering of 1947; should we deny a few tears for the sufferers of militancy-era Punjab?

Today's talking heads are still talking but now their favourite phrase is TINA: There Is No Alternative. This means 'all the abuses, all the falsehoods, all the failures of parties, leaders and governments—remember it all, forget it all. It doesn't matter; either way nothing is going to change'. The Vedic seers intoned *neti, neti, neti* meaning 'not this, not this, not this'. Now the seers are stuck on TINA, TINA, TINA.

How can they be so sure that nothing is going to change? Look at America, supposedly a country with an optimal democratic system and lots of transparency and accountability. Citizens are not overwhelmingly cynical when it comes to the honesty and even moral rectitude of their representatives. When a system is pretty good, one would expect that it would remain highly stable and if it changes, it changes so that it better reflects the aspirations of all citizens. How could the politics of fear-mongering and manipulation arise? And yet we see gender, racial, religious and economic divides are increasingly problematic and America's parties and politicians are having a difficult time coping.

In 2008, Barack Obama rallied supporters with the slogan 'Change!'; eight years later, Donald Trump promised 'Change!' to his supporters. He was going to shake up Washington and drain the swamp. Sure enough, change they got. Be careful what you wish for.

Things *can* change … They can change for the worse. In a democracy, it is basically up to the citizens to prevent things from changing for the worse, but will they make the effort if memory spans shrink to one news cycle or less? Between 1991 and 2018, 272 people, many of them children, lost their lives in mass shootings. A few days of outrage followed each horrific incident, and then … forgotten. The media spotlight moves on.

As dangerous as forgetting is remembering things that were not so, or that were only selectively so, or remembering a digestible *little* history when the big history is too rotten to consume. Sit through a film about a 1940s German manufacturer who saves 1,200 people from gas chamber extermination and come out of the cinema hall feeling that the World War II wasn't all bad.

The question of remembering and forgetting underlies our examination of post-militancy Punjab. The book is meant to hold up a mirror to developments in Punjab with regard to political parties, government policies, the operation of the courts and police, responses of the union and state governments, activist responses, cultural responses (particularly films) and 'opportunist' responses, since many people found troubled waters ideal for fishing.

Preface

Notes

1. Hiram W. Johnson, staunchly isolationist senator for California, to the US Senate in 1917.
2. Thukral, 'Punjab Borrows', *The Tribune*.

Interestingly, three Prime Ministers, Mr P. V. Narasimha Rao, Mr H. D. Dev Gowda and Mr Inder Kumar Gujral, promised to waive the loan completely. But all they could do was to meet the demand in parts. But the government led by Mr Atal Bihari Vajpayee has done little to honour its commitment.

Vinayak, 'Narasimha Rao's Punjab Visit', *India Today*.

Congress Prime Minister P. V. Narasimha Rao, speaking at a political rally in Ludhiana, promised that if Congress were returned to power, he would ensure that ₹5,800 crore, the cost of the 10-year battle against militancy which Punjab owed the Centre would be waived off.

India Today, 'I.K. Gujral Writes Off'.

At a specially-convened meeting, attended by Chief Minister Parkash Singh Badal and Central government secretaries, Gujral overruled the objections from the finance officials with a crisp order: 'No more recoveries from Punjab. It's not Punjab's but the nation's debt'. Punjab Finance Minister Captain Kanwaljit Singh explained. 'Since the state no longer has to shell out ₹750 crore every year to the Centre, for the first time in a decade it will have ₹600 crore as extra funds for its annual plan outlay'.

Singh, 'Govt Term', *The Telegraph*.

Badal had approached Advani last year to get ₹274 crore—the sum the Punjab government owed to the Central Reserve Police Force for using its services during the terrorism era—to be waived. Advani, however, refused to budge and instead, asked Badal to provide the accounts. Government sources said the Centre had never intended to implement the decision taken by Gujral as is clear from the decision to refer the matter to the Eleventh Finance Commission for providing the state appropriate debt relief.

'Even after the moratorium on payment of the loan till 2005, if the Centre had any intention of waiving off the amount, it could have easily modified the finance commission's recommendations before placing its report along with the action-taken report in Parliament which it did not do. Instead, on July 24, 2000, the Centre conveyed to the accountant general and the state government that it had been decided not to effect recovery of the further instalment and interest payment on the special term loans', the official explained.
3. Preet, 'Centre Rejects Punjab Plea', *The Sunday Guardian*.

Preface

The three-member committee, headed by Secretary Expenditure Sushma Nath, was formed by the Union Finance Ministry to suggest restructuring or waiving the loans of Punjab, West Bengal and Kerala. The committee conveyed last week to the Central government that it is not in favour of the idea. The committee is reported to have said that this would set a bad precedent and encourage fiscal mismanagement.

Punjab traces its heavy debt liability and interest burden to its struggle with terrorism in the 1980s and early 1990s, a period when it was primarily under Central rule. The fight against insurgency left a deep hole in the state's finances, leaving it in heavy debt that has only grown over the years. The debt burden on Punjab currently stands at over ₹69,000 cr. The state pays annual interest of more than ₹5,000 cr to service this debt, even as the Central government had waived off parts of loan amounting to ₹6,772 cr in two instalments. Punjab expected to be at least partially waived off of the liability.

4. Kundera Milan: *The Book of Laughter and Forgetting* (1979) Part 1: Lost Letters, p. 7

Milan Kundera: born April 1, 1929, Brno, Czechoslovakia (now the Czech Republic); lives in Paris.

Kundera, along with other reform communist writers such as Pavel Kohout, was involved in the 1968 Prague Spring of 1968. In 1975 he fled to France. He has lived there since.

In 1978, Kundera wrote *Kniha Smíchu a Zapomnění*. As might be expected, the Czech government forbade its publication so the book was first published in French as *Le livre du rire et de l'oublie* (Editions Gallimard, Paris,1979). It was subsequently translated into English (*The Book of Laughter and Forgetting*) and published in the United States (Alfred A. Knopf, New York, 1980). Fresh translation by Aaron Asher (Harper Collins, New York, 1996).

5. Hobbes, *Leviathan*, 391.

Acknowledgements

Primarily, this book is concerned with the violation of human rights and civil rights. In two chapters, 'Due Process: Punjab' and 'Due Process: Delhi', the focus is on the 35-year struggle to get justice in specific cases as well as the general struggle to see the rule of law upheld in general. The struggle required persistence and courage.

This book and, more importantly, the improved situation for the rule of law in Punjab and Delhi would not have been possible without the efforts of men and women who took the risk of documenting wrongdoing, speaking out and supporting victims who filed and pursued cases in the courts. A bow in gratitude is owed to all of them; we name only a few.

The late Jaswant Singh Khalra paid with his life. The Punjab Police saw to it that he did not live to complete his human rights mission but was to be their own undoing. His habeas corpus case eventually came before the Supreme Court, which ordered a CBI investigation and the fallout of this investigation was hundreds of cases of extra-judicial killing and illegal cremation.

Two Chandigarh-based groups began in the mid-1980s and remain active to this day. They are the Chandigarh-based Punjab Human Rights Organisation (PHRO) and the Movement Against State Repression (MASR). Among their active members were Justice Ajit Singh Bains, Baljeet Kaur, Rajwinder Singh Bains, Bhai Ashok Singh Bagrian, Mohinderjit Singh Sethi, Sukhjeet Kaur, late Lt Col Partap Singh and late Maj Gen (Ret.) Narinder Singh. One of the authors of this book, Inderjit Singh Jaijee, remains active in MASR.

Acknowledgements

The ashes of the Delhi riots were still warm when the Delhi-based People's Union for Democratic Rights (PUDR) began to investigate and take up the cause of riot victims. An allied organization was People's Union for Civil Liberties. Professor Rajni Kothari, Justice Rajinder Singh Sachar and journalist Kuldip Nayar are no more, but their work is not forgotten.

After Punjab's 1997 Assembly election, the Committee for Coordination on Disappearances in Punjab (CCDP) was set up with Ram Narayan Kumar as coordinator. The People's Commission on Human Rights Violations in Punjab emerged from this committee. The Committee was banned, but the CCDP continued its work, producing valuable documentation.

Ram Narayan Kumar is no more, but the work of the CCDP has been carried forward by Ensaaf, a group based in the USA. Ashok Agrwaal, Amrik Singh and Jaskaran Kaur of Ensaaf published their findings in 2003 in *Reduced to Ashes: the Insurgency and Human Rights in Punjab*. To the present date, Ensaaf volunteers continue to document cases at the grassroots level and present their findings on their website, Ensaaf, a Mission to End Impunity (https://ensaaf.org/).

1
Normalcy

'Normal' in the Rear-view Mirror

April 1979, a conference was held at the Punjabi University, Patiala: Three hours of talk, talk, talk; a near-death experience with boredom as the lethal agent. The convenor was down to his final thank yous, and the distinguished invitees were rousing up in anticipation of lunch when two fellows ran in from the back of the hall and jumped on the dais. They shouted their rejection of the Constitution of India, flung a few scraps of paper into the air and ran out as quickly as they ran in. Lunch was the usual.

But the next day ... Newspapers carry signed editorials only if a quake throws Mumbai under the sea or India wins the World Cup, so readers of *The Tribune*, Punjab's leading English daily, were shaken to see one in the next morning's paper. Prem Bhatia, the paper's oracle-in-chief, told readers that the university conference incident was extremely serious and he used a word that many readers had never heard or before, *Khalistan*.

The word was not in common usage and even after it began to appear in print now and again, people took a sceptical view of the whole idea. It was five years before Bluestar. Who knew?[1]

About 15 years later, after most of the gunfire had ceased, 'normalcy' replaced the word 'Khalistan'. To be precise, 'returning to normalcy'—as though, by making a simple U-turn, the state would find itself in some pleasant place of bygone days. It sounded good, provided you didn't actually dredge up memories of the late 1970s and early 1980s.

Political Lead-up to Turmoil

1979. With the Lok Sabha election looming, Congress Prime Minister Indira Gandhi was in do-or-die mode. No sooner was she back in the saddle in January 1980, than she declared war on every state non-Congress government. She knew the states would pack the Rajya Sabha with non-Congress MPs, so the non-Congress state governments had to go. With one midnight order, she swept away nine such governments.

When Gurcharan Singh Tohra split from the Akali Dal, Indira had the pretext she needed to dismiss the Akali government of Punjab. The state was put under President's Rule and Punjab was frog-marched to the Vidhan Sabha poll in May 1980. Congress was voted in, but setting up a Congress government in Punjab required more Indira-muscle. Giani Zail Singh, the previous Congress Chief Minister of Punjab, was dragged to the Union Cabinet to keep him from lunging for the throat of his bête noire, Darbara Singh, who was Indira's choice for Chief Minister.

Meanwhile the automatic switch built into every politician flipped to the out-of-power setting. The switch is described as *'jeetenge to lootenge, harenge to kootenge'* (If we win, we will loot; if we lose, we will hammer). The Akalis began to hammer the Centre: *'rasta roko, rail roko, nahar roko'* (road block, rail block, canal block). The Centre's answer was to stall and keep talking without giving anything. The more the Centre stalled, the harder the Akalis hammered.

The pre-Bluestar days, marked by Mrs Gandhi's desperation to hold every state government bound, gagged and under her heel might have been somebody's idea of 'normal', but it was hardly an attractive time-travel destination. Not that it matters; it is not possible to revisit even the most idyllic political landscape.

Economic Lead-up to Turmoil

Ditto for the economic landscape of years past. The state's economy looked bright in the Green Revolution Days of the 1960s but even before Bluestar, the revolution was at its last gasp. By the time the militancy era came to a close, the state's industrial base had shrivelled, agriculture was faltering, unemployment was endemic and foreign investors wanted nothing to do with Punjab.[2]

In 1996, the general election resulted in a hung Parliament. India saw fragile coalitions and three short-lived prime ministers in less than two years. If Punjab was abnormal during the previous decade, the Centre too entered an abnormal phase. But normal, or not, Punjab stumbled forward. The state election in the following year brought the Akalis back ... and back in a never-before tried alliance. The perfect partner for Sikh chauvinist Akali Dal turned out to be Hindu chauvinist Bharatiya Janata Party (BJP). They have been happily married ever since.

After 1997, the state has had two Congress governments and three Akali governments.

Punjab's present political leaders are old men, survivors of Indira days. One wonders what they remember. How do they tally up those 15 bad years?

The Akalis, for all their agitations, got nothing: neither just share of river waters nor Chandigarh as the state capital nor greater state autonomy.

Parkash Singh Badal came out ahead; he managed to stay alive, outlive challengers within his party and finally scrabble to the top of the Akali heap. A one-time, temporary Akali, Capt.

Amarinder Singh, also came out ahead ... by a Congress *ghar wapsi* (home coming).

In her 1984 electoral gamble, Indira Gandhi played Punjab as a 'card'. Election won, life lost. Her party still carries the blot of Bluestar and the failure to support justice and recompense for the victims of those lawless days.

Both parties were diminished by the events of 1984–1994, and yet the Akalis and Congress persist. They are superficially different, yet in motive and manner indistinguishable. They rotate in and out of office but bring little tangible benefit to the vast majority of Punjabis.

Installed or Just Plain Stalled?

Politics is a struggle for power. Constitutions are supposed to set limits on how this struggle is conducted; but wherever you look, it is seen that politicians understand their limits to be whatever they can get away with until somebody stops them.

Power for what? A common remark about politicians is that 'they are out to line their pockets'. Long observation tells us that this is true, but it is a little unfair. After all, who would go into politics if there were no money in it? The really objectionable behaviour is lining the pocket but doing nothing for the state. When we observe the stagnation that has gripped Punjab since the 1980s, clearly the type of power sought has not been power to revive the economy or enhance human capital and the quality of life.

The politicians and political parties have not raised their sights higher than capturing power for the sake of perpetuating themselves. Whether an Akali has been in the saddle or a Congressman, the horse has not moved.

Normalcy

The Science with No Formulas

Punjab's political fortunes have been closely studied, particularly during the militancy era and to a lesser extent thereafter. It's no wonder that political scientists love Punjab. It's a state that has everything: distinct regions, linguistic and religious divisions, almost no long-term experience of peace in its 4,000-year history. It's a state that is both a minority and a majority at the same time, in the sense that the state's core community, the Sikhs, are a minority vis-à-vis India, but a majority in Punjab itself. The gap between Punjab's very rich and very poor is wide and getting wider; but at the same time, a poor man in Punjab is better off than a poor man in states such as Odisha or Jharkhand. And if all that weren't enough, one Punjabi in three belongs to a Scheduled Caste (SC). Punjab has the highest proportion of SC citizens in the country. And here's another plus: the population of Punjab's SC is growing faster than other demographic groups.[3]

So, what's not to like? It's as though this state, with its numerous conflicts, contradictions and paradoxes, was made for scholarly analysis. Books, theses, articles in academic publications have propelled hundreds of students to PhD status and elevated similar numbers of humble college lecturers to exalted professorships.

When it comes to political developments in Punjab, a very long shelf of detailed studies is available, particularly for the decade that followed Bluestar. Many historians and political scientists have assembled blow-by-blow accounts, thick with footnotes. (See reading list.)

Science is predictive. Combine X with Y at so many degrees Celsius and you get Z. Happens every time. Let's say that the workings of politics in Punjab before the militancy era were 'normal' and we have a political scientist with a thorough grasp of how Punjab politics worked at that time. On the basis of pre-Bluestar politics, would that scholar be able to predict the workings of Punjab politics in later years, say from 1996 onward?

Yes and no.

'No' because politics is human behaviour which is never very scientific, hence never entirely predictable. Were that so, no pollster or media pundit would ever have to eat humble pie after an electoral upset that nobody saw coming. The return of the Akalis in 2012 for instance. Everybody knew that the voters of Punjab had never returned an incumbent government to power but … Voila, there was the SAD–BJP combine with 68 seats; well over an absolute majority in the 117 member House!

And 'yes' because political science is largely political history and the study of history is a search for patterns. While patterns are rarely replicated exactly over time, broad outlines have a way of persisting.

Standard Practice

If this were a bet, our money would be on the diligent scholar. Writing of the past couple of decades, he would dust off that wise old saw from Talleyrand: 'They learned nothing and they forgot nothing'.

The practice of politics in Punjab has certainly displayed a predictable pattern. Let's summarize it.

1984–2006 Timeline

1984	Operation Bluestar: attack on the Sikh faith's holiest shrine, the Golden Temple, at Amritsar.
1985	'The Boys' (i.e., Sikh militants) take the lead from establishment Akalis, Congress assumes power but not legitimacy.

Normalcy

	Lok Sabha poll in Punjab: Akalis – 7, Congress – 5, BJP – 1.
	July 24: Longowal Accord signed. August 20: Longowal assassinated. September 25: Combined Lok Sabha and Assembly election.
	SAD outscores Congress in both; Surjit Singh Barnala forms government.
1986	IPS Julio Ribeiro takes over as DGP. Upswing in fake encounters.
	Militants declare Khalistan independence. Black Thunder I: Golden Temple stormed; no casualties but counter-productive.
	SAD splinters.
1987	Barnala government out; President's rule imposed (in force until 1992).
	Militants eclipse moderates.
1988	K. P. S. Gill takes over as DGP, posted out same year. Black Thunder II.
1989	Lok Sabha election: radical SAD–Mann – 6, independents – 3, other parties marginalized.
1990	K. P. S. Gill returns as DGP. Violence increases, human rights violations.
1991	Rajiv Gandhi assassinated. Punjab Lok Sabha election cancelled 24 hours before polling. 23 candidates killed. Congress boycotts poll.
1992	Assembly elections. Militants warn against voting, SAD boycotts. Congress led by Beant Singh voted in on mandate of less than 10% of voting population.
1993	Panchayat elections: 80 per cent turnout.
1994	Akali radicals merge as SAD United. Advocate restructuring India on federalist principles (Amritsar Declaration).
	December 25: Death of former President of India Giani Zail Singh following an accident.

(continued)

The Legacy of Militancy in Punjab

(continued)

1995	Beant Singh assassinated. Harcharan Singh Brar becomes the Chief Minister.
	Municipalities elections: 82 per cent turnout.
1996	Lok Sabha poll: Akalis—8, BSP—3, Congress—2.
	Akali Dal Moga Convention: Membership opened to all irrespective of religion, thus conforming to Election Commission rule that only those parties may contest elections that accept Constitution and secularism.
	Congress revolt dumps Harcharan Singh Brar; installs Rajinder Kaur Bhattal as the Chief Minister.
	SGPC election: Badal's group wins nearly all seats.
1997	Capt. Amarinder Singh de-radicalizes, relaunches SAD (Panthic) which then merges with Congress. Congress dumps Bhattal; installs Amarinder Singh.
	Assembly Elections: SAD wins most seats ever. SAD has absolute majority but recognizes BJP as coalition partner.
1998	Lok Sabha poll: SAD—8, BJP—3, Congress—0.
	Badal SAD splits: Rival and SGPC president G. S. Tohra forms splinter party. Badal-controlled SGPC dumps Tohra.
1999	Lok Sabha poll: Congress—8, SAD–Badal—2, SAD–Mann—1, BJP—1, CPI—1.
2002	Assembly election. Congress led by Capt. Amarinder Singh wins.
	SAD–Badal sweeps SGPC election.
	Supreme Court directs Punjab to complete the SYL canal within a year.
2003	Tohra and Badal reconcile. Prakash Singh Badal and son Sukhbir Singh jailed in corruption case.
2004	SGPC president and Akali politician G. S. Tohra dies.
	Lok Sabha poll: SAD-Badal—8, BJP—3, Congress—2.
	SAD-Badal sweeps SGPC election; main opponent, hardline Panthic Morcha, alleges rigging.

Normalcy

	Punjab rejects river water agreements with neighbouring states. Rejects Supreme Court directive.
2005	Militancy era debt: moratorium on repayment ends. Punjab owes ₹6,800 crore to Centre.

Come to power on populist promises and, once in power, devote all energies to:

1. Crippling the rival (usually with corruption cases)
2. Buying off/slapping down/eliminating challengers within the party
3. Enjoying the fruits of victory such as:
   a. Contracts (liquor, construction)
   b. Licences and permits (bus/truck transport, mining)
   c. Wink-and-nod for dubious practices in recruitment to government service and business. 'Business' can be just about anything—maybe real estate, or cable TV services or import–export. Regarding the latter, an example of import might be heroin smuggling, while an example of export might be *kabooter-baazi* (pigeon-flying), as human trafficking is described in Punjab.

Their Honest Earnings: What Punjab Legislators Get Paid

Post	Monthly Salary (₹)	Item	Amount
Chief Minister	1 lakh	A report in *Jagran* gave a somewhat different breakdown. Figures under the headings of Office, Telephone, Secretariat and Daily match the figures carried in the *Hindustan Times* report but *Jagran* mentioned some additional allowances.	
Dy Chief Minister, Speaker, Dy Speaker, Leader of Opposition and Dy Leader of Opposition	50,000		
Chief Parliamentary Secretaries	40,000		
MLA basic salary + allowances	93,000	MLA's basic salary	25,000
Allowances Monthly		**Allowances Monthly**	
Constituency	25,000	Light	25,000
Office	10,000	Computer subsystem	5,000
Telephone	15,000	Expenditure	3,000
Secretariat	10,000	Water and electricity	1,000
Daily	1,500	Road mileage	15 per km

Allowances Annual	
Annual free travel facility	3 lakh
Ex-gratia amount	5 lakh

Source: *Hindustan Times*, 20 March 2015. https://www.hindustantimes.com/chandigarh/budge1t-session-punjab-mlas-united-on-pay-hike/story-gBeC6rp40oMTSdLbFl8aUP.html

Source: *Jagran*, 15 December 2018. https://www.jagran.com/punjab/chandigarh-preparation-to-increase-salary-and-allowance-of-mlas-in-punjab-despite-of-severe-economic-crisis-18750533.html

The pension is sweet too. The amount of basic monthly pension, as per the notification issued on 26 October 2016, is ₹15,000 for the first term and ₹10,000 for each subsequent term and a 50 per cent dearness allowance comes with that (https://www.tribuneindia.com/news/punjab/punjab-mlas-pension-grows-with-every-additional-term-rti/703204.html). This is for an ordinary MLA; ministers get more.
Not to forget lifelong free railway pass, medical care and loans at 6 per cent per annum interest (https://www.jagranjosh.com/).
So the MLA is paid ₹93,000 per month in return for attending the Assembly. In each financial year, the Assembly must sit for three sessions—Budget, Summer/Monsoon and Winter. Generally Monsoon and Winter sessions are three days each, and Budget session goes up to 10 days; a total of 16 days in a year (https://examupdates.in/mla-salary-india/).

We refer to *enjoying* the fruits of victory but actually, these fruits serve a higher purpose than simple enjoyment: Fruit deficiency makes politicians and parties weak and helpless. From the very day of election, an elected politician must start getting ready for the next election. He must prepare a war chest that will see him through the next campaign. Woe to the aspirant who starts thinking about the campaign war chest only a few months before a forthcoming poll.

War chests can only be fattened with the blessings of the Supremo. Naturally, the Supremo blesses only worthy partymen— the devoted, loyal, capable and useful. Ability to feed or starve war chests is what makes a Supremo a Supremo.

A ruling party can hope to be re-elected only if it practices sound financial management. State funds must not be spent during the first four years in power because this money will be needed shortly before elections are announced. Utilizing it two or three months before the election code of conduct comes into force, the Supremo helicopters from village to village granting *darshan*[4] to common people and scattering largesse.

Aside from war chests and darshan tours, election preparation has a third vital element, namely, perpetuation. Veteran politicians must see to it that a party ticket goes to their son/daughter or other close relative. One family member in the Assembly is good, two are better. If he has upheld his obligation to family, then when the inevitable day comes, the elder politician will be able to pass on calmly and be at peace, knowing that his descendants have inherited a place in the party and a good chance to occupy his Assembly or Lok Sabha seat too.

An analysis of membership of all the parties shows that while the inheritance of party tickets is not guaranteed, most political families stay in the game generation after generation. When party leaders talk about inducting 'new blood', they don't mean giving a chance to just any youngster with political potential. They mean 'passing the baton'. The youngsters are generally started out in zila parishad and block samiti elections and graduate to the Assembly within a few years;[5] so in that sense, they 'rise through the ranks', but they were eligible for political baptism solely on the strength of their heritage (see box: 'The House of Lords').

Seen from the outside, it appears that election time is when politicians come forth to battle and their opponents are candidates of other parties. Actually, the most intense political fighting does not take place between parties, but within the party. It's the hottest at the time of ticket distribution or when cabinet members are being chosen. State politics is where the action is. If national parliamentary elections are 'the dog' and state elections are 'the tail', then the tail wags the dog.

Political campaigning has patterns that show up in the behaviour of both ruling and opposition parties. Electoral defeat has its pattern too: The ruling party is brought down at the ballot box through its own greed and malfeasance rather than any positive merit on the part of its rival. The voters get fed up. One bunch of crooks is driven into the wilderness and another bunch of crooks jostle up to the feed trough.

When something rarely or never shows up over a long period, that too is a pattern. For example, for years and years, the obvious needs of the state and its people receive lip-service once every five years at election time and neglect thereafter. Fat on promises, thin on policy directed at long-term improvement. About this last, politicians are likely to object that no candidate has ever been elected because voters liked his policies. Politicians campaign on promises because that is what voters want and understand.

Old Blood, New Blood

All these patterns were seen before militancy and continue unchanged to this day. But given the intensity of Punjab's trauma, *something* must have changed.

The Legacy of Militancy in Punjab

Bluestar and the Delhi riots horrified people, particularly the Sikhs—so much blood spilt—men, women and children killed. These events also horrified the long-established actors in Punjab's established formal political parties: The cart had been tossed upside down and every single apple was rolling in a different direction. They had lost control and knew that regaining it was far from a foregone conclusion. The upset of 1984 could only be compared to the upset of 1947 in terms of total disruption.

As mentioned earlier, political party leaders, both Congress and Akali, have long trotted out the pious intention of 'bringing in new blood'. The years of militancy challenged established politics to such an extent that, at the peak point of disruption, it looked like the old blood of Punjab politics might be literally flushed away. A politician may get depressed if he fears that the future will consign his name to 'the dung heap of history', but he gets positively jittery at the thought that a bullet might consign him to the cremation ground.

The militants were 'new blood', unrelated to any of the state's entrenched political lineages. In their brief lifespans, 'the boys' came close to breaking Punjab's political closed shop. What if a large number of these boys had gone into electoral politics? Would they have changed the way the game is played or would the game have changed them? Would they have been worse than those they replaced?

We will never know. A few died deaths that earned their photographs a place in memorial galleries. Others died with not even a name recorded—cremated as unclaimed with family and friends to guess at their fate. Some came out alive but crippled, physically, mentally and perhaps sorry to still draw breath.

For years now, the state, with its Akali–Congress rotation, has been sitting 'idle as a painted ship upon a painted ocean'. Any breeze would be welcome.

Failed Experiments: Broom and Gloom

Between 2014 and 2017, it seemed a fresh wind was picking up. These were the years of Punjab's experiment with the Aam Aadmi Party (AAP). AAP, whose party symbol was a broom, was welcomed enthusiastically by an electorate that had long sought in vain for political representatives who would be clean, sincere and dedicated to the welfare of the state. Enter AAP proclaiming 'swaraj' and boasting an elaborate organization designed to get down to the grassroots. It took the party barely two years to demonstrate that it was fully as false, arrogant, autocratic, power-hungry and venal as the Akalis and the Congress. Maybe more so.[6]

Sadly, AAP now belongs to the category of failed experiments. But it was not the only failed experiment. Long before AAP came along, Marxist parties failed and the Bahujan Samaj Party, a party that represented SC people, also failed.

Lonely on the Left

Histories of Leftist movements in pre-Independence Punjab are plentiful. Many books have been written about the Ghadar Movement, the Naujawan Bharat Sabha (meaning Bhagat Singh and his comrades). The Praja Mandal and the Muzarra Movement, both localized in Punjab's princely states, are well documented. (Although the single issue of tenant rights was at the heart of both these movements, they could be considered proto-leftist.) What's hard to find are works focused on leftist parties in Punjab just before, during and after the militancy era. The only three that come to mind are *Insurrection to Agitations: The Naxalite Movement in Punjab* by Paramjit Singh Judge, Gurharpal Singh's *Communism in Punjab* and *Communist Party in Punjab: The Politics of Survival* by Jasmail Singh Brar.[7]

The Legacy of Militancy in Punjab

The Naxalites (there were several mutually antagonistic strands) had no use for bourgeois democracy—meaning elections, alliances, campaigning, etc. Their high point came in the early 1970s. At that time, they had a noticeable presence in Punjab campuses; they dominated the Punjab Students Union and resurrected the Naujawan Bharat Sabha, which had been moribund since 1931 when Shaheed Bhagat Singh was hanged in Lahore Central Jail.

The state government (at that time, an Akali government led by Parkash Singh Badal) came down on the Naxalites with take-no-prisoners fury. Torture and disappearances were standard practices in this anti-Naxal campaign, but then they were standard in the time of the Mughals and probably before them as well. Some say that the anti-Naxal years introduced one new procedure: The Punjab Police are said to have discovered the beauty and convenience of the fake encounter at this time. The fake encounter became famous during the militancy era and has since spread to all parts of India.

The high point for Punjab Left parties' electoral performance came in 1977. In that year, the CPI won seven Vidhan Sabha seats and the CPI(M) won eight. The CPI had done even better in 1972 (10 seats) but the CPI(M) could get only one. Year 1980 was the last year that the Left parties made a reasonable showing: nine for the CPI and five for the CPI(M). Since then, the CPI(M) has been completely out of the running. The last time the CPI got anything (two seats) was in 1997. A party that goes 20 years without an electoral victory is wiped out (see box: 'Election Statistics').

Recollecting the years before Khalistan, every village had its Comrade—at least one and maybe a little gaggle of them. They were addressed as such: 'Comrade Sahib'. They were often Sikhs and tended to be good Sikhs, able to quote from scripture at length, particularly those verses that denounced the accumulation of wealth and caste pride.

Normalcy

Just before militancy hit Punjab, the Communist parties—the CPI and the CPI(M)—were visible but marginal. They were master organizers of marches and rallies and could assemble a veritable sea of red flags. But somehow, when election time rolled around, they simply could not turn the flags into more than a small handful of elected MLAs or MPs. Urban voters went with the Congress or (to a lesser extent) the BJP. Big landholders held sway in the villages where landholder factions vied for dominance. If Rival A aligned with the Akalis, then Rival B aligned with the Congress. Religious identity was the basis of voter mobilization for both the Akalis and the BJP. Countering this was not easy even for the Congress party with all its national party resources. Class identity was the only mobilizer available to the Communist parties, but class just didn't fire up the voters nor did the communist parties have financial resources to buy votes or hire enough thugs to capture enough polling stations.

The Khalistan militants agreed with Mao about power growing out of the barrel of a gun but disliked the Maoists and Marxists all the same. A gun barrel was often the last thing a village comrade saw.

Electoral statistics make it plain that the CPI(M) was never much of a force in Punjab. The CPI fared better, thanks in part to money pumped in by the national level CPI. In the 1980s, Punjab's never-robust leftist parties were declining; the militants merely hastened the end. After the breakup of the Soviet Union in 1991, the national-level CPI was out of rubles and in no position to help the Punjab CPI regain a space in the state's electoral landscape.

The political space once occupied by the Left in Punjab is now somewhat filled by the multitude of kisan unions. Small as they are, these little unions have a talent for crowd mobilization and visibility. Their leaders bargain for crumbs with political parties but are too small and poor to venture into electoral politics.

The Legacy of Militancy in Punjab

Bloc Busters

The history of the left in Punjab goes back to more than a century (the Ghadar Party was launched in 1913, several years before the Bolshevik revolution in Russia). The Bahujan Samaj Party (BSP) is of much more recent vintage; it came into being in 1984 and from the start declared itself to be the voice of the Scheduled Castes. But its lifespan in Punjab has been shorter than that of the Leftist parties.

How could the BSP fail? Population was in its favour and its founder, Kanshi Ram, belonged to Punjab. The peculiar circumstances of 1992 provided the party its only tiny taste of state power.

First, a word about Punjab demography. State-wide, Punjab's SC population is about 32 per cent; the percentage crosses 42 per cent in the districts of Muktsar, Ferozepur and Shaheed Bhagat Singh Nagar districts with Faridkot and Jalandhar at 39 per cent. Even SAS Nagar, the district with the lowest percentage of SC population, still has 22 per cent. By way of contrast, the Jat caste accounts for only about 21 per cent of Punjab's population. The strength of various castes is a major consideration when Indian political parties formulate their electoral strategies, so you would think that the BSP, which claims to represent the interest of Punjab's numerically strong SCs, would win a large number of seats in the State Assembly, maybe enough to form the government.

Elections statistics tell a different story: The only time the BSP has won Vidhan Sabha seats was in 1992 (nine seats). The Akali parties boycotted the 1992 elections and many others backed away fearing death at the hands of either militants or police. In elections to the Lok Sabha, the BSP record has been just as dismal: one seat in 1985, one seat in 1992 and three seats in 1996. In more than 20 years, the BSP in Punjab has won not a single seat either in the Vidhan Sabha or the Lok Sabha.

One very big problem before the BSP is that the 'Scheduled Castes' is not *one* thing: 39 such castes exist in Punjab. Caste consciousness and caste hierarchy does not disappear simply because one's caste is listed on a 'Schedule'. In order to stay out of trouble, let's go with English surnames: If there were a concept of ritual purity in England then a *Potter* might hold himself several notches higher than a *Thatcher* and a *Thatcher* might feel superior to a *Shepherd* or a *Gardner*. Getting Potter, Thatcher, Shepherd and Gardner and 30 other listed surnames to pursue common benefit by voting en bloc is difficult if it means that the whole bunch accepts equality among themselves. This sentiment may be developing, but it is developing slowly.

In a thesis, Inderjit Singh provides an insightful grassroots view of the party and gets right to the heart of the party's failure to turn demographics into votes. Here is his ready reckoner to the BSP's failure in Punjab.[8]

Organization:

- Organizational structure of the BSP is very weak at the state level in Punjab. Coordination among the various organizational bodies of the party is absent. No regular meetings of any organization are held.
- Mayawati takes all the decisions. Office bearers including the State President, State in-charge and Vidhan Sabha and Lok Sabha Committee in-charges are handpicked by the party supremo Mayawati. BSP has no inner party democracy.

Party strategy:

- In Uttar Pradesh, the BSP realized that sticking to the Dalit-card alone would not provide a support base sufficient to come to power, so they devised a 'social engineering' strategy. This has never been earnestly tried in Punjab; 80 per cent leadership of Punjab BSP comes from the Dalit

community and the party has never tried to appeal to non-Dalit voters.
- Punjab politics revolves around Congress and Akali Dal. All other political parties in Punjab, including BSP, can win only if they contest in alliance with Congress or SAD. The majority of BSP leaders reject forming an alliance because when there is an alliance, the BSP supporters vote for the allied party but the supporters of the allied party do not vote for BSP candidates.
- Leaders from other parties joining BSP are fewer than the number of BSP leaders joining other parties. From other parties, only those leaders join the BSP who face discrimination in their original party. They join if the BSP gives them a ticket to contest an election and then they work as spoilers of those parties which they have left. After some time, especially after defeat in elections, they leave BSP. This trend discourages long-time committed BSP workers.

Leadership:

- Punjab BSP leadership is poorly educated and unable to communicate the party's message either to voters or party workers. The educational qualification of approximately 70 per cent of leaders was up to 10+2 level.

Dissatisfaction within the BSP:

- Many old workers have left the party.
- BSP leaders complain that after Kanshi Ram's death, it has become a one-person party.
- Majority of the Punjab BSP leadership complain that the national party focuses only on Uttar Pradesh.

- Presently there are six factions of BSP. Out of these three factions are more active viz BSP, BSP(A) and DBSM. Dalit votes get divided among these factions.

Voters' perception:

- Because of the influence of Sikhism and the Arya Samaj movement, the caste system is weaker in Punjab than in other states. It is thus more difficult to play the Dalit card.
- Punjab Dalits have representation in the Akali Dal, the Congress and even the BJP. Each of these parties woos the Dalit vote. Punjab Dalits have not felt a party of their own to be an urgent need.
- Elections 'pay off' for the voter only if he bets on the winning horse. To get his work done, a voter needs a sitting representative. A BSP candidate is seen as having little chance of winning, hence a vote for BSP is deemed 'thrown away'.
- BSP leaders have failed to impress ordinary Dalit voters. Voters perceive all political leaders, including those of the BSP, to be equally false, indifferent and self-serving—appearing at election time only.
- BSP has not been able to attract and mobilize youth. Congress and SAD have greater hold on young voters.
- The party has been unable to attract support from non-Dalits, and electoral failure has resulted in even Dalits drifting away from the party.

Reincarnations

The militancy period saw a great deal of violence but not everyone who was opposed to the Government of India took to arms. Many radical outfits had both a shooting wing and a talking wing.

Those wielding the guns were new names, and the names of those wielding the press notes were also new. However, the familiar names did not go away. The problem of somehow remaining credible in a radicalized environment compelled establishment politicians to repackage themselves, not once but again and again (see box: '1984–2006 Timeline').

For example, Punjab's present Congress Chief Minister, heir to the throne of Patiala, Captain Amarinder Singh, shed his skin thrice: from Congress to Akali, from moderate Akali to radical Akali, from radical Akali to Congress. He was one of the signatories of the 1994 'Amritsar Declaration' which described the subcontinent as a collection of different cultures, all of which should be free from central government straight-jacketing and, for this, a confederation was the most just and agreeable arrangement. The Declaration concluded, 'If the Government of India fails to restructure the Indian polity into a federal structure, the Akali Dal would be left with no alternative but to wage a struggle for a sovereign Sikh state'. Among the signatures on that document, we read not only Amarinder Singh's name but the names of Badal, Tohra, Barnala and Simranjit Singh Mann. Captain Amarinder Singh became the president of the radical Shiromani Akali Dal, Amritsar.

New groups took birth, old names were resurrected. Among the repackaged lot, each of them claimed to be 'the real Akali Dal'. In other words, they declared that they were not turning away from the Akali Dal but cleansing it and returning it to purity.

Splinters and Fringes

For the moment, set aside the backdrop of Punjab in crisis and Sikhs in crisis. The political history of India, both before and after independence … all of India, Kashmir to Kanyakumari … is a history of splintering, negotiating, converging and splintering again.

This is easy to explain.

India is extremely heterogenous, cobwebbed with fault lines, right down to village level. Look anywhere and you will find some distinct identity around which to crystalize support. In fact, you are most likely to find several such identities.

Walking out as a strategy for gaining control of a situation was discovered long ago, all over the world. Feeling undervalued, Karna sulks for 10 days on the sidelines of Kurukshetra. A beautiful captive is denied to Achilles so he tells Agamemnon that he is taking his soldiers and going home. Battle flag, slave girl, party ticket, cabinet berth ... same thing.

Indians are no better than anyone else when it comes to pride and a desire for self-aggrandisement. Satan's soliloquy in *Paradise Lost* perfectly suits every *neta* breaking away from his party: 'Better to reign in Hell than serve in Heaven'.

Splinter groups or front organizations amplify political resources. There are several ways that this can work.

Communication is vital to advancing a political cause. This is true for all parties, but let us imagine a 'fringe' party. When this fringe party holds a press conference, it will be lucky to get two paragraphs on Page 5. But suppose you have two fringe parties of similar views; one holds a press conference and the other, howsoever briefly, blocks traffic outside the Secretariat. In the next morning's paper, perhaps they will have made their presence felt to the extent of 10 paragraphs. Small outlay, impressive profit. For maximizing media exposure, two fringe parties are better than one. Political genius lies in knowing the point at which multiplication of fringe parties becomes a losing game.

Rebel/radical/fringe parties can be very useful to a major party or party leader. In a contest in which Party A is at a disadvantage vis-à-vis Party B, victory can be achieved if Party A can split Party B's vote. Party A need not wait for alternate parties to arise on their own.

There is strong evidence that Congress leader Giani Zail Singh propped up Sikh radical Sant Jarnail Singh Bhindranwale to weaken (a) his fellow Congress leader and bête noire Darbara Singh and (b) the Punjab Congress Party's bête noire, the Akali Dal. (Numerous books and newspaper/magazine articles have put forward this claim. It appears in documented detail in *A Centenary History of the Indian National Congress, Vol V.*)[9]

A third way that rebel/radical/fringe parties can be useful is in driving a centrist or moderate party to a more extreme position. It works like this: The moderate party's rival secretly creates a radical party or faction tasked with whipping up public sentiment on emotive issues and hammering the centrists. The idea is to make moderate party leaders fear that a substantial chunk of their voters is being lured away by radicals. Should the moderate party remain centrist and lose the radicalized vote or shift to a more extreme position and risk losing the centrist vote?

Try, Try Again?

We have strolled through the genealogical gallery of Punjab's political families and scrapped moss off the tombstones of dozens of parties that came and went during the past 30 years. What to do with this knowledge? Would we better off without the brain-clutter? If we remember and put it all together, should it add up to something? What?

Let's go back to Talleyrand. When he wrote 'They learned nothing and they forgot nothing', he was referring to the monarchical government imposed on France after the defeat of Napoleon. A few years later, the French political elite chucked out the British-imposed Bourbon Dynasty princes and then they imposed an Orleans Dynasty prince. Less than 20 years later, this prince was also chucked out and replaced by a nephew of Napoleon. This fellow was elected but, rather than stepping down when his term was over, he declared himself the emperor. France was stuck in an autocracy rut and replacing heads of state came down to 'same old shop, new name'. Talleyrand was probably right about the ruling elite learning nothing, but he doesn't tell us what it took for France to stop searching for better autocrats and instead search for a better system.

The House of Lords

To conjecture what 'game change' could have meant in Punjab, one must know something about the Ancien Régime. Except that is not the right term—it implies a set of people who have passed into history. Punjab's regime may be 'ancien', but it's still doing fine, thank you. Its members are interchangeably Congressmen and Akalis. When Party Tweedle-dee denies one of them a ticket, he calls the press to witness a grand show in which he defiantly joins Party Tweedledum and vice versa. Some have bounced back and forth between parties several times.

Those who live in Punjab are well acquainted with the genealogical web that connects nearly all the names on ballot-sheets year after year. For those who need a backgrounder, here it goes.

Aristocrats

Patiala

Capt. Amarinder Singh has been the Chief Minister of Punjab twice: elected in 2002 and in 2017. He is the son of Patiala Maharaja Yadavinder Singh. He is married to Preneet Kaur Kahlon, a three-term MP and Minister of State for External Affairs in the Manmohan Singh government. She is the daughter of Gyan Singh Kahlon ICS, long-ago Chief Secretary of Punjab. Preneet Kaur is the sister of Geetinder Kaur Kahlon, wife of Simranjeet Singh Mann, founder and head of SAD (Amritsar), a hard-line Sikh political party that now consists of Mann's friends and relatives. Simranjeet Singh Mann is the son of Bhupinder Singh Mann, member of the Constituent Assembly who refused to accept the proposed Constitution on the grounds that minorities were inadequately protected.

Amarinder's son, Raninder, has contested for both Lok Sabha and Assembly elections: defeated both times.

More princely-political connections. Nirvan, Amarinder's grandson (son of daughter Jay Inder and Gurpal Singh), in 2017, married Mriganka (her paternal grandfather was Kashmir Maharaja and Union Minister Karan Singh; her maternal grandfather was Gwalior Maharaja and Union Minister Madhavrao Scindia). Another grandson of Amarinder, Angad, is married to Aparajita, daughter of erstwhile Bushahr Maharaja and Himachal Pradesh Chief Minister Virbhadra Singh.

Badals

Raghuraj Singh Dhillon (big landlord of Village Abul Khurana, near Malout in Muktsar district, Punjab) had two sons—Prakash Singh and Gurdas Singh. Badal is the name of a village near Abul Khurana. Both sons preferred to be called 'Badal' rather than Dhillon.

Parkash Singh has a son, Sukhbir Singh. He was Deputy Chief Minister when his father was chief minister, and is now the president of the SAD. Parkash Singh's daughter, Parneet is married to Adesh Partap Kairon, Adesh Partap, now an Akali, belongs to a distinguished Congress lineage. Father: Surinder

Singh Kairon, MP and MLA; Grandfather: Partap Singh Kairon, Chief Minister of Punjab 1956–1964. Sukhbir is married to Harsimrat Kaur. Harsimrat is the daughter of Satyajit Singh Majithia, long-ago Union Deputy Defence Minister, and granddaughter of Surjit Singh Majithia MP and long-ago ambassador to Nepal. Her brother is Bikram Singh Majithia, Akali and ex MLA and minister.

Gurdas Singh Badal's son, Manpreet Singh, also went into politics. First elected as an MLA as an Akali and became Finance Minister. Formed his own short-lived Punjab People's Party and endured a couple of years in the wilderness. In 2017, he returned to the Vidhan Sabha as a Congressman and is again the Finance Minister.

Ex-Akali MLA and minister Janmeja Singh Sekhon is related to Parkash Kaur, late wife of Parkash Singh Badal. Another cousin, politician Mahesh Inder Singh, is on the Congress side of the fence.

Kairons

Nihal Singh Kairon, Raj-era Singh Sabha activist and women's education proponent, was not a politician but close enough to political activity to point his son Partap Singh in that direction. Partap Singh (Nehru era) ultimately rose to be Congress Chief Minister of Punjab.

Partap Singh's son, Surinder Singh, became an MP, initially as a Congressman, later as an Akali. Another son, Gurinder Singh, swore off politics after his maiden campaign on the Congress ticket ended in defeat.

Pratap Singh Kairon's niece, Gurbinder Kaur, married Harcharan Singh Brar, who later became Congress Chief Minister of Punjab.

Partap Singh is the grandfather of Adesh Partap Singh (see Badals) and Raman Kaur, wife of Congress ex MLA Jassi Khangura.

Brars

Balwant Singh Brar was a big landlord of Village Sarai Naga in District Muktsar. His son, Harcharan Singh Brar joined the Congress and was returned to the Vidhan Sabha five times. He rose to become the Chief Minister of Punjab and Governor of Odisha and Haryana.

Harcharan Singh had a son, Adesh Kanwarjit Singh Brar (known as Sunny), who became Congress MLA, and a daughter Kanwaljit Kaur (Bubli), who unsuccessfully contested for a Vidhan Sabha seat in 1996. Sunny's widow is Karan Brar, also a Congress MLA. Karan Brar is the sister of Harpriya Kaur, wife of Malvinder Singh, brother of Capt. Amarinder Singh (see Patiala). Karan Kaur's son, Karanbir Singh, is the sarpanch of the Brar's ancestral village and likely to swiftly rise in the ranks of the Punjab Congress Party.

All the above belong to the Jat caste.

Squires and Gentry

Punjab's active politicians who are not the children, nephews/nieces, spouses of MP/MLA parents are the exception in Punjab. This is exactly the problem when it comes to enumerating Punjab's political scions. Although scores are named, yet others may be inadvertently omitted. If they are left off the list, they are sure to take it to heart.

Out of the 117 members of the Vidhan Sabha who were elected in 2017, 43 MLAs (36.75%) are closely related to persons who are or were MLAs or MPs. Candidates belonging to politically connected families who were defeated in the 2017 Assembly election have been ignored. Also, no mention for MLAs, who, as per media reports, are pushing to get tickets or party posts for their kin. Including those categories would produce a list longer than Methuselah's whiskers.

Members of Punjab Legislative Assembly Elected in 2017 (29.25% hail from political families)

S. No.	Constituency	Name	Party	Connection
1.	Sujanpur	Dinesh Singh	BJP	–
2.	Bhoa	Joginder Pal	INC	–
3.	Pathankot	Amit Vij	INC	s/o Anil Vij, Punjab Congress Committee member
4.	Gurdaspur	Barindermeet Singh Pahra	INC	grandson Kartar Singh Pahra, Akali MLA
5.	Dina Nagar	Aruna Chaudhary	INC	daughter-in-law of Jai Muni Chaudhary, MLA
6.	Qadian	Fatehjang Singh Bajwa	INC	Brother of Pratap Singh Bajwa MP & s/o Satnam Singh Bajwa, three-time Punjab MLA and Minister
7.	Batala	Lakhbir Singh Lodhinangal	SAD	–
8.	Sri Hargobindpur	Balwinder Singh Laddi	INC	–

(continued)

(continued)

S. No.	Constituency	Name	Party	Connection
9.	Fatehgarh Churian	Tript Rajinder Singh Bajwa	INC	s/o Gurbachan Singh Bajwa, minister in Bhargava government
10.	Dera Baba Nanak	Sukhjinder Singh Randhawa	INC	s/o Santokh Singh Randhawa, one-time Punjab Congress Chief
11.	Ajnala	Harpartap Singh	INC	s/o Harcharan Singh Ajnala, MLA speaker
12.	Raja Sansi	Sukhbinder Singh Sarkaria	INC	s/o Narinder Singh Sarkaria, veteran Congress politician
13.	Majitha	Bikram Singh Majithia	SAD	Satyajit Singh Majithia MP ex Dy Defence Minister, younger brother of Bathinda MP, Harsimrat Kaur Badal and brother-in-law of ex Dy CM Sukhbir Singh Badal. Married to Ganieve Grewal, niece of Radha Soami sect guru
14.	Jandiala	Sukhwinder Singh Danny	INC	s/o Sardool Singh MLA
15.	Amritsar North	Sunil Dutti	INC	–
16.	Amritsar West	Raj Kumar Verka	INC	–
17.	Amritsar Central	Om Parkash Soni	INC	–

Normalcy

S. No.	Constituency	Name	Party	Connection
18.	Amritsar East	Navjot Singh Sidhu	INC	–
19.	Amritsar South	Inderbir Singh Bolaria	INC	s/o Raminder Singh Bolaria, MLA
20.	Attari	Tarsem Singh D.C.	INC	–
21.	Tarn Taran	Dr Dharambir Agnihotri	INC	–
22.	Khem Karan	Sukhpal Singh Bhullar	INC	s/o Gurchet Singh Bhullar MLA, minister
23.	Patti	Harminder Singh Gill	INC	–
24.	Khadoor Sahib	Ramanjeet Singh Sahota Sikki	INC	–
25.	Baba Bakala	Santokh Singh	INC	–
26.	Bholath	Sukhpal Singh Khaira	AAP	s/o Sukhjinder Singh Khaira MLA, minister
27.	Kapurthala	Rana Gurjit Singh	INC	–
28.	Sultanpur Lodhi	Navtej Singh Cheema	INC	s/o Gurmail Singh Cheema MLA
29.	Phagwara	Som Parkash	BJP	–
30.	Phillaur	Baldev Singh Khaira	SAD	–
31.	Nakodar	Gurpratap Singh Wadala	SAD	s/o Kuldip Singh Wadala MLA
32.	Shahkot	Ajit Singh Kohar	SAD	–

(continued)

(continued)

S. No.	Constituency	Name	Party	Connection
33.	Shahkot (bypoll in May 2018)	Hardev Singh Ladi	INC	–
34.	Kartarpur	Chaudhary Surinder Singh	INC	Nephew of Santokh Singh Chaudhary, Congress MP
35.	Jalandhar West	Sushil Kumar Rinku	INC	–
36.	Jalandhar Central	Rajinder Beri	INC	–
37.	Jalandhar North	Avtar Singh Junior	INC	s/o Avtar Henry, MLA & minister
38.	Jalandhar Cantt	Pargat Singh Powar	INC	–
39.	Adampur	Pawan Kumar Tinu	SAD	–
40.	Mukerian	Rajnish Kumar Babbi	INC	s/o Kewal Krishan, MLA, ex speaker & minister
41.	Dasuya	Arun Dogra	INC	s/o Ramesh Chander Dogra, MLA & ex Dy Speaker
42.	Urmar	Sangat Singh Gilzian	INC	–
43.	Sham Chaurasi	Pawan Kumar Adia	INC	–
44.	Hoshiarpur	Sunder Sham Arora	INC	–
45.	Chabbewal	Dr Raj Kumar	INC	–

S. No.	Constituency	Name	Party	Connection
46.	Garhshankar	Jai Krishan	AAP	–
47.	Banga (SC)	Sukhwinder Kumar	SAD	–
48.	Nawanshahr	Angad Singh	INC	s/o Gur Iqbal Kaur Babli (MLA) & Parkash Singh (MLA), who was nephew of Dilbagh Singh (MLA)
49.	Balachaur	Darshan Lal	INC	–
50.	Anandpur Sahib	Rana K. P. Singh	INC	–
51.	Rupnagar	Amarjit Singh Sandoa	AAP	–
52.	Chamkaur Sahib	Charanjit Singh Channi	INC	s/o Dilbagh Singh, MLA
53.	Kharar	Kanwar Sandhu	AAP	–
54.	SAS Nagar	Balbir Singh Sidhu	INC	–
55.	Bassi Pathana	Gurpreet Singh	INC	–
56.	Fatehgarh Sahib	Kuljit Singh Nagra	INC	–
57.	Amloh	Randeep Singh	INC	–
58.	Khanna	Gurkirat Singh Kotli	INC	Grandson of Beant Singh Punjab CM
59.	Samrala	Amrik Singh Dhillon	INC	–
60.	Sahnewal	Sharanjit Singh Dhillon	SAD	–
61.	Ludhiana East	Sanjeev Talwar	INC	–

(continued)

(continued)

S. No.	Constituency	Name	Party	Connection
62.	Ludhiana South	Balvinder Singh Bains	LIP	Simarjit Singh Bains' brother
63.	Atam Nagar	Simarjeet Singh Bains	LIP	Balwinder Singh Bains' brother
64.	Ludhiana Central	Surinder Kumar Dawar	INC	–
65.	Ludhiana West	Bharat Bhushan Ashu	INC	–
66.	Ludhiana North	Rakesh Pandey	INC	s/o Joginder Pal Pandey, MLA
67.	Gill	Kuldeep Singh Vaid	INC	–
68.	Payal	Lakhvir Singh Lakha	INC	Protégé of Tej Parkash Singh, ex Congress minister, son of assassinated CM Beant Singh
69.	Dakha	Harvinder Singh Phoolka	AAP	–
70.	Dakha	Bypoll TBD		–
71.	Raikot	Jagtar Singh Jagga Hissowal	AAP	–
72.	Jagraon	Saravjit Kaur Manuke	AAP	–
73.	Nihal Singhwala	Manjit Singh	AAP	–
74.	Bagha Purana	Darshan Singh Brar	INC	–

Normalcy

S. No.	Constituency	Name	Party	Connection
75.	Moga	Harjot Kamal Singh	INC	–
76.	Dharamkot	Sukhjit Singh Kaka Lohgarh	INC	–
77.	Zira	Kulbir Singh	INC	s/o Inderjit Singh Zira, Congress Kisan Cell Chief
78.	Firozpur City	Parminder Singh Pinki	INC	–
79.	Firozpur Rural	Satkar Kaur	INC	w/o Jasmail Singh Laddi Gehri, member Ferozepur zila parishad
80.	Guru Har Sahai	Gurmeet Singh Sodhi	INC	–
81.	Jalalabad	Sukhbir Singh Badal	SAD	s/o Parkash Singh Badal, MLA, MP & CM
82.	Fazilka	Davinder Singh Ghubaya	INC	s/o Sher Singh Ghubaya, MP
83.	Abohar	Arun Narang	BJP	–
84.	Balluana	Nathu Ram	INC	–
85.	Lambi	Parkash Singh Badal	SAD	–
86.	Gidderbaha	Amrinder Singh Raja Warring	INC	–
87.	Malout	Ajaib Singh Bhatti	INC	s/o Late Comrade Arjan Singh, CPI cadre, contested from Nihasinghwala

(continued)

(continued)

S. No.	Constituency	Name	Party	Connection
88.	Muktsar	Kanwarjit Singh	SAD	–
89.	Faridkot	Kushaldeep Singh Dhillon	INC	s/o Jasmat singh Dhillon, MLA
90.	Kotkapura	Kultar Singh Sandhwan	AAP	Zail Singh's grandnephew
91.	Jaitu	Baldev Singh	AAP	–
92.	Rampura Phul	Gurpreet Singh Kangar	INC	–
93.	Bhucho Mandi	Pritam Singh Kotbhai	INC	–
94.	Bathinda Urban	Manpreet Singh Badal	INC	Ex CM Parkash Singh Badal's nephew
95.	Bathinda Rural	Rupinder Kaur Ruby	AAP	–
96.	Talwandi Sabo	Professor Baljinder Kaur	AAP	–
97.	Maur	Jagdev Singh	AAP	–
98.	Mansa	Nazar Singh Manshahia	AAP	–
99.	Sardulgarh	Dilraj Singh	SAD	s/o Balwinder Singh Bhundar, MLA & MP
100.	Budhlada	Budh Ram	AAP	–
101.	Lehra	Parminder Singh Dhindsa	SAD	s/o Sukhdev Singh Dhindsa, MLA, MP, & minister
102.	Dirba	Harpal Singh Cheema	AAP	–
103.	Sunam	Aman Arora	AAP	d/o Bhagwan Dass, MLA

Normalcy

S. No.	Constituency	Name	Party	Connection
104.	Bhadaur	Pirmal Singh Dhaula	AAP	–
105.	Barnala	Gurmeet Singh Meet Haher	AAP	–
106.	Mehal Kalan	Kulwant Singh Pandori	AAP	–
107.	Malerkotla	Razia Sultana	INC	w/o Md Mustafa, Director General of Police (DGP) Punjab
108.	Amargarh	Surjit Singh Dhiman	INC	–
109.	Dhuri	Dalvir Singh Goldy	INC	–
110.	Sangrur	Vijay Inder Singla	INC	s/o Sant Ram Singla, MP and MLA
111.	Nabha	Sadhu Singh	INC	–
112.	Patiala Rural	Brahm Mohindra	INC	–
113.	Rajpura	Hardial Singh Kamboj	INC	–
114.	Dera Bassi	Narinder Kumar Sharma	SAD	–
115.	Ghanaur	Madan Lal Jalalpur	INC	Lal Singh' nephew, Congress ex-minister, present Chairman Punjab Pradesh Congress Committee (PPCC), Election Management Committee & Mandi Board

(continued)

(continued)

S. No.	Constituency	Name	Party	Connection
116.	Sanour	Harinder Pal Singh Chandumajra	SAD	s/o Prem Singh Chandumajra, MLA & MP
117.	Patiala	Amarinder Singh	INC	–
118.	Samana	Rajinder Singh	INC	s/o Lal Singh, MLA & minister
119.	Shutrana	Nirmal Singh	INC	Retired HC judge; Akali MP Paramjit Kaur Gulshan's husband, who is the daughter of Dhanna Singh Gulshan, Akali leader and union minister

Punjab Lok Sabha 13 Seats Total

1977 General Election 6th Lok Sabha		1980 General Election 7th Lok Sabha		1985 General Election 8th Lok Sabha		1989 General Election 9th Lok Sabha		1992 General Election 10th Lok Sabha		1996 General Election 11th Lok Sabha		1998 General Election 12th Lok Sabha		1999 General Election 13th Lok Sabha		2004 General Election 14th Lok Sabha		2009 General Election 15th Lok Sabha		2014 General Election 16th Lok Sabha	
Turnout 70.1%		Turnout 62.7%		Turnout 67.4%		Turnout 62.7%		Turnout 24.0%		Turnout 62.2%		Turnout 60.1%		Turnout 56.1%		Turnout 61.6%		Turnout 69.8%		Turnout 70.6%	
BLD	3	INC	12	INC	5	BSP	1	BSP	1	BSP	3	BJP	3	BJP	1	BJP	3	BJP	1	BJP	2
CPM	1	SAD	1	SAD	7	INC	2	INC	12	INC	2	IND	1	CPI	1	INC	2	INC	8	INC	3
SAD	9			BJP	0	IND	1	Others	3	SAD	8	JD	1	INC	8	SAD	8	SAD	4	AAP	4
						JD	1					SAD	2	SAD	2					SAD	4
						SAD-M	6					INC	0	SAD-M	1						

Source: Wikipedia [Year] Punjab General Election

Undivided Pb: 154 seats		Punjab Vidhan Sabha: 117 Seats																				
1962		1967		1969		1972		1977		1980		1985		1992		1997		2002		2007		2012		2017	
Turnout 63.44%		Turnout 71.18%		Turnout 72.27%		Turnout 68.63%		Turnout 65.37%		Turnout 64.33%		Turnout 67.5%		Turnout 23.4%		Turnout 68.7%		Turnout 65.1%		Turnout 75.5%		Turnout 78.6%		Turnout 76.6%	
Congress	90	Congress	48	SAD	43	Congress	66	SAD	58	Congress	63	SAD	73	Congress	87	SAD	75	BJP	3	BJP	19	Congress	46	Congress
SAD	19	Akali Dal Sant Fateh Singh	24	Congress	38	SAD	24	Janata Party	25	SAD	37	Congress	32	BSP	9	BJP	18	CPI	2	Congress	44	SAD	56	AAP
CPI	9	Jan Sangh	9	Jan Sangh	8	CPI	10	Congress	17	CPI	9	BJP	6	INC	6	CPI	14	Congress	62	SAD	48	BJP	12	SAD
Jan Sangh	8	CPI	5	CPI	4	CPI-M	1	CPI-M	8	CPIM	5	CPI	1	CPI	4	CPI	2	SAD	41	IND	5	IND	3	BJP
Socialist Party	4	CPI-M	3	CPI-M	2	IND	3	CPI	7	BJP	1	IND	4	IND	4	IND	6	IND	9					LIP
Swatantra Party	3	Republican Party of India	3	Socialist Party	2			IND	2	IND	2			Others	7	Others	2							NOTA	0.7%
Haryana Lok Samiti	2	Akali Dal Master Tara Singh	3	Janta Party	1																				
IND	18	Socialist Party	1	Praja Socialist Party	1																				
		IND	9	Swatantra Party	1																				
				IND	4																				

Source: Wikipedia [Year] Punjab Legislative Assembly Election

Notes

1. Author's personal recollection.
2. Tripathi, 'Punjab's Slowing Economy'.
3. http://www.insafbulletin.net/archives/604
4. Auspicious sight of a deity or a holy person.
5. Singh, 'Kin of Former, Serving MLAs'.
6. For a meticulously detailed and authoritative account of the Punjab's AAP adventure, see Ram, *Third Alternative in Punjab*.
7. Judge, *Insurrection to Agitations*; Singh, *Communism*; Jasmail Singh Brar, *Communist Party in Punjab*.
8. Singh, *Bahujan Samaj Party in Punjab*.
9. Mukherjee, *A Centenary History*. Former President of India Pranab Mukherjee is the Chairman of the Editorial Board.

2

Due Process: Punjab

India has the benefit of being a very big country, and the government has been lucky so far: In the 70-year history of modern India, it has had to deal with uproar in only one or two corners at a time. In the early 1980s, the uproar corner was Punjab and to a lesser extent Assam; political games were the order of the day. In Punjab, reckless talk escalated and acts of violence and provocation became more severe and more frequent. When the Golden Temple was attacked, it wasn't a game anymore.

The gamers found themselves facing more than a crore of people whose religious sensibilities were outraged. The misguided and heavy-handed mopping up that followed Operation Bluestar radicalized more young men than Bhindranwale ever had.[1] As the situation deteriorated, the government concluded that it would take a whole lot more than the Indian Penal Code to get the lid clamped on again. The end justified the means. The problem is that dictatorial means inevitably diminish the legitimacy of a democratic government. But, at that time, crisis management was top priority and legitimacy occupied a very distant back seat.

In Punjab, between 1984 and 1994, the provisions of 'terrorist' laws, proclamations and ordinances encouraged police and other security forces to believe that they could literally get away with murder. But the story of a crime does not end in the mortuary, it passes on to a whole new life in the courts. To this day, cases of murder, abduction, rape, extortion and wrongful arrest are still dragging through the courts. The accused are not militants, they are the police. For many victims of that era, the 'Punjab problem' is not over and it's not fixed.

Freedom of Repression

To start from the beginning, although the union government enjoyed overwhelming force vis-à-vis militants, it knew that insurgency succeeds if it is able to make people doubt whether the government's writ runs or not. The longer a conflict goes on, the greater the chance of that doubt taking root. The provisions of the Indian Penal Code involve many niceties of due process: restrictions on how long a person can be held without charge, insistence on production before a magistrate, provisions for bail and narrow view of what constitutes reasonable cause for arrest.

Shaken by the rage loosed by Bluestar, the union government was convinced that unfettered freedom of repression was the need of the hour and the government would have it if it had to trample every provision of the Constitution to get it. By ordinance and by legislation, one draconian measure after another came into existence.

Democracy and the Law

It is possible to get all the way through school, college and university without ever hearing of John Locke, 17th-century philosopher and the Big Daddy of Democracy Theory. Even highly educated people may be unable to tick off the characteristics that define and give legitimacy to a democratic political system. But you don't need a PhD to understand that when the government gives itself the power to deprive *someone* of fundamental rights and the protection of law, *everyone* becomes vulnerable.

The minute the citizen gets the chance to vote out an imperious and over-reaching government, he will. From 1975 to 1977, civil liberties were swept aside and the then Prime Minister Indira Gandhi assumed dictatorial powers. The Emergency ended with a general election in 1977 in which voters drove her and her party from power. But draconian measures did not disappear with Mrs Gandhi's Emergency. Rather, over the past 40 years, the government has expanded its powers, all at the cost of constitutional protection to the citizen and legitimacy of the government itself.

Elected representatives swear to uphold the Constitution, that is, protect the rights of the citizens and the rule of law. If they fail in this duty, the citizen looks to another wing of the government, the judiciary. Rule of law, implemented, upheld and protected by a respected and credible judiciary is the anchor of a democratic government. The role of the judiciary was enunciated more than 250 years ago by a French philosopher, Montesquieu. He said,

> The court holds not only individuals but also the government and its agencies accountable under law. It has the power to stop any illegal or unconstitutional act committed by parliament, or any governmental agency. It protects even the humblest and may not turn away from any man. It is bound to protect fundamental rights, including the security of life and property. Its trials are open and, so that the law be made clear and known to all, every judgment is a public record. The court is independent: any attempt to influence the court is itself an offense.

What happens if public trust in judges and the judiciary in general is eroded? A judge may be intelligent and well versed in the law but who will accept his judgements if he is widely seen as biased, partisan and corrupt? When the credibility of the judiciary goes, democracy gives way to brute force—the police state, martial law, goonda raj.

However, a citizen can't relax just because there is 'rule of law'. Dictators promulgate laws to stifle any challenge to their rule, including challenges that are purely symbolic. For example, in 1989, Deng Xiaoping ordered the army to remove pro-democracy students from Beijing's Tienanmen Square. The initial crackdown was brutal and subsequent suppression of dissent was intense. The dissenters fell silent but did not cease; rather, they became devious. The name Xiaoping sounds like another Chinese word meaning 'small bottle'. Small broken bottles began to appear on street corners as an expression of contempt for Deng. A law was soon in place to take care of suspected bottle-breakers. Since the repressive laws of a dictatorship are applied uniformly across society, such governments claim to be enforcing 'rule of law'. Years behind bars for breaking a bottle? There is no law that says a law has to be reasonable. The law can be insane and still be the law.

Big Stick: TADA and POTA

The first of these laws was the Terrorist and Disruptive Activities (Prevention) Act, or TADA. It came into effect on 23 May 1985, was renewed three times and finally allowed to lapse in 1995 after TADA abuses became too flagrant to ignore. You didn't have to actually do anything to fall into the TADA net; it was enough to directly or indirectly advocate insurrection or secession.

TADA provisions went far beyond normal law. While the police was still obliged to produce a detainee before a magistrate within

24 hours and seek police remand, TADA stipulated that the detainee might be held in police custody up to 60 days (greater risk of torture). Moreover, the detainee need not be produced before a judicial magistrate; an executive magistrate was good enough. An executive magistrate is an official of police and administrative service and not answerable to the High Court. Earlier the maximum remand could be only of 15 days. Under the IPC, an accused has a right to bail if no chargesheet is submitted within 60 or 90 days depending on the category of the crime—but even for murder, the accused has a right to bail after 90 days. Under TADA, the period was increased to 180 days and allowed a further 180 days with permission of the court. In other words, a person could be held for 360 days without even knowing what evidence the police had against them. That made it almost impossible to even file a bail application. The cases were heard in special TADA courts and the trials could be held in camera with the identities of the witnesses kept secret. Confessions made to police officers were admissible as evidence, with the burden of proof being on the accused to prove his innocence. A person found guilty could appeal only to the Supreme Court. Police officers were empowered to attach the properties of the accused.

Hussein Zaidi writes that during TADA's decade of operation, 76,161 people throughout India were arrested under its provisions.[2] Twenty-five per cent of these cases were dropped by the police without any charges being framed. Only 35 per cent of the cases were brought to trial, of which 95 per cent resulted in acquittals. Less than 2 per cent of those arrested were convicted.

Looking at just one year (1990) in Gujarat, 5,000 were arrested under TADA (most of them Muslims); in Punjab, the number was 1,600; and in Jammu and Kashmir, it was 2,000.

TADA was replaced by Prevention of Terrorism Act (POTA), 2002. This Act was initially defeated in the Rajya Sabha and could only get through when it was put before a joint session of parliament.

POTA took over most of the TADA provisions but expanded the definition of terrorist act to 'intent to threaten the unity, integrity, security or sovereignty of India'. TADA vaguely referred to 'intent to overawe the government'. POTA also swept up anyone who was a member of an 'unlawful association'.

Bigger Stick: UAPA

POTA lasted only two years but was replaced by an even more repressive law: the Unlawful Activities Prevention Act (UAPA). Initially, UAPA was introduced in 1967 to bring India closer to the security paradigm set out by the international Financial Action Task Force (an intergovernmental organization keeping watch over money laundering and terrorism funding). With one amendment after another (all enacted during Congress regimes), it has become the ideal instrument with which to suppress legal dissent. Lacking the checks that characterize regular criminal law, it does much more than simply allow the state to deal with terrorism-related acts that threaten the country's territorial sovereignty. UAPA is all of TADA, all of POTA, plus it broadened the definition of terrorist act still further. Now it's any act that makes use of 'bombs, dynamite … or any other substances … of a hazardous nature', or 'any other means of whatever nature'. Speak, write, publish, organize, mobilize … aren't all these activities 'likely to threaten' the government or 'likely to strike terror in (certain segments of) the people'. The word 'likely' is a veritable barn door through which anything can pass.

You can be arrested by any officer on the basis of his 'personal knowledge', or information furnished by another person, or information 'from any document, article or any other thing which may furnish evidence of the commission'.

Police can hold you without charge for six months.

You can be denied bail if the court believes that accusations against you are prima facie true. (The purpose of a bail hearing is not to pre-judge the accused but to determine whether the accused will run away or commit another crime while on bail.)

When you are interrogated and when you stand trial, you do *not* have the right to remain silent.

UAPA grants immunity from prosecution to central and state governments and their employees.

UAPA is not a time-bound Act and allows only limited judicial review by the judiciary. It's permanent.

Given its sweeping provisions, it is the best possible law to invoke when the government wants to crack down on activists, lawyers, writers or anyone who openly, loudly and persistently disagrees with it.

The government takes the plea that the *extra*ordinary provisions of the UAPA are required by *extra*ordinary threats facing the nation. What has become ordinary over the years is the resort to Stalinesque laws to bypass due process and the Fundamental Rights set out in the Constitution.

Water under the Bridge?

For those who think that by now Punjab's troubles are long forgotten, it would be reasonable to suppose that over the past 35 years all the cases would be cleared up one way or another. But here's a little collection of headlines from just last year:

> Operation Bluestar Jodhpur 'detainees': 34 yrs on, ₹4.5 cr compensation for 40 Sikhs, Punjab agrees to pay half but Centre files challenge (*Hindustan Times*, 19 June 2018)
>
> Will compensate Jodhpur detainees if Centre fails to pay its share: Captain (*Hindustan Times*, 19 June 2018)
>
> Operation Bluestar: Amarinder urges Centre to withdraw appeal in compensation case (*Business Standard*, 20 June 2018)

'Jodhpur detainees' might not ring a bell for the average reader. Briefly, 375 unarmed men, women and children were found in the

Golden Temple when the Army entered on 6 June 1984. These people did not look dangerous, but the Army took no chances and had them all arrested anyway. In his book, *My Life as a Police Officer*, Julio Ribeiro (Punjab DGP 1986–1989) explained:

> Many of them were not connected with Bhindranwale or the terrorists. They were there merely to offer prayers on the occasion of the anniversary of the martyrdom of the sixth Sikh guru. It was unfortunate that the operation was undertaken on that very day. Yet, since those who were arrested had been found by the Army in the temple, they were all bracketed together in a conspiracy case and charged with 'waging war against the State.' As it was not possible to separate the accused at a late stage of the investigation after the charge sheet had been filed, even the innocent were kept in custody along with the hard-core extremists.

All 375 of them were sent to Jodhpur Central Jail, and there they remained for the next 4–5 years. They were released in three batches, between March 1989 and July 1991. That's a minimum of four years behind bars for the crime of being in the wrong place at the wrong time.

Of these, 224 detainees had appealed for compensation in the lower court, alleging 'wrongful detention and torture', but they failed to get any relief in 2011. Out of these, 40 of the detainees went in appeal to the District and Sessions Court, Amritsar, and, in April 2017, were awarded ₹4 lakh each as compensation with 6 per cent interest (from the date of filing of the appeal to payment of compensation). The compensation for all the 40 petitioners, including interest, worked out to ₹4.5 crore. The Punjab government gave an undertaking to the court to pay half the amount, but the Central government appealed against the order in the Punjab and Haryana High Court.

In July of that year, the Centre withdrew its appeal.[3] In the absence of any further news coverage, it is not known whether the victims finally got compensation.

Due Process: Punjab

One of the things that swung the case in the detainees' favour was lack of evidence that any warning had been given. In his ruling, the Amritsar District and Sessions Judge Gurbir Singh termed the arrests 'illegal'. He wrote:

> There is no evidence that army made any announcements asking ordinary civilians to leave Golden Temple complex before launching the operation in 1984 ...There is no written record of any public announcement by the civil authorities requesting the people to come out the complex. No log of vehicle used for making such announcements is there.... The event underlines the human rights violations by troops during the operation.[4]

An additional bit of information. More than 100 of the Jodhpur detainees got speedier justice in the highest court of all, meaning they died before an earthly court could find in their favour.

A Slap on the Wrist

Quiz Time. In the Preamble to the Constitution of India, what is Number 1 on the list of things that 'We, the people of India,... secure to all its citizens'? The answer is 'justice'. But like the other shining ideals promised in the Preamble, justice isn't handed out for the asking.

In Punjab, there are around 100 cases of abduction and murder in which the accused are officers of the Punjab Police. As reported in *The Tribune* on 3 September 2018, 'Data gathered from the police shows that the Central Bureau of Investigation (CBI) booked 188 cops between 1993 and 1998'.[5] The charges against them include abduction, murder, extortion and rape, and wrongful arrest.

From the 2018 judgement on the Jodhpur detainees, we see how long and difficult the pursuit of justice has been. It is not just two or three cases either. If we were to examine every case before the court as of 2019, the resulting book would be fatter than a volume of the

All India Recorder and just as heavy going. Instead, we present a small number of representative cases. A certain amount of small detail cannot be avoided, but we have tried to keep explanations as concise as possible.

Death of a Sarpanch

Kuljit Singh Dhatt was not an impulsive youngster looking for trouble. He was the Sarpanch of his village, the director of Bhogpur Sugar Mill, and on the boards of a school and a college. He was also a relative of Shaheed Bhagat Singh. To be specific, Kuljeet Singh's brother Harbhajan Singh was married to the daughter of Parkash Kaur. Parkash Kaur was the younger sister of Shaheed Bhagat Singh.

Dhatt disappeared in 1989, and, for the next 30 years, his family fought a legal battle to bring those responsible to justice.

- Thirty years in the courts, appeals in the case are still being heard
- Twenty three years to reach a judgement
- Five years imprisonment; this is the sentence handed down to policemen found guilty of murder

Here's how it unfolded.

1989. July 23: A police party led by Deputy Superintendent of Police (DSP) Ajit Singh Sandhu burst into a house in Village Garhi and took away Kuljit Singh Dhatt and several other men. They claimed Kuljit Singh had concealed some weapons, and he would be made to reveal their hiding place. A witness informed Kuljit's brother Harbhajan, who traced him to Gardiwala Police Station. There he met DSP Ajit Sandhu who told him, 'We have let the rest go. We have done with Kuljit Singh, what we wanted to do.... We aren't going to return the body. Do what you want'. Harbhajan turned to Superintendent of Police (Operations) or SP(O) S. P. S. Basra, but the SP(O) said, 'Did you not understand what Ajit Singh said'. The police repeated these admissions to Harbhajan Singh on 29 July.

September: After appeals to government officials fell on deaf ears, Kuljit's wife Gurmeet Kaur and Parkash Kaur, filed a habeas corpus petition with the Supreme Court, calling for an inquiry and suspension of the accused police officers.

1990. Supreme Court ordered the Punjab and Haryana High Court to appoint a commissioner to probe Dhatt's disappearance and report in three months.

1991. Retired Justice H. L. Randev was appointed. At the first hearing, the Dhatt family told him that police officials threatened to kill them if they did not withdraw from the inquiry. Commissioner requested transfer of the police; police fought the commission at every step. After an eight-month battle and another petition to the Supreme Court, the policemen were transferred.

1992. Commission began collecting evidence.

1993. Randev report concluded that Dhatt was murdered by Ajit S. Sandhu (who committed suicide in 1997, after serving as Senior Superintendent of Police [SSP]), Jaspal Singh (currently serving life imprisonment for murder of human rights activist Jaswant Singh Khalra), Sardool Singh (died in 2008), S. P. S. Basra (retired in 2013 as Deputy Inspector General) and constable Sita Ram.

1996. Supreme Court accepted Randev Commission findings, rejected State of Punjab on account of minimal information, rebuked State of Punjab for lack of seriousness, and ordered investigation by a DIG. The job fell to DIG J. P. Birdi.

All this time, as per police record, Dhatt was an accused in a murder case. Even though Dhatt was abducted, no FIR was

The Legacy of Militancy in Punjab

registered regarding his abduction or murder or disappearance. It was only in 1996, after the Supreme Court directed inquiry found evidence against the police officers and the Supreme Court accepted the report, that directions were given to register an FIR for Dhatt's disappearance.[6] S. P. S. Basra, Ajit Singh Sandhu and Jaspal Singh were suspended, Sita Ram was in judicial custody for another case, and Sardool Singh had retired. Months later, Harbhajan Singh Dhatt's affidavit told Supreme Court the following:

1. The DIG Birdi's charge sheet substituted Section 365 (kidnapping/abducting with intent to secretly and wrongfully confine the person) for Section 364 (kidnapping/abducting with intent to murder) as 365 carries maximum sentence of seven years and 364 carries maximum life sentence.
2. The DIG didn't question the accused police officers or members of the alleged police team that went for recovery of weapons, and thus failed to identify additional accused. The five police officers were arrested and released on bail.

1997. Sessions court allowed Dhatt family application for summoning additional accused but accused appealed to the High Court. This application remains stayed to date.

1998. Additional Sessions Judge, Hoshiarpur, framed charges under Section 364 and other sections. Before witnesses could begin testimony, accused contested sanction to prosecute on the grounds that the state was under Punjab Disturbed Areas Act, and only the central government could sanction. (Under law, sanction by either government was unnecessary, since the police officials committed crimes that were not recognized as part of their official duties.) Punjab and Haryana High Court stayed the trial.

13 Years

2011. Supreme Court granted Dhatt family petition for speedy trial; asked Punjab and Haryana High Court to render judgment by March. In August, High Court dismissed policemen's petition.

2012. Trial started in Hoshiarpur Sessions Court.

2014. Witnesses completed their testimony. Judge who heard the testimony got transferred and new judge found three living police officials guilty. They were sentenced to five years imprisonment. Convicted men appealed against conviction. Dhatt family appealed against light sentences. After 6 months in jail, ret. DIG S. P. S. Basra and ex-Inspector Sita Ram were released on bail.

2019. Judgements on the appeals are awaited and the convicted men are free on bail.

Two mysteries remain in the Dhatt case: What did the police do with the victim's body (it was never found) and why did DSP Ajit Sandhu go after Dhatt in the first place. Courts sifted the evidence in this case for more than 20 years, and it was never averred that Dhatt had committed any terrorist crime, harboured terrorists, financed terrorists or sympathized with terrorists. The Dhatts were a well-to-do family; they not only farmed but also ran a school and a college in their village. Incidentally, these institution were confiscated and never been returned to the family. Was Dhatt's murder an extortion gone wrong? Another CBI case in which DSP Ajit Singh Sandhu was charged lends weight to that suspicion.

In August 1992, two years after the murder of Sant Chanan Singh of Village Thathian, district Tarn Taran, the Punjab and Haryana High Court heard the petition of his wife. She said that her late husband paid ₹10 lakh to Ajit Singh Sandhu to spare his family, and, when he could not pay more, Sandhu had him tortured and killed along with his three brothers and two brothers-in-law.[7]

Chanan Singh was known as the 'karsewa sant' because he was involved in the construction of gurdwaras all over the country. Since he managed all the donated building funds, it's easy to see why he might be regarded as a 'plump pigeon' by an extortionist.

The CBI was called in to investigate, and, in August 2001, it presented five challans against 13 police officials including Tarn Taran SSP Ajit Singh Sandhu, and several deputy superintendents of police, inspectors, sub-inspectors and assistant sub-inspectors posted in Tarn Taran in 1992–1993. The CBI probe not only supported the wife's accusation regarding the murder of Sant Chanan Singh and his brothers but also found that the police took away and sold 40 trucks of wheat and a tractor from Sant Chanan Singh's gurdwara.[8]

The CBI also found that Chanan Singh was only one of many well-to-do victims. According to the report, Sandhu would falsely implicate them in cases relating to illegal possession of arms and then force them to shell out huge sums to have the cases dropped. Some of these extortion victims were killed.

The Sant Chanan Singh case is still before the Punjab and Haryana High Court. Since 8 August 2016, there had been a stay on framing of charges, but, on 25 March 2019, the High Court refused to quash the CBI FIR and charge sheet filed against the Punjab policemen. Now, the accused cops will face prosecution in the special CBI court.[9]

Kuljit Dhatt was also picked up on suspicion of possessing illegal arms. Was extortion the motive? Ajit Singh Sandhu is not around to deny it. He had been dead 14 years by the time the Dhatt trial actually began. Sandhu figures in many cases and this is as good a place as any to provide some background on him.

The Terminator

Ajit Singh Sandhu, SSP of Tarn Taran from 1988 to 1993, was the prime accused in 43 cases of extrajudicial and custodial killing, abduction, torture, extortion and destroying evidence, but he did not live to face a single trial. On 23 May 1997, Sandhu was found dead on the Chandigarh–Ambala railway tracks near the village of Lalru, with a suicide note in his pocket, written, according to the police, days before the incident.

He was not an Indian Police Service officer but a recruit to the subordinate services. In fact, at the time of his death, he was the President of the Punjab Police Officers' Association, a body of non-IPS policemen. The IPS–non-IPS tension apparently rankled throughout his career.[10]

He climbed a veritable mountain of corpses in his rise from assistant sub-inspector to SSP, each killing serving to endear him even more to DGP K. P. S. Gill, who rewarded him with out-of-turn promotions.

The first big kill came in 1988—a Khalistan Commando Force (KCF) General Labh Singh. This brought him the SSP's pips. He went on to kill almost all the deputies of Gurbachan Singh Manochahal, Manochahal's entire family, including the aged parents, and Manochahal himself. He also eliminated the family of KCF head Paramjit Singh Panjwar (Panjwar himself escaped and is still alive in Pakistan).

Sandhu was transferred to Ropar in October 1993, but, within months, Gill sent him back to Tarn Taran. It was at this time that human rights activist Jaswant Singh Khalra was killed. The lingering consequences of the Khalra case is outlined later in this chapter.

But mid-1990s, Sandhu's stars were on the wane. Too many cases were piling up against him. Harcharan Singh Brar, the successor of the assassinated Punjab Chief Minister, Beant Singh, was unwilling to be dictated by the police, and, during his brief tenure, he saw both K. P. S. Gill and O. P. Sharma into retirement. (The DGPs who followed—Choudhry Sube Singh and P. C. Dogra—were both officers of the Punjab cadre and could not afford to antagonize the local population in a big way.)

With Gill and Sharma gone, Sandhu had no one to protect him. In any case, considering the number and gravity of the cases against him, protection would have been difficult. Sandhu was famous throughout Punjab for his boast: 'I never allowed the fish in the Hussainiwala barrage to starve'.[11] (What he fed them one can well guess. It is known that a large number of bodies were thrown into rivers and canals.)

An instrument which is useful for a particular time and purpose becomes a liability when times and purposes change. Then it is expedient to discard it. Just who did the discarding? Sandhu and other officers, including K. P. S. Gill, were beginning to defend themselves by pointing the finger upwards. How high up?

Twenty-eight years after Sandhu's death, a retired Punjab Police Director General asserted that Sandhu's death was faked and in fact he was living under a false name in Canada.[12]

Insider's Story

Courts were not readily convinced about police guilt even when the account of crimes comes from one who was himself a policeman. This is illustrated by the story of Satwant Singh Manak. The Manak case is still before the court.

In 1985, Manak was recruited by the Punjab Police as a constable and was posted to the town of Moga. For the next seven blood-spattered years, he served without complaint, but on April 1992, an incident happened that turned him around. He was a member of a police party that killed two teenagers, Kulwant Singh, a resident of Village Ghumaria, District Faridkot, and Baldev Singh, a resident of Village Karamati, District Ferozepur. According to Manak, they were brutally tortured for three days, then slain and their bodies thrown into Rau Kae canal near Moga. The police falsely reported the killings as 'encounter deaths'.

News stories quote Manak as saying that after agonizing over the consequences, he got the courage to denounce the policemen involved. Instead of taking action against the culprits, the seniors in whom he confided came down on him. The Punjab Police accused him of carrying an unlicensed weapon, theft and firing on a police party with intent to kill—all false charges, according to Manak. He was kept in illegal detention for 42 days and tortured.

By 1994, he had been dismissed from service. In October of that year, when he was released on bail, he filed a petition in the Punjab and Haryana High Court asking protection as he feared for his life.[13] The bombshell element of the petition was the names of 11 Punjab Police officers and the claim that they had tortured and killed for the sake of earning cash rewards and out-of-turn promotions. Manak furnished information about 11 deaths in custody.

He went into hiding for several years, but his whole family could not hide. Manak's father was detained and, according to Manak, severely tortured.

Fourteen years later in 2008, a judge of the Punjab and Haryana High Court heard his petition and pronounced the instances related as cases of fake encounters. Holding that it would be impossible for the Punjab Police or any special team to conduct fair investigations, the judge asked the CBI to probe the charges.[14] In the long interval since filing the original petition, the families of 10 of the police victims named by Manak had joined his petition. The Punjab government immediately appealed the decision and a division bench had stayed the order of inquiry. Another gap followed but this time for only five years.

When the appeal was heard in November 2013, different High Court judges took a U-turn and decided that Manak was motivated by 'personal grievance' against his superiors. They threw out his case and ordered him to pay costs of ₹2,000 to each of the officers named. What was most unusual about this judgement was that the division bench, in no uncertain terms, lambasted the judge who had heard the case in 2008.[15]

Manak didn't give up. On 2 April 2014, he appealed his case to the Supreme Court. The petition was supplemented later by a detailed affidavit, describing Manak's personal experiences of police torture and his father's death as a result of police torture. In response, the Supreme Court granted Manak and the victims' families leave to appeal the High Court judgement that had denied them a high-level inquiry into the killings.

But the Supreme Court is yet to rule on the Manak case as such. As of now, no independent probe has been conducted and no charges are framed against accused policemen. It is possible that they will be completely exonerated like Sub-Inspector Sita Ram of Tarn Taran in the Surjit Singh Valtoha case.

It Only Looked Like Murder

The details of the Sita Ram case are committed to black-and-white public judicial record; so astounding as this case is, we must believe that it really happened.[16]

In the wee hours of 30 October 1993, at the Village of Ram Singh Wala under Valtoha Police Station, police shot two men who were apparently coming from Pakistan. The bodies were taken to Civil Hospital, Patti, for a post-mortem at 6:30 AM. However, one of the men was found alive and could talk. He said he was Surjit Singh, son of Harbhajan Singh Dhand of Valtoha, and asked for the staff nurse, Baljeet Kaur, who was from his village. Instead of Baljit, her husband, Mahavir Singh, came to the hospital and saw Surjit Singh receiving treatment. He left the hospital to find a vehicle for taking Surjit Singh to a hospital in Amritsar where there were surgeons. Meanwhile, Valtoha Station House Officer (SHO) Sub-Inspector Sita Ram forcibly took away the injured Surjit Singh in a police vehicle.

On learning that Surjit had been taken away, Mahavir Singh and a local lawyer Surinder Pal Singh immediately wired the President of India and the Chief Justice of India. Both telegrams said,

> Dead body of Surjit Singh was brought in Civil Hospital, Patti at 6 AM. 30 October. When his body was being kept in the mortuary, he was found alive. He was admitted to the hospital for treatment by doctors. The Valtoha police came to the hospital and take away forcibly injured Surjit Singh, after about 1–1/2 hours. I fear Surjit Singh would be killed in a false encounter. Mahavir Singh, Civil Hospital, Patti, District Amritsar.[17]

After about half an hour, Sub-Inspector Sita Ram and his companions returned to the hospital with Surjit Singh; this time well and truly dead. The body was cremated as unclaimed on the same day. Many people witnessed what happened at the hospital. The police report however omitted any mention of the post-mortem 'confusion'. FIR 69, dated 30 October 1993, was registered at Police Station, Valtoha, under IPC Section 307/34 and Section 25 of the Arms Act and Section 5 of the Terrorist of Disruptive Act reported only that the two terrorists died in the encounter when the police fired in self-defence.

The Supreme Court took a serious view: 'If the news is correct, it is a most heinous offence against the penal laws of the country as well as humanity'. The court directed the Amritsar Chief Judicial Magistrate to visit Patti and Valtoha, seize the police record, hospital record, take witnesses' statements, complete his report before 2 November 1993, and forward all the papers to the Supreme Court.[18] With the report in hand, the Supreme Court directed the CBI to register a case against Sita Ram and other police officers.

Five years later, the Amritsar District and Sessions judge found Sita Ram guilty and sentenced him to 10 years imprisonment. Sita Ram appealed the conviction and the Punjab and Haryana

High Court overturned the verdict of the Sessions Court.[19] The judges pulled up the Chief Judicial Magistrate for sloppy investigation but also agreed that there were many unanswered questions including the following:

- Why the ambulance was not used?
- Why did the doctor not accompany Surjit Singh?
- Why were there cuttings in the bed-head ticket?
- Why was the medical record forged?
- Why was the body cremated as 'unclaimed' when the identity was known?
- Why didn't the hospital or the police inform the family of the victim?

While granting that the questions pointed to the sordid state of affairs at Patti, the court ruled that even if the answers went against Sita Ram, all of it was circumstantial evidence since no witness saw Sita Ram 'finish off' Surjit Singh after taking him from the hospital. Sub-Inspector Sita Ram was a free man ... at least in this case.

In 1998, the Punjab and Haryana High Court was cautious about circumstantial evidence and rightly so. It was more cautious than the Supreme Court had been in 1985 when Kehar Singh was convicted and sentenced to hang. Kehar Singh was the man found guilty in the Indira Gandhi assassination case. It was shown in court that some days before the crime, he spent 15 minutes on the roof of a house talking with one of the men who actually pulled the trigger, although nobody heard what they spoke of.

Manak is not the only policeman who has approached the court with details about fake encounters. Rather than repeat similar stories, here are very brief summaries of two such stories and links to full information on the Internet.

The Tribune, 6 December 2015.²⁰

Pinky, alleged terrorist-turned-police cat, claimed to have witnessed 50 killings and referred to the unsolved mystery behind 2,300 unidentified bodies cremated during the days of terrorism. He gave graphic details of killings committed by senior police officers who rose many ranks via such acts. He claimed to have paid ₹50 lakh bribe to a top police officer, still in service, for reinstating him in May this year as head constable after he was released from jail where he was serving a life term for murdering Ludhiana youth Avtar Singh Gola.

Hindustan Times, 9 July 2013.²¹

The Punjab and Haryana high court on Tuesday refused to entertain a petition seeking the arrest of suspended Tarn Taran Sub-Inspector Surjit Singh who had confessed to killing about 83 persons in fake encounters in Punjab during the days of militancy and compensation to the victims' families.

A Generation Later

With every passing year, age makes witnesses more reluctant to 'ask for trouble', or they die. Accuser and accused die. Back in 2015, commenting on a case involving Tamil Nadu politician, J. Jayalalithaa, Supreme Court Justice Madan B. Lokur observed that 'a case spanning 15 years is a classic illustration of what is wrong with our criminal justice delivery system. It is the system that comes out the loser and something drastic has to be done to remedy it'.

What would Justice Lokur say about cases that drag on for more than 25–30 years?

In 2018 and 2019, judgements were finally pronounced in some of the fake encounter cases. These were cases that came to light in the course of probing the death of human rights activist, Jaswant Singh Khalra.

Khalra revealed the police practice of cremating bodies as 'unidentified' and was able to document more than 2,000 such cremations. A spin-off of the investigation into Khalra's death was the investigation of the 'unidentified bodies'. Convictions in the case of Khalra's own death came in 2011.[22] In December 1996, the Supreme Court asked the National Human Rights Commission to probe further. CBI investigators were again put on the job. Out of 2,097 bodies, 1,513 were identified. Of these 1,513 bodies, 109 involved young men who were in police custody when killed and were later disposed of as unidentified. After the CBI discovered who the men were and what happened to them, the next step was to charge those who had abducted and killed them. This has taken years and involved overturning stay after stay obtained by the police.

The press has duly reported the twists and turns in these cases.

Hindustan Times, 14 July 2012.[23]

The Supreme Court stayed a Punjab and Haryana High Court ruling as well as further proceedings pending before Patiala's special CBI court against Punjab police personnel—serving as well as retired—facing charges of fake encounters while fighting terrorism. The Punjab government had challenged the 14 May 2012 ruling of Justice Mehinder Singh Sullar of the Punjab and Haryana High Court, wherein the high court had rejected 35 criminal petitions of the cops and had directed the trial court to start proceedings on a day-to-day basis

The high court had pointed out that the tendency of the police personnel charged by the CBI for the offences such as 'criminal conspiracy, illegal detention, kidnapping and murders, etc.' to delay the disposal of criminal cases on one pretext or the other had been increasing day by day.

The judgements that have come out in the past two years are only the beginning. More are expected in the next couple years.

There are many common elements in these cases. Rather than going into details of all of them, here are summaries and Internet links of three recent cases:

Hindustan Times, 28 February 2019.[24]

The CBI court convicted Harjinder Pal Singh, the then SHO of Ropar (Sadar), of murdering Gurmail Singh and Kuldeep Singh. The police claimed that SHO Harjinder was taking Kuldeep and Gurmail (who were in police custody) to make recovery of arms when they were ambushed by unidentified persons near Bhadal village in Ropar, and Gurmail and Kuldeep were killed in crossfire. The CBI investigations pointed out that the police showed recovery of 42 shells of AK-47 and 14 shells of .315 rifle from the encounter site, but only 42 shells were deposited. Moreover, although Gurmeet and Kuldeep were killed, none of the cops sustained any injury. In such cases, the police preserve the blood-stained clothes of the slain men, but this had not been done and there was nothing to support the police version. The police had cremated Gurmail and Kuldeep as 'unidentified'.

The Tribune, 27 September 2018.[25]

CBI court convicted Raghbir Singh, the then SHO of Beas police station, and then Sub-Inspector Dara Singh, of murdering 15-year-old Harpal Singh. In September 1992, the 15-year-old was abducted from his home, kept at the Beas Police Station for four days and then killed at Village Nijjar. Police version of 'encounter' was proven false. Another teenager, Harjeet Singh, picked up at the same time, was killed after 16 days. In both cases, the bodies were cremated as unclaimed. The convicted policemen have been sentenced to life imprisonment.

The Tribune, 1 October 2018.[26]

CBI court convicted Sub-Inspector Narinder Singh Malhi and former Inspector Gian Singh of the murder of Harjit Singh, alias Gora in November 1992. When Malhi and Gian Singh picked up Harjit Singh (around 20 years) and his father Balbir Singh from their home in Village Patti Balol (Amritsar), they falsely claimed that they wanted to know the whereabouts of Kuldeep Singh, alias Kala, another son of Balbir Singh. In fact, the policemen had killed Kuldeep Singh on 6 November 1992 in a fake encounter. Balbir Singh was released after 20 days' illegal detention. CBI found that Harjit Singh was last seen in the custody of Sub-Inspector Narinder Singh Malhi. The judgement said, 'It was not a simple case of abduction.... It was a conspiracy by those whose duty is to prevent crime. When the police engage in a conspiracy to kill citizens, they are perverting their role'.

How to Make Money in Government Services

One recent case brings out a new angle and is worth mentioning in detail. But before reading the details of this case, learn a little bit about an American gangster of the 1930s.

Al Capone made most of his money from prostitution and selling illegal liquor during the Prohibition era (1920s). His nickname was Scarface, and he didn't get that moniker by being a kind old gentleman. He eliminated other gangsters who wanted to make money the same way he did and often firebombed illegal booze dens that refused to purchase liquor from him. As many as 100 people were killed in such bombings. His relationship with then Chicago mayor William Hale Thompson and the city's police was mutually profitable. After he and his gang gunned down seven rivals in the heart of the city in broad daylight, public outcry against him became impossible to ignore. Still, he was protected by local law enforcement. Witnesses dared not testify and no criminal charge against him was ever proved. Finally, federal authorities hit on a way to put Capone behind bars: They prosecuted him in 1931 for tax evasion. He was convicted and sentenced to 11 years in federal prison.

Capone's story makes a nice foil for the story of retired SSP Surit Singh Grewal. In December 2017, the Punjab Vigilance Bureau booked him for allegedly possessing disproportionate assets worth ₹10 crore.[27] 'During preliminary investigation, it was found that Grewal had net income of ₹2.12 crore in 15 years, but during same time, he purchased properties (moveable and immoveable) worth ₹12.19 crore', the FIR stated.

In the two years since the disproportionate assets case was filed, SSP Grewal has been doing his best to stay out of custody and avoid interrogation. When the Punjab and Haryana High Court turned down his bail plea, he moved the Supreme Court.

In March 2018, the Supreme Court rejected his plea.[28] The Vigilance Bureau had a lot to say at the Supreme Court hearing. In its submission, the Punjab Vigilance Bureau told the Supreme Court that during his tenure as an SSP, he does not only bought *benami* (without name) land at different places across the state but also laid up around ₹25–30 crore in fixed deposits and stashed 40 kg of gold in bank lockers. At the moment, all this is just the prosecution case; it still has to be proved in court.

Before acquittal in the fake encounter case, SSP Grewal had been indicted for framing a Ferozepur district patwari in a corruption case involving missing paddy.[29]

The Legacy of Militancy in Punjab

On 12 April 2019, with all chances of getting bail gone,[30] SSP Grewal surrendered and was taken into custody. Custody may not be all that bad. Photographs of Capone's jail cell at Alcatraz show a spacious interior, tastefully furnished with a large bed, chairs, side-tables, lamps, ornate wooden armoire, writing desk and Persian carpets. Just because you are in jail, it doesn't mean you have to stop running your companies.

It would be interesting to know how much SSP Grewal paid for the various pieces of land that he bought. Were the owners persuaded to sell cheaply? Did Grewal have special bargaining strategies? Did he make them offers they couldn't refuse? On his property-purchase expeditions, did Grewal's reputation precede him?

Kulwinder Kid Case

SSP Grewal started building his reputation 30 years ago. Twenty-year-old Kulwinder Singh Kid was the son of a Kharar (a small town just outside of Chandigarh) high school principal. He was also a member of the All India Sikh Students Federation and therefore naturally of great interest to the Punjab Police. Beginning in 1985, he was picked up on one charge or another. Between 1986 and 1988, he was held in High Security Prison, Nabha. After he was released, he went into hiding.

Then the police apparently changed their mind about Kulwinder. In early 1989, they told his father, Tarlochan Singh Sidhu, that no cases were pending against his son and he could return home. No more trouble.

In March that year, the DSP of Pinjore (Haryana) was shot dead and the police came after Kulwinder again. A large number of witnesses saw the police arrest him from his house in Mohali. A couple of days later, the police announced that two men had been killed in an encounter near Village Sohana.[31]

Tarlochan Singh feared that one of those killed might be his son but when he went to identify the body, the police prevented him from doing so. He contacted Human Rights activists (Justice Ajit Singh Bains and Inderjit Singh Jaijee) and gave them a description of his son. They went to Ropar Hospital where the bodies were lying in the mortuary, but the police barred their entry. They then approached the Deputy Commissioner of the District D. S. Bains, who granted permission to see the bodies and informed the hospital to allow the human rights workers into the mortuary. But before the Human Rights team could reach the hospital, the police had removed the bodies.

Later it was learnt that the police took the bodies to Kharar and handed them over to the municipal committee, which cremated them as 'unknown persons'. It took years before Tarlochan Singh gave up hope that his son might be alive somewhere.

For all the remaining years of his life, Kulwinder's father pounded the doors of the courts: He fought a habeas corpus case, then a case to get an inquiry, then a case to get suspected policemen charged and then to get a trial. Finally, in May 2012, the CBI court decided that Surjeet Singh Grewal (then SSP, Moga) and six other policemen deserved the 'benefit of doubt' and acquitted them.[32] The father appealed against the acquittal. The appeal is still pending but Tarlochan Singh Sidhu died in 2012 shortly after the acquittal verdict.

Lesson for Judges

It was not only the shock of terrorist incidents that convinced the government to replace normal laws and due process with Acts and Ordinances worthy of a medieval despot. Application of the normal law could embarrass the government.

Equally undesirable is the existence of stickler judges—judges, who despite even broad hints, insist on carrying out their responsibilities honestly and thoroughly. The story of the judges and Ladda Kothi shows how the State of Punjab and Union Ministry of Law and Justice handled the problem.

In 1984, the judge of the Patiala District and Sessions Court was Justice Tara Singh Cheema. This posting was considered the exact opposite of 'plum'—no judge wanted to occupy that Bench mainly because this court had to deal with cases of prisoners lodged in the Maximum Security Jail at Nabha.

One of the duties of a district judge is to inspect prisons, so it was that Justice Cheema went to the jail at Nabha. He was accompanied by Justice S. S. Sodhi. There, the judges found several prisoners who were unable to walk. They told the judges that they had been taken to Ladda Kothi in batches and there they were tortured. The police hoped to make them name others as militants. The jail superintendent confirmed that Ladda Kothi was an interrogation centre, and the police regularly took prisoners there.

Once a prisoner is taken into judicial custody—in other words, sent to jail by the court—the law does not permit the police to take him out again except by order of the court. The Ladda Kothi excursions were in violation of the law.

Justice Sodhi directed Justice Cheema to file his report. The salient points were as follows:

1. The police were illegally taking prisoners out of the jail.
2. These prisoners were being tortured at Ladda Kothi.

Justice Sodhi forwarded the report to the Chief Justice of the Punjab and Haryana High Court to be placed on the judicial file. The report was a very hot potato indeed, and High Court judges refused to hear this matter so the report was referred back to Justice Sodhi.

Sodhi then asked Dharmvir Sehgal, then president of the Punjab and Haryana High Court Bar Association (later he became a judge) to assist in presenting the case.

Due Process: Punjab

Angered by Justice Cheema's report, the Punjab Police prevailed upon the state government and got Ladda Kothi notified as a jail. No court order was needed to transfer a prisoner from one jail to another.

But the report was 'out there' and somehow the government had to make it go away. Advocate General Bhagwant Singh Siddhu announced that a magisterial inquiry would be instituted. This move was outflanked when Justice Sodhi announced that he would hold the inquiry himself. After getting instructions from the state government, Justice Sodhi suggested that Advisor to the Governor S. S. Dhanoa, IAS, investigates the charges.

But before Dhanoa could take over the inquiry, Surjit Singh Barnala's government came in. Barnala appointed retired Justice C. S. Tiwana to hold an inquiry under the Commission of Inquiry Act.

The government's hopes were dashed. In his report, Justice Tiwana confirmed the findings of Justices Cheema and Sodhi, and, in addition, he named 25 police officers who had tortured prisoners. He recommended compensation for the tortured prisoners and transfer of the prisoners to Jodhpur Jail.

Justice Tiwana's report was picked up by Amnesty International, and its account mentioned the names of both Justice Sodhi and Justice Cheema.[33] The international exposure upset the government even more than the original report.

Justice Tiwana was already retired but Justices Sodhi and Cheema were still serving. They paid the price.

With effect from 1 May 1990, Justice Cheema became the senior most district and sessions judge in Punjab; he had an excellent record of service but, still smarting from the 'embarrassment' of the Ladda Kothi Case, the police got their chance to get back at Cheema.

An adverse report of the Intelligence Bureau (IB) disqualifies a judge for appointment to the High Court or Supreme Court. The IB is a wing of the police. This department's report on Justice Cheema went from calumny to calumny and dubbed him 'unfit' for the High Court Bench on account of his 'pro-Sikh leanings'.

Jatinder Vir Gupta was the Chief Justice of the Punjab and Haryana High Court at this time, and he took the plea that he would not recommend Cheema's promotion because he wanted to appoint a woman as judge. When the Union Ministry of Law and Justice was approached, it cited the motivated IB report.

Around the same time, the Supreme Court collegium consisting of Justices Ahmedi, Kuldeep Singh and J. S. Verma recommended Justice Sodhi for elevation to the Supreme Court.

No such report would have been made had Justice Cheema not had the audacity to report the third degree methods of the police ... and yet, by taking cognizance of the prisoners' woeful conditions, he had simply discharged his duties as a judicial officer.

Justice Sodhi was also sidelined. His name was among those accepted by Justices Kuldeep Singh and Jagdish Sharan Verma. But then, behind the back of the other justices and without their knowledge, Justice Ahmedi sought the opinion of Justice Madan Mohan Punchhi, then Chief Justice of the Punjab and Haryana High Court and Justice Vishnu Sahay of the Allahabad High Court. Both Punchhi and Sahay had a grouse: Sodhi had not recommended one judge's son nor had he recommended the judge's junior counsel when he was a lawyer. Both Punchhi and Sahay gave a negative report against Sodhi and the appointment was denied.[34]

And what happened to Ladda Kothi itself? The place was a princely edifice with ornate towers and wide verandas, originally built by the Maharaja of Jind as a hunting lodge. It still stands and is still in the hands of Punjab Police. And there is still little doubt that Punjab Police interrogation methods are hazardous to the health of the accused.

Due Process: Punjab

Justice for Siso

All the cases discussed so far have been 30-year sagas of stays and delays that often ended in acquittal or in punishments that hardly amounted to more than a mild irritant. It is easy to see why people who have been wronged may come away from the courts feeling intensely frustrated and bitter. After this chapter, even the reader, unscarred by personal experience, may regard the courts with cynicism. Knowing this, we have saved for last a case that shows the judicial system working at speed, expertly sifting truth from lies and delivering a justice for a woman with no money and no influence, who dared to complain against three policemen. This was a case of gang rape and in all such cases, the name of the victim is not revealed. However, the case is well known as The Siso Case; Siso being the victim's nickname.[35]

The convicted men made appeal after appeal—the last one to the Supreme Court in 2007—but their conviction has not been reversed.

Siso's trouble started in February 1989. The principal of a school in the small town of Balachaur had been shot dead. Police heard a rumour that some 'outsider' had visited the house of Gurmail Singh and his wife, Siso, who was a midwife. Siso was alone in the house when three policemen came and took her away to the police station along with a nurse, Kamaljit Kaur. In the course of questioning, the two women were beaten. The president of the local paramedics union came to the police station and persuaded the cops to release Kamaljit Kaur but Siso remained. That night, the three policemen, Charanjit, Kashmiri Lal and Radha Krishna, drugged and raped her.

They released her the next morning on the intervention of the panchayats of Villages Paili, Otal Majarh and Unaramour. She was bruised and bleeding profusely. On reaching home, she told her husband and a neighbour what had happened. Over the next week, she found her courage and decided that she would tell the highest

The Legacy of Militancy in Punjab

authority what happened. This illiterate woman got someone to write a letter to the Governor of Punjab. Then she waited.

When no action was taken against the three men, she went to Hoshiarpur and filed a criminal complaint before the Chief Judicial Magistrate, repeating her accusations. The Magistrate recorded the preliminary evidence of the complainant and took cognizance of the offences under Sections 323 and 504 read with Section 34 of the IPC. He issued summons to Charanjit, Kashmiri Lal and Radha Krishan. By now, it was July and the wheels of justice were set in motion.

The accused policemen filed a petition to quash the complaint as well as the summons. The court rejected their petitions and ordered the magistrate to investigate. The magistrate's report found Siso's story credible. The magistrate also found that Siso had on her own gone to the Balachaur Civil Hospital and later to a hospital at Village Sarao and asked for a medical examination but the doctors refused out of fear of the police. The magistrate recommended prosecution.

The case was transferred to the Sessions Court in Chandigarh. As cases go, this one skipped right along. No merit was found in the account offered by the accused. By 1995, a verdict of guilty was handed down and the policemen got 10 years in prison. The trial court accordingly convicted Charanjit, Kashmiri Lal and Radha Krishan under Sections 323/34, 504/34, 376(2)(a) and 376(2)(g) of IPC and sentenced them to rigorous imprisonment for various periods which were to run concurrently, the maximum being 10 years for the offences under IPC Sections 376(2)(a) (rape in custody) and 376(2)(g) (gang rape).

In 1997, the High Court dismissed the appeals of the convicted men, and, in 2007, their appeal went before the Supreme Court but by then the guilty men had served their time.

The people of Balachaur could not believe that anyone could get a conviction against the police, no matter what the crime. Siso is still living there … a local hero.

Happy ending! (One, anyway…).

Due Process: Punjab

Notes

1. Stevens, 'With Punjab the Prize'.
   There have never been more than about 500 of them, the authorities say. Most are in their late teens or early 20s. Most are religious militants but some are ordinary criminals who have seized an opportunity. A few are old-line Maoist revolutionaries whose main movement in India was crushed more than a decade ago.
   Anderson, 'Punjab's Cycle of Violence'.
   'In July, police counted 141 citizens and 128 militants killed. They estimate that rebel groups still have more than 1,400 members armed with 1,625 AK-47s, 110 rocket-propelled grenade launchers and more than 3,500 pounds of explosives'.
2. Zaidi, *Black Friday*.
3. Sura, 'Centre Agrees to Pay'.
4. https://www.hindustantimes.com/punjab/33-yrs-on-compensation-for-40-sikhs-held-illegally-from-golden-temple-no-proof-of-announcement-for-civilians-before-op-bluestar/story-LbmSYkl36g00lkUNifeouJ.html 2017 May 12|Hindustan Times|Surjit Singh 'No proof of announcement for civilians before Op Bluestar': 33 yrs on, court orders relief for 40 Sikhs.
5. Singh, 'Punjab DGP for Relief'.

In the Dock				Committed Suicide	
Rank	No.	Rank	No.	Name	Date
IG	1	ASI	36	SP Ajit Singh Sandhu	23 May 1997
DIG	1	Head Constable	32	SP Vivek Mishra	20 May 2007
SP	12	Constable	4	DSP Swaran Singh	2 Feb 2008
DSP	16	SPO	1	Inspector Mohan Singh	1 April 2011
INSP	59	Home Guard	1	Inspector Jagsir Singh	27 June 2013
SI	25	Total	188	**3 Died during Pendency**	
80 of them are more than 70 years of age 28 of them have been convicted				ASI Prithipal Singh	19 March 2014
				Home Guard Jagsir Singh	30 April 2016
				SP Ram Singh	30 March 2018

At meetings with the Union Home Department and the Solicitor General recently, Punjab DGP Suresh Arora, who retires next month, reportedly pleaded for a 'sympathetic' view, stressing that these policemen had been charged for 'acts committed while on duty during anti-terror operations'....

Activist Jaspal Singh Manjhpur, who has been fighting for the release of Sikh detainees, said the move smacked of double standards. '20 Sikh detainees are still languishing in jails. The question is why has the trial of these cops started so late, or not started at all? It's because the government has been shielding them', he claimed.

6. Personal communication from Punjab and Haryana High Court advocate Rajwinder Singh Bains.
7. Khanna, 'CBI Exposes Cops'.
8. Walia, 'Warrants Issued'.
9. Sura, 'No High Court Reprieve'.
10. In his interview in this now defunct news magazine, *Sunday*, Sandhu said, 'I was not the only SSP of Tarn Taran, there were IPS officers before me. Why pick only on a non-IPS officer? Is it because we do not have batch-mates in the Home Ministry, or the CBI or the IB?' ('Interview with Ajit Singh Sandhu', *Sunday*, 4–10 May 1997.)
11. Walia and Sudan, *Genesis of State Terrorism*.
12. Kant, 'Ex-DGP: "Dead" Cop'.

Former Director General of Police (DGP), Jails, Shashi Kant today alleged a senior Punjab Police officer infamous for atrocities committed by him during the days of militancy and who was said to have committed suicide, was alive and living in Canada....

He later faked his suicide and moved to Canada where he is leading a conformable life. Certain government and security officials and even those who prepared his medical record after his 'death' had played role in his escape.

13. *The Tribune*, 'Cops Killed Eleven'.
14. Singh and Dhaliwal. 'Fake Encounters'.
15. *The Tribune*, 'HC "Raps" Ex-judge'.
16. Punjab–Haryana High Court/*Sita Ram vs State of Punjab*, 17 March 2009/Crl. Appeal No. 285 DB of 1998; *The Tribune*, 'Killed Once, Twice'.
17. This was written in a Punjab & Haryana High Court judgement: Punjab-Haryana High Court / *Sita Ram vs State of Punjab* on 17 March, 2009 / Crl. Appeal No. 285 DB of 1998 Initial report of the event: 1993, Nov 1 | The Tribune | Killed once, twice ...,
18. Punjab–Haryana High Court/*Sita Ram vs State of Punjab*, 17 March 2009. https://indiankanoon.org/doc/64928994/

19. Malik, 'Cop Acquitted'.
20. Singh, 'Witnessed 50 Fake Encounters'.
21. HT Correspondent, 'Fake Encounters'.

    The Punjab and Haryana high court on Tuesday refused to entertain a petition seeking the arrest of suspended Tarn Taran sub-inspector Surjit Singh who had confessed to killing about 83 persons in fake encounters in Punjab during the days of militancy and compensation to the victims' families.

22. Express News Service, 'SC Upholds Life Term'.

    The Supreme Court on Friday upheld the life imprisonment awarded to ... Prithipal Singh (head constable), Satnam Singh (sub-inspector), Surinder Pal Singh (sub- inspector), Jasbir Singh (sub-inspector) and Jaspal Singh (DSP), all posted at the Taran police district (Punjab) in 1995. Another accused in the case, Ajit Singh Sandhu, the then SSP, Taran (Punjab), committed suicide in 1997 before the court could frame any charges against him....

    At the time of the murder, Jaswant Singh Khalra had been actively probing the alleged unauthorised cremation of bodies by the Punjab police. He was picked up from his residence on September 6, 1995, allegedly at the behest of the then Punjab Police officials. The activist was allegedly tortured at the Jhabal police station before being shot dead and his body disposed of near the Harike Bridge on the Sutlej river. It was only on a petition filed by Khalra's widow, Paramjit Kaur, that the Supreme Court in 1996 ordered that the case be handed over to the CBI.

    The Tribune, 'Key Witness'.

    Kuldeep Singh Bachre, a key witness in the murder of human rights activist Jaswant Singh Khalra, died of heart failure last night at his native village Bachre, 4 km from Tarn Taran. Shortly before his death he had gone missing from his home but Batala police traced him and brought him back to the village.

23. Sharma, 'SC Stays Further Trial'. Also see, Tondon, 'Punjab Mass Cremations-1'; 'Punjab Mass Cremations-2'.
24. HT Correspondence, '1993 Ropar Fake Encounter'.
25. Tribune News Service, '26 Yrs on, 2 Ex-cops Get Life Term in Fake Encounter Case'.
26. Ibid.
27. Singh, 'Punjab Vigilance Bureau'.
28. Sirhindi, 'Supreme Court Rejects Interim Bail'.
29. Rambani and Singh, 'Former VB SSP'.
30. https://www.ptcnews.tv/former-punjab-ssp-surjit-singh-grewal-surrenders/sl-185/

31. Crossette, 'Killings by Police'.
32. Express News Service, 'Kid Murder Case'.
33. Amnesty International, *Human Rights Violations in Punjab*; See also, Shan, *An Indian Torture Chamber*.
34. Sodhi, *The Other Side*.
35. Supreme Court of India, *Charanjit & Ors vs State of Punjab & Anr*, 4 July 2013. https://indiankanoon.org/doc/169026887/?type=print

3

Due Process: Delhi

The Fallen Tree

On 31 October 1984, two Sikh guards posted at the house of Indira Gandhi shot her dead. One of these guards was killed on the spot and one was tried and hanged about three years later. If Mrs Gandhi's death was a shock, the bloodbath that followed was horrifying.

For three days, mobs organized and led by Congressmen went on the rampage, looting, killing and burning. Most of the carnage reported pertained to Delhi, but later attempts to piece the whole story together reveal that incidents occurred in 18 states and 100 cities.[1] Estimates for Delhi alone vary from a low of 372 (official figure) 2,733 (Ahooja Committee figure), 3,872 (People's Union for Civil Liberties) or a minimum of 8,000 (estimate of Delhi Gurdwara Prabandhak Committee).

In spite of appeals made to the PM-designate Rajiv Gandhi and to Home Minister P. V. Narasimha Rao, the Army was not called in although a force of around 5,000 soldiers was standing by in the Meerut Cantonment. On the third day, Home Minister P. V. Narasimha Rao remarked to his aides, '*Ab bahut ho gaya*' (now it is enough). Thereafter the Army took over and the carnage stopped the same day.[2]

Much has been written about the massacre of Sikhs in Delhi and elsewhere. *When a Tree Shook Delhi* by Manoj Mitta and H. S. Phoolka[3] is meticulously researched, full of eyewitness accounts and written with details sufficient to chill the blood. Just as powerful is *I Accuse...: The Anti-Sikh Violence of 1984* by Jarnail Singh.[4] He was an 11-year-old school student in Delhi in 1984 and writes what he lived through.

The murderous rampage itself was unspeakable, but what added to the repugnance was a softly spoken remark. On 9 November 1984, Rajiv Gandhi addressed a rally at the Boat Club. This was the occasion on which he referred to the riots that followed the assassination of his mother: 'When a big tree falls, the earth trembles'.

When Mahatma Gandhi was shot dead by a Maharashtrian Hindu assassin, the 'earth' didn't 'tremble' for Maharashtrian Hindus. Was he a smaller 'tree' than Indira? When Tamil separatists killed Rajiv Gandhi, no riots against Hindu Tamils broke out either.

Undeniable

Commissions and committees and special investigation teams (SITs) have gone into various aspects of the killings and detailed cases of victims have been published, bit by bit, over the past 35 years. Many of the reports and cases can be easily accessed thanks to the Internet. In book after book, article after article, the main points that emerge are as follows:

- The riots were organized and not spontaneous. Mobs were transported into and around Delhi (often using buses of the municipality). They were provided weapons, kerosene and inflammable white phosphorus (a substance available from a limited number of sources that would have had to have been procured specially).
- At the head of the mobs were Congress leaders, recognized and named by the victims.
- The mob leaders had pre-determined the location of Sikh homes in given areas, and they came with voters lists to ensure that every Sikh home was attacked.

- The mobs were given a free hand to loot.
- The Delhi government and the Union Home Ministry were complicit in the riot since they stood by passively during three days of lawlessness.[5]
- The Delhi Police (which reports directly to the Union Home Ministry) were complicit, either by inactivity or by active assistance. Not only did policemen fail to protect Sikhs but they also disarmed them, and, when Sikhs gathered in places such as gurdwaras for protection, the police ordered them to disperse and return to their homes where they could be attacked easily. After the rioting stopped, the Delhi Police bungled the First Information Reports, making them vague and nameless. They ensured that the names of influential political leaders were never mentioned.
- There are rumours but no proof that Rajiv set the riots in motion in the first place. Certainly, the Congress leaders who led the mobs hoped to benefit by pleasing Mrs Gandhi's heir apparent.
- The 'successful' organization of the Delhi riots led to both the Congress and the BJP, adopting the same pattern in subsequent riots (notably Mumbai 1993 and Godhra 2002).

Out of the vast amount that has been written, *some* material might be exaggerated, unverified or based on rumour, *some* writers may be biased, but they can't *all* be fabricating the appalling story. Too many fingers point towards the Congress party, the home ministry, the local administration and the local police. There are even some incidents that show the judiciary in a bad light.

Getting at the Truth: Justice Nanavati's Findings

For those who demand the most sober, dispassionate and credible observations, the best choice is the Nanavati Commission Report.

The Legacy of Militancy in Punjab

Justice G. T. Nanavati was a retired Judge of the Supreme Court of India, and his report, in two fat volumes, is heavy going.[6]

The terms of the Nanavati inquiry were sweeping:

- Investigate the causes and course of the criminal violence and riot targeting members of the Sikh community in Delhi and other parts of the country;
- Establish whether crimes could have been averted and whether there were lapses or dereliction of duty on the part of authorities;
- Examine the adequacy of the administrative measures taken to prevent and to deal with the violence;
- Recommend measures to give justice to the victims and
- Anything else 'found relevant in the course of the inquiry'.

Nanavati concluded that then Delhi Lt Governor P. G. Gavai didn't move to control the riots until it was all over, and held the then Delhi Police Commissioner S. C. Tandon responsible for not putting down the riots at the first sign of trouble and making no sincere effort to protect the Sikhs thereafter.

He looked at accusations that senior Delhi Congressmen Jagdish Tytler, Sajjan Kumar and H. K. L. Bhagat instigated the mobs and found sufficient evidence to recommend prosecution. However, by the time Nanavati submitted his report, the BJP government at the Centre had been voted out and Congress was ruling again, Bhagat and Tytler were Cabinet Ministers, and Sajjan Kumar was an MP.

Nanavati's report was the impetus for Prime Minister Manmohan Singh to stand before parliament and say 'sorry'.[7] Words are cheap and no substitute for justice.

Here are two paragraphs from the Commission's conclusion, lightly edited for brevity:

31 October 1984.

Cars in the entourage of President Giani Zail Singh were stoned at AIIMS.

Death of Smt. Indira Gandhi announced on All India Radio.

Crowds gathered in several parts of Delhi and became violent. Sikhs were beaten and their vehicles burnt. Till then, the attacks were made by persons who had collected on the roads to know what had happened and what was happening. They were stray incidents and the attacks were not at all organized. The mobs till then were not armed with weapons or inflammable materials. With whatever that became handy, they manhandled Sikhs and burnt their vehicles. Stray incidents of damaging houses or shops of the Sikhs.

Evidence shows that either meetings were held or the persons who could organize attacks were contacted and were given instructions to kill Sikhs and loot their houses and shops.

1 November 1984.

Nature and intensity of the attacks changed. Other forces moved in to exploit the situation.

After about 10:00 AM on that day, mobs raised slogans like '*khoon ka badla khoon se lenge*' (we'll avenge blood with blood).

Rumours were circulated which had the effect of inciting people against the Sikhs and prompting them to take revenge.

At some places, the mobs indulging in violent attacks had come in DTC buses or vehicles.

They either came armed with weapons and inflammable materials like kerosene, petrol and some white powder or were supplied with such materials soon after they were taken to the localities where the Sikhs were to be attacked.

The attacks were made in a systematic manner and without much fear of the police, almost suggesting that they were assured that they would not be harmed while committing those acts and even thereafter.

Many affidavits indicate that local Congress (I) leaders and workers had either incited or helped the mobs. But for the backing and help of influential and resourceful persons, killing of the Sikhs so swiftly and in large numbers could not have happened.

In many places, the riotous mobs consisted of outsiders, though there is evidence to show that in certain areas like Sultanpuri, Yamunapuri, where there are large cluster of jhuggis and jhoparis, local persons were also seen in the mobs.

Outsiders in large numbers could not have been brought by ordinary persons from the public. Bringing them from outside required an organized effort. Supplying them with weapons and inflammable material also required an organized effort.

There is evidence to show that outsiders were shown the houses of the Sikhs. Obviously, it would have been difficult for them to find out the houses and shops of Sikhs so quickly and easily.

There is also evidence to show that in a systematic manner, the Sikhs who were found to have collected whether at a gurdwara or at some place in their localities for collectively defending themselves were either persuaded or forced to go inside of their houses.

Material on record shows that at many places, police took arms away from Sikhs with which they could have defended themselves.

After they were persuaded to go inside their houses on assurances that they would be well-protected, attacks on them started.

What speaks most loudly for Nanavati's credibility is that the Congress party denounced it as too much and the BJP denounced it as too little.

Judges Speak Out

There are many plain-spoken judgements on record.[8] Here's one from 1996 handed down by Justice Om Prakash Dwivedi.

> In State v Kishori & Ors. (Karkardooma, Delhi S.C. No.53/95, FIR No.426/84)[9]:
>
> Law and order machinery was completely paralysed because of inaction/connivance of the police. This is apparent from the fact that for hundreds of murders that took place in the area of PS Kalyan Puri only one single FIR i.e.426/84 was registered and that too did not contain any specific details regarding the names of the persons killed or the names of the rioters who took part in the killings.

Here's another delivered by Justice Shiv Narain Dhingra in 1996:[10]

> It is apparent that Kanak Singh and Ram Pal Saroj were the local Congress I leaders, they seem to have silently encouraged the riots and perhaps they were also part of conspiracy, then a conspiracy on the part of local leaders, local police. They allowed no outside help to reach block no. 32, nor sent any police force there to protect the innocent persons. It would not have been possible for any group of rioters to wipe out almost 200 Sikhs adult male members living in block no.32 and to burn their houses systematically. Accused, therefore got benefit of police and

state apathy towards 1984 riot and the state's lack of interest in investigating the conspiracy part of the riots.

If a judge, trained in the laws of evidence, lambasts the police and talks of conspiracy between the police and Congress (I) leaders, there must be something to it.

Tipped Off: An IAS Officer's Recollection

A senior IAS officer—retired, with nothing to gain or lose—should enjoy high credibility. Writing in *Caravan*, journalist Hartosh Bal, narrated the recollection of Avtar Singh Gill, IAS (ret.), a former secretary in the Union Ministry of Petroleum.[11]

> The mention of Arun Nehru led Gill to relate his personal experience of the aftermath of Indira Gandhi's death. On 1 November, he went to his office. 'Lalit Suri of Lalit Hotels, who used to come and see me often, dropped by. He was the errand boy for Rajiv Gandhi, and since he often needed some work done, he was close to me. He came to me in the ministry and said, "Clearance has been given by Arun Nehru for the killings in Delhi and the killings have started. The strategy is to catch Sikh youth, fling a tyre over their heads, douse them with kerosene and set them on fire. This will calm the anger of the Hindus"'.

Suri, Gill continued, 'told me that I should be careful even though my name is not on the voters' list, the Delhi gurdwara voters' list. They have been provided this list. This will last for three days. It has started today; it will end on the third'.

A detail in Gill's story also helps solve one piece of a long-standing puzzle. The lawyer H. S. Phoolka has been at the forefront of the legal battle to secure justice for the victims of the 1984 violence. When I told him about my conversation with Gill, he immediately seized upon the mention of the gurdwara voters' lists, which contain the names of people eligible to vote in elections to the Delhi Sikh Gurdwara Management Committee. 'We had always wondered how government voters' lists were sufficient to tell a Sikh from anyone with the last name Singh', Phoolka said. 'But, of course, the ease with which Sikh houses were identified would make sense if gurdwara voters' lists were available'.

Delhi was not the only place where Sikhs were killed: Bokaro, Daltonganj, Hazaribag, Dhanbad, Ranchi, Kanpur, Lucknow, Ghaziabad, Ratlam, Rewa, Sonipat, Panipat and scores of other towns went through the same thing, and it was seen that the same methods were employed. Those who led the mobs often had lists of ration card holders in their hands to make sure that they did not miss a single Sikh household.

At this point, would it be possible to accurately establish exactly how many Sikhs were killed during the first week of November in 1984?

Tell-Tale Claims

Goods transport operations in those days were mainly in the hands of Sikh operators. Thousands of trucks, waylaid en route, were burnt and the crew killed. The government refused to disclose how many trucks and truckers perished despite the fact that insurance companies have exact figures.

At least some of the persons killed at that time would have had life insurance so there is another record that can be dredged up. Such records would also reveal something about cases of arson. A man is likely to insure his business even when he doesn't insure his life.

Many Sikhs were slaughtered in trains. Since Indian Railways is liable to pay compensation to those killed or injured in incidents involving trains, it maintains detailed records of all such persons. The Railway Police also record death and injuries as well as incidents of lawlessness. It is likely that the figures from the first week of November 1984 are gathering dust on some shelf.

George Fernandes, Union Minister for Railways in the Chandrashekhar government, inquired into the matter belatedly and unofficially confirmed that 600–700 Sikhs killed in the trains had been identified until then. This was in deference to a letter of introduction and request for help in getting the information sent by the then Punjab Governor Nirmal Kumar Mukarji.[12]

Many of the Sikhs killed in trains were soldiers. The Army, with its strict pension rules, would be obliged to give the victim's pension to his widow or parents, so the Army too would know exactly who died, and how and where. The list exists but remains confidential.

Figures from Ahooja

Here are the figures we *do* have: The Ahooja Committee[13] put the death toll at 2,733 for Delhi. The number of deaths covered by the cases registered by the police in the immediate aftermath was 1,419.[14] For these 1,419 deaths, the Delhi police eventually filed only 587 FIRs.[15] Out of these, the police closed 241 cases without investigation, claiming inability to trace evidence. Subtracting 1,419 from 2,733 gives us 1,314. That's 1,314 people whose murders have not even been acknowledged by the police, much less investigated.

Now let's subtract the number of cases closed from the number of FIRs filed, which gives us 346 investigated cases. Out of these 346 cases, the number of persons convicted for murder is 52 and eight police personnel have faced disciplinary action. After appeals, the number of persons who could not manage to slip out of the net were only 30.[16] These convictions were handed down only for crimes in Delhi; no one has been found guilty of murder outside of Delhi. In terms of all convictions, as reported by PTI and carried in *The Quint* on 23 December 2015, the Minister of State for Home

Haribhai Parathibhai Chaudhary informed the Rajya Sabha that 442 people have been convicted so far by various Delhi courts in connection with the anti-Sikh riots of 1984.[17]

The Aftermath: Year by Year

The individual human details of what happened tend to absorb all attention. Who suffered, how many suffered, who did what. But obsession with details can obscure the bigger picture. To get that, we need to step back and take in developments over a long span of time. The coming and going of commissions and committees need to be juxtaposed with coming and going of governments and the progress of petitions and appeals in the courts. Since this is a lot to juggling all at once, it may help to lay it out in a calendar.

Between 1984 and 1989, the Congress party was ruling at the Centre and, except for 593 days, Punjab was under President's Rule and Delhi had no Assembly.

During this period, the Justice Ranganath Misra Commission was appointed and this commission in turn set up three committees. Misra exonerated the Congress party, glossed over the performance of the police, set the number of victims at less than 3,000, and recommend measures for rehabilitation that were rejected.[18] Its proceedings were entirely in camera, and it excluded a citizens' group that was supposed to be part of the inquiry. The terms of reference of the commission placed the burden of proof on the riot victims; they were not allowed to testify before the commission otherwise.[19]

In 1989, the Janata Party of V. P. Singh was voted to power at the Centre. A year later, the successor government of Prime Minister Chandrashekhar appointed the Poti–Roshan Committee. On the basis of affidavits originally submitted to the Misra Committee, this committee held the police in dereliction of duty and recommended action on some 30 affidavits, including cases against H. K. L. Bhagat,

Jagdish Tytler and Sajjan Kumar. A 1990 incident arising out of the Poti–Roshan Committee's charge against Congress leader Sajjan Kumar is revealing.[20]

Excerpt from interview with Justice S. N. Dhingra:

Q. Who failed the riot victims?

A. *It is the failure of the entire state machinery, including the investigating agencies, the government and the judiciary.*

Q. So you are saying the judiciary must share the blame?

A. *I am saying that the judiciary must share equal blame. The Sajjan Kumar that you are talking about, I remember when many years ago [1990] the CBI went to arrest him early one morning, he managed to gather his supporters and prevent the CBI from arresting him. In the meantime, he called his lawyer, RK Anand, who moved the Delhi High Court for anticipatory bail. Now, there is a legal process to followed while disposing of an anticipatory bail application – the prosecution has to be given a notice, has to be heard and only then a final decision can be given. In Kumar's case, the high court opened at 10.30 and by 11, the then registrar of the Delhi High Court had communicated to the CBI officers still waiting outside Kumar's residence that anticipatory bail has been granted. Who instructed the registrar to directly communicate the orders to the CBI? Now, what will you call this – support of the judiciary to the victim or the accused? What is the message that the high court sent to trial courts?*

Poti and Roshan quit when their six-month term expired, but they had by then put in place a system of dealing with the laborious task of ascertaining whether the police had probed all the complaints of the victims. They were replaced by Jain and Aggrawal. These two worked their way through more than 1,000-odd victims' affidavits. The affidavits resulted in more cases registered against Sajjan Kumar and H. K. L. Bhagat who by then were high up in the Congress Party.

In 1991, the Congress took power at the Centre again under P. V. Narasimha Rao. Never again does the Congress appoint any commission, committee or SIT to review anything about the November 1984 riots. Between 1956 and 1993, Delhi was a Union Territory without a Legislative Assembly. The BJP swept the election to the 1993 Delhi Assembly. It is not true that BJP workers remained entirely innocent during the riots. The names of 49 of them figured in FIRS.[21] Nevertheless, Madan Lal Khurana, the new Chief Minister of Delhi, not only appointed the Narula Committee to go into riot cases but also personally fought with the Central Government to get affidavits from the Misra Commission released so that action on them could be taken. A year later (1994), a Delhi trial court had again initiated proceedings against Sajjan Kumar and 12 others.

The year 1996 was another busy year in the Delhi courts, but no more commissions or committees were formed until 2000. The general election in 1999 brought the BJP to power at the Centre. This government appointed the Nanavati Commission. This commission sat for nearly five years and received a lot of fresh evidence, but ultimately re-opened only four cases. By the time the Nanavati Commission submitted its report in 2005, the Congress was in power at the Centre again and had the majority in the Delhi Government. In that year, frail and demented, H. K. L. Bhagat went to his eternal reward. There followed another long period of no inquiry, no review. In the courts, nothing could be pinned on accused Congress leaders, although in 2007 a few of those who did the actual dirty work were convicted of murder.

Congress denied tickets to Sajjan Kumar and Jagdish Tytler to contest the 2009 Lok Sabha poll. In the wake of the 2008 attack on

Mumbai, plenty of genuine emotion was available and directed against Pakistan so it was unnecessary to whip up artificial emotion. Year 2009 brought Congress to power at the Centre. The issue of justice for Delhi riot victims slept before the elections and continued sleeping afterwards. Elections to the Punjab Vidhan Sabha came and went in March of 2012 with the incumbent Akalis returning to power to the vast surprise of the Congress.

From 2012, many court cases moved forward; the Sajjan Kumar case came under repeated scrutiny. In 2013, both the Congress and the BJP got a jolt when, in February 2013, the fledgling AAP captured power in the Delhi Assembly. Year 2014 brought another Lok Sabha election. In the last month of 2013, the Congress party talked of additional compensation to kin of 1984 riot victims. With BJP victory, the Modi government enhanced compensation (₹5 lakh) to next of kin of Delhi riot murder victims.[22]

This was done barely a month before the Delhi Assembly elections. The AAP came to power in Delhi and Chief Minister Arvind Kejriwal handed out ₹5 lakhs to riot victims' next of kin.

In 2015, another election to the Delhi Assembly loomed. The BJP remembered the suffering of Delhi's Sikh residents. In the last month of 2014, the BJP central government appointed Justice Mathur to advise it on reinvestigating the 1984 riots. In February of 2015, the same month as the Delhi Assembly poll, the central government acted on Justice Mathur's advice and appointed the Pramod Asthana SIT to look into *all* 1984 riot criminal cases. Asthana got six months to do so. The committee was to re-open cases and file charge sheets. AAP won the Delhi Assembly poll. By appointing the Asthana SIT, Delhi's AAP government was blocked from appointing any such SIT or committee of their own for the same work. By June 2016, out of 241 cases closed by Delhi Police for lack of evidence, the Asthana SIT had re-opened 75 cases pertaining to Delhi and other states.

	1984 Election Year	1985 Election Year	1986	1987	1988	1989 Election Year
Lok Sabha	8th Lok Sabha **Dec** Congress majority Rajiv Gandhi is PM					9th Lok Sabha **Dec** Janata Party majority V. P. Singh is PM
Punjab Assembly		**Sept** Akali majority S. S. Barnala is CM				
Delhi Assembly	Didn't exist	Didn't exist	Didn't exist	Didn't exist	Didn't exist	Didn't exist
Commission/ Committee/SIT	**Oct 31** Mrs Gandhi shot dead **Nov** Delhi riots **Marwah Commission** Probes role of police On appeal of Delhi Police Dy Commissioner, Delhi HC stays investigation on grounds that it violates Police Act	**May Marwah Commission** told to cease and hand over to **Misra Commission** Probes organized violence charge, all proceedings in camera **Dhillon Committee** Recommends rehab measures urges settlement of insurance claims but this is rejected		**Misra Commission** submits report Names 19 mob leader Congressmen but clears Congress Party **Feb Kapoor–Mittal Committee** Probes police conduct Kapoor and Mittal disagree. Govt doesn't allot Kapoor staff or office so nothing done. Mittal completes report but Delhi Admn demands joint report **Jain-Bannerjee Committee** Delhi HC quashes appointment notification on grounds that it violates Police Act. Recommends murder case against Congress MP Sajjan Kumar **Ahooja Committee** Set up to determine the exact number of deaths: 2,733		
Court Cases	Central Govt grants ₹20,000 to next of kin of Delhi riot murder victims. Allows ₹2,000 compensation to injured	**Jul** Congressman **Lalit Maken** (son-in-law of late Pres S. D. Sharma) allegedly led rioters. Shot dead				**Jan** Mrs Gandhi's killers hang

	1990	1991 Election Year	1992 Election Year	1993 Election Year	1994	1995
Lok Sabha	**Nov** Coalition Chandershekhar is PM	10th Lok Sabha **May** Congress majority P. V. Narasimha Rao is PM				
Punjab Assembly			**Feb** Congress majority Beant Singh is CM			
Delhi Assembly		Didn't exist	Didn't exist	**Dec** BJP majority Madan Lal Khurana is CM		
Commission/ Committee/SIT	**Poti-Rosha /Jain-Aggarwal Committee** Re-examines affidavits, FIRs from Misra Committee. Hold police derelict. Urges cases against **H. K. L. Bhagat, Jagdish Tytler,** and **Sajjan Kumar** No action taken Delhi Admin sets up **Jain-Aggarwal Committee** to take over from Poti-Rosha Submits a detailed report Goes into how police scuttled cases. Urges action against several police officials for lapses			**Narula Committee** Appointed by Delhi BJP Govt urges charges against Congress leaders **H. K. L. Bhagat, Jagdish Tytler** and **Sajjan Kumar.** Centre balks at Delhi request to let police take action on 21 affidavits against **H. K. L. Bhagat** and **Sajjan Kumar.** Centre sends affidavits after Khurana threatens to complain to National Human Rights Commission		
Court Cases					**Dec** Sultanpuri killings: CBI chargesheets **Sajjan Kumar** and Nathu Pradhan, Brahmanand Gupta, Udal Singh, Shishram, Jai Bhagwan Gupta, Peera Ram, Hanuman Prasad, Satyaveer Singh, Mahender Singh, Islam, Rajendra Singh and Jai Kishen for multiple murders	

	1996 Election Year	1997 Election Year	1998	1999 Election Year	2000	2001
Lok Sabha	11th Lok Sabha **May** BJP majority~ A. B. Vajpayee is PM		12th Lok Sabha **Mar** Coalition Dev Gowda is PM	13th Lok Sabha **Oct** BJP majority A. B. Vajpayee is PM		
Punjab Assembly		**Feb** Akali majority P. S. Badal is CM				
Delhi Assembly	**Feb** BJP majority~ Sahib Singh Verma is CM		**Oct** BJP majority Sushma Swaraj is CM **Dec** Congress majority Sheila Dixit is CM			
Commission/ Committee/SIT					**Nanavati Commission** Appointed by BJP govt to probe causes of criminal violence; identify lapses, dereliction of duty. Slams low-level Congress leaders and police but clears Rajiv Gandhi, other Congress big shots. Gets hundreds of fresh affidavits from victims and prominent persons e.g. I. K. Gujral, Khushwant Singh, Kuldip Nayar, Jagjit Singh Aurora urges re-opening only 4 o 241 closed cases	
Court Cases	Delhi HC orders Delhi Govt to hike compensation to murder victims' kin to ₹3,5 lakh ard compensation to injured to ₹1,25 lakh. **Aug** Out of 107 held for rioting, arson in Trilokpuri area of East Delhi 88 convicted **Sep** Delhi court orders. **Sajjan Kumar et al** to stand trial for Sultanpuri killings: East Delhi rultiple murders. FIR registered against **H. K. L. Bhagat**		**Dec** East Delhi multiple murders: Chargesheet filed against **H. K. L. Bhagat**		**Sep** East Delhi murders: **H. K. L. Bhagat** case dismissed. Delhi court accepts police report 'his presence could not be established'. Summons for other five other co-accused	

	2002 Election Year	2003 Election Year	2004 Election Year	2005	2006	2007 Election Year
Lok Sabha			14th LS **May** Congress majority Manmohan Singh is PM			
Punjab Assembly	**Feb** Congress majority Amarinder Singh is CM					**Mar** Akali majority P. S. Badal is CM
Delhi Assembly		**Dec** Congress majority Sheila Dixit is CM				
Commission/Committee/SIT						
Court Cases	**Dec** Sultanpuri multiple murders. Delhi court acquits **Sajjan Kumar** for lack of evidence			**May** Delhi HC directs Delhi govt to pay ₹1.23 lakh compensation' Central Govt raises murder compensation to kin to ₹7 lakh Congressman **Sajjan Kumar** among six charged with murder of 5 Sikhs. CBI alleges that Kumar and police conspired so that Kumar's name omitted in police records **Oct** **H. K. L. Bhagat**, dies of old age	**Jan** Since 2005 High Court judgments yet to be implemented, Central Govt package incorporates enhanced compensation for injury. Adds job for one member of each affected family and pension to aged	**Mar** Delhi court convicts 3 for East Delhi multiple murders

	2008	2009 Election Year	2010	2011	2012 Election Year	2013
Lok Sabha		15th LS **May** Congress majority Manmohan Singh is PM				
Punjab Assembly					**Mar** Akali majority P. S. Badal is CM	
Delhi Assembly	**Nov** Congress majority Sheila Dixit is CM					**Dec** AAP majority Arvind Kejriwal is CM
Commission/ Committee/SIT						
Court Cases		**Mar** CBI clears Sajjan Kumar but Congress denies him and Tytler tickets for Lok Sabha	**Jan** CBI files 2 chargesheets against six, including **Sajjan Kumar**, in multiple murder case. **Apr** Court accepts CBI report that Congressman **Jagdish Tytler** not present when 3 Sikhs murdered at Pul Bangash	**Jan** Massacre at Hondh Chillar village near Gurgaon is revealed	**Feb** Outcry forces Delhi Gov Sheila Dixit to rescind parole decision of Lt-Gov Tejendra Khanna, based on Sentence Review Board nod for parole to 1984 multiple murder convict **Kishori Lal** (in jail since 1996)	**Apr** Delhi court convicts Delhi Municipal Councillor Balwan Khokhar, Capt Bhagmal and Girdhari Lal of multiple murder but acquits **Sajjan Kumar** Delhi Sessions Court refuses to accept clean chit to **Jagdish Tytler** as per 2009 CBI closure report, Orders re-examination of –witnesses **Dec** Ahead of 2014 Lok Sabha poll, Congress Party vows additional compensation kin of 1984 riot victims.

	2014 Election Year	2015 Election Year	2016	2017 Election Year	2018	2019 Election Year
Lok Sabha	16th LS **May** BJP majority Narendra Modi is PM					17th LS **May**
Punjab Assembly				**Mar** Congress majority Amarinder Singh is CM		
Delhi Assembly		**Feb** AAP majority Arvind Kejriwal is CM				
Commission/ Committee/SIT	**Dec** **Mathur Committee** BJP Union govt-appoints Justice Mathur to advise on 1984 riots re-investigation	**Feb** **Pramod Asthana Committee** Mathur Committee recommends SIT. Union govt appoints Pramod Asthana, IPS, and 2 others to look into *all* serious 1984 riot criminal cases, re-open cases, file charge sheets. Given 6 months to do so, including filling charge sheets, in nearly 30-yr-old cases	**Jun** **Asthana Committee** re-opens 75 cases pertaining to Delhi and other states, Delhi Police had closed 241 cases citing lack of evidence		**S. N. Dhingra SIT** Set up to examine 186 closed cases	
Court Cases	**Dec** CBI again files closure report, exonerating **Jagdish Tytler** **Oct** Ahead of 2015 Delhi Assembly poll, BJP Central govt announces ₹5 lakh relief for Delhi riot victims. 3,000 people likely to benefit.[i]	**Mar** Lawyer representing riot victims learns of CBI clean chit to Jagdish Tytler. Objects as closure report was filed secretly **Nov** Delhi CM Arvind Kejriwal distributes ₹5 lakh to riot victims' families	**Nov** Union Govt tells Supreme Court to re-investigate 286 riot cases. Govt is '*determined to render speedy justice to affected families*'.	**Apr** Fresh summons to multiple murder convicts Naresh Sehrawat and Yashpal Singh **Sep** Supreme Court to scrutinise SIT decision to close 199 riots related cases **Feb** BJP Govt re-announces ₹5 lakh compensation to Delhi riot victims, previously granted in 2014.[ii]	**Apr** Delhi Court gives CBI more time to probe **Jagdish Tytler** charges **Oct** Delhi Court convicts 2 murder accused: Yashpal Singh to hang, lifer for Naresh Sherawat **Nov** Delhi HC dismisses 22-year old appeals by 88 people convicted in 1996 by trial court for involvement in Nov 1984. Hands down 5-year sentence to all 88 but only 47 appellants still alive **Dec** **Sajjan Kumar** convicted of multiple murders, gets lifer	

Four months later, the BJP central government told the Supreme Court to reinvestigate all 286 riot cases as the government was 'determined to render speedy justice to affected families'. In February 2017, the BJP central government announced compensation of ₹5 lakh each to the kin of Delhi riot victims. Apparently, this was the same relief announced in 2014. By September 2017, Supreme Court announced that it would review the Asthana SIT decision to close 199 riot-related cases, and, by January 2018, the Supreme Court had appointed another SIT headed by Justice S. N. Dhingra to examine 186 closed cases.

As of April 2019, this SIT had yet to submit its report and the Supreme Court had extended the deadline for doing so.

This complicated 35-year retrospective is summed up with a little aphorism:

'The cloud of political calculation forever dims the sunshine of justice'.

Haryana Post Script

Year 2011 brought a surprise. Just when it seemed that surely every story connected with the riots had been told, an entirely new episode of savagery came to light.

On January 22 of that year, Manwinder Singh Giaspur, an engineer working in Gurgaon, struck up a conversation with a delivery boy who came to his office. The youngster spoke of a 'deserted village of Sardars' near his own village. When the boy began talking about arson, Giaspur realized he was talking about the 1984 anti-Sikh pogrom. The boy told him that people went to the abandoned village of Hondh Chillar to steal wood and bricks from the crumbling houses.

On 23 January 2011, Giaspur drove to Chillar, found the site and clear evidence of massacre. He photographed it and put the pictures on Facebook. Then he contacted Punjabi language

The Legacy of Militancy in Punjab

newspapers to investigate and preserve the site. When the Shiromani Gurdwara Parbandhak Committee (SGPC) remained silent, Giaspur contacted the All India Sikh Students Federation and Sikhs for Justice. Within days, the national press picked up the story.

His employers found it unsettling to have one of their employees at the heart of something that would attract attention certainly and controversy probably, so by 13 March 2011, Giaspur was asked to resign from his position as General Manager of V&S International Pvt Ltd.[23]

Giaspur did not fight the company for sacking him. Instead, he plunged in to investigate further. He found that an FIR (No. 91) had been registered in the Jatusana Police Station of Mahendergarh district (now Rewari district). The FIR had mentioned that on 2 November 1984, an unknown number of persons were killed by a mob comprising unknown accused. Shockingly, after about five months (5 March 1985) the police file was closed as untraceable. At this time, Haryana had a Congress government, headed by Chief Minister Bhajan Lal.

But there were some who survived the incident. They fled the village, took shelter elsewhere and kept quiet for 27 years.

A Congress government was in power in Haryana in 2011 with Bhupinder Hooda as the Chief Minister. Responding to the outcry over Hondh Chillar, the Haryana government set up an inquiry commission, under Justice T. P. Garg, a retired judge of the Punjab and Haryana High Court.

It wasn't long before two more incidents—in Gurgaon and in Pataudi, a town in Gurgaon district—also came in to light. The same commission was assigned to inquire into these two cases as well.

In 2015, after seven extensions, Justice Garg submitted his report. It was established that 32 Sikhs were killed at Hondh Chillar, 30 in Gurgaon and 17 in Pataudi town, a total of 79 deaths. Garg recommended compensation to the victims of the Hondh Chillar,

Gurgaon and Pataudi violence. Most of the affected families have been traced and the state has paid out a total compensation of ₹12.07 crore. Justice Garg also held that the police had been derelict in performing their duty. Named in his report were the then Superintendent of Police Satender Kumar, then Jatusana DSP Ram Bhaj, then Jatusana police SHO Ram Kishore and investigation officer head constable Ram Kumar. All of them are now retired.[24]

Looking the Other Way

Punishing those guilty is another matter. No FIRs for murders have been filed in response to the deaths in Hondh Chillar or other places in Haryana.

In 2017, Giaspura petitioned the Punjab and Haryana High Court to direct the state of Haryana to act against the police officials. So far, the case has not moved forward. Last year, the state government told the court that the question of police culpability is under consideration in the state Home Department, and, as of April 2019, there the matter rests.[25]

Meanwhile, Giaspur has not sat idle. In January 2019, Using the provisions of the Right to Information Act, he asked the Haryana government about the deployment of police in Gurugram (formally known as Gurgaon) district during November 1984. Surprisingly, the answer showed that the police were present wherever Sikhs and their houses or gurdwaras were attacked. Where there was no police deployment, there was no attack.

At a press conference in January 2019, Giaspur said that on the basis of information supplied in response to his RTI query, he could only conclude that Sikhs were targeted with active connivance of the police. 'A total of 79 Sikhs were killed in Haryana during November 1984, but no culprit was ever brought to book and all the cases were closed'. He noted that the Garg Commission had recommended action against the police and accused Haryana's present BJP government of backpedalling.[26]

If the Hondh Chillar incident could come to light purely by chance decades after the village was burned and its inhabitants murdered, could similar attacks be waiting for discovery in other obscure little hamlets?

Template for Riots

Two long chapters—'Due Process: Punjab' and 'Due Process: Delhi'—have dealt with how victims of crime fought to get justice through the courts. In Punjab, in instance after instance, the perpetrators of the crimes were policeman, employees of the state government. These 'upholders of the law' believed that they had carte blanche to do anything, that they would never be punished, that the state would ignore or outright condone, any 'excess' they committed.

In the case of the November 1984 riots, several categories of perpetrators were active: senior ministers of the Government of India and the highest authorities in the Administrations of Delhi and some other cities, politicians (ranging from men in the very high inner circles down to mohalla organizers), and the Delhi Police from top to bottom. Even some of those in the judicial system failed to live up to expected standards.

If the 'what' and 'how' of the November 1984 riots are sickening, the 'why' stinks to high heaven. That is because the 'why' is still completely operational and guides politicians and parties today no less than 35 years ago.

Riots can be Profitable

Shortly after I (Dona Suri) moved to Bangalore in 1970, a Hindu–Muslim riot broke out in Chikkaballapur, a small town to the north.

I don't remember whether deaths were many or few; the big story in all the papers was that whole neighbourhoods were burnt to the ground.

At a party some months afterwards, I met a DIG of the Karnataka Police. His friends were urging him to take a vacation after all his recent hard work. He had been the Chikkaballapur riot inquiry officer and had just submitted his report. They managed to draw the inquiry conclusions out of him but then they asked 'what really happened'.

I was very young at the time, and it had never occurred to me that an official report would be anything besides the full, plain truth.

What really happened was that a very large area in the heart of the town, favourably situated in front of the railway station, was home to hundreds of small workshops devoted to woodwork, both plain and fancy. The craftsmen were Muslims, the workshop owners were Muslims, the units were both residence and factory and they had occupied the congested Chikkaballapur 'old city' from the time of Haider Ali. All of them earned just about enough to get by.

The police official explained, 'You can't have low-income people occupying high-income real estate'. The influential people of the town (Hindu businessmen) coveted that area, minus the Muslims. They had enough political clout to get some sort of renewal scheme for the town, but acquiring the land legally would have been tied up in the courts for years. The faster method was to engineer a disturbance, blow it up into a riot, burn out the workshops and then stand back and let the state government compensate, and resettle the Muslims somewhere on the periphery of the town. This is in fact what happened.

The DIG confidently predicted that in the very near future, visitors to Chikkaballapur would see wide streets lined with cinema halls and big showrooms where once the dingy little workshops stood.

Riots didn't begin with the November 1984 bloodbath, and they haven't ended there either. Another '1984 riot' could be around the corner for some group, somewhere in India. This will be a fact of life so long as riots are an instrument for gaining political advantage. We have been down the road too often to imagine that riots just happen and political patronage has nothing to do with them.[27]

Political parties patronize riots, but why would a party be satisfied with merely 'patronizing'? Only if party members themselves are actively involved can the party feel confident of getting value for money. If the story of the Delhi riots has any lesson to impart, it is surely that, while care must be taken to see that nothing suspicious splatters onto the leader's pristine white kurta, political parties are perfectly okay with lower-level party workers getting their hands bloody.

Come to think of it, 'riot in theory and practice' is a really hot topic, virtually shouting out to be studied properly. How long before some institute of management scholar comes forward?

Teaching Lessons

Currently, life-and-death struggles to protect constitutionally guaranteed legal rights are playing out in Jharkhand, Chhattisgarh, Telangana, Odisha, Madhya Pradesh and parts of Maharashtra. Last August, police from Pune fanned out to different cities of the country to arrest 'trouble-makers'. Nine such people were on their list, but they could only grab five. Four slipped away or were able to foil the police plan. These were not people sneaking around in the dead of night with AK-47s, they are lawyers and human rights activists and even one elderly poet.[28] Many lawyers and activists have been jailed for long periods under the provisions of the UAPA. Police cite one suspicion or another, but the lawyers' actual crime was to take up cases involving people's land rights or forest rights. Writing in *Scroll*, an Internet news magazine, Indira Jaisingh very powerfully expressed the present danger:

> We are going through times when lawyers who are on the front lines taking up unpopular causes are being maligned, attacked, arrested and held in prolonged detention, and/or even killed. If this does not stop, one day there will be no one to defend the rule of law, since there will be no rule of law to defend.[29]

Price of Indifference

The midnight knock ... death-by-burning-tyre ... so long as it is not happening to me, or my relatives, my friends or immediate neighbours, I remain indifferent. People are focused on their personal lives. Some people will wake up if their city or their state is overtaken by lawlessness or if civil and human rights abuses are flagrant and deadly. But for so long as my own home, neighbourhood, city or state is spared the worst, I can easily remain oblivious to lawlessness and abuses elsewhere. India is a very big country, if, at a given time, most places offer at least a semblance of rule of law, the places where rule of law and civil rights are eclipsed are remote and not too troubling. The locus of conflict shifts from one corner to another, and the news media spotlight maintains a very narrow beam so that at any given time great swathes are deprived of journalistic light.[30]

The problem is that what you don't know *can* hurt you. There is no greater threat to a democracy than ignorance and lack of concern. We need an awareness that is both temporal and spatial. In other words, by remembering abuses and crimes that happened decades ago, we become alert to their re-occurrence and are motivated to prevent a repetition. To be aware of what is happening now in places far from us, or to people unlike us, makes us alert to safeguard the place where we live. It also makes us remember what every Indian school student recites every morning: 'India is my country and ALL Indians are my brothers and sisters'.

No one should stand silently by while the government oppresses *any* brother or sister and deprives them of constitutionally guaranteed rights and the protection of the law.

Notes

1. ET Bureau. 'US Court Summons Congress'.
2. Stevens. 'Indian Army Goes into 9 Cities'.
3. Mitta and Phoolka, *When a Tree Shook Delhi*.
4. Singh, *I Accuse*....
5. Economic & Political Weekly Correspondence, 'Who are the Guilty?'
6. The full report of the Nanavati Commission is available at the following URLs:
   http://www.mha.nic.in/hindi/sites/upload_files/mhahindi/files/pdf/Nanavati-I_eng.pdf
   https://justiceprojectsouthasia.files.wordpress.com/2013/08/nanavati-commission-1984-anti-sikh-riots-vol-2-annexures.pdf
   An extended synopsis of the Nanavati Commission Report may be read at https://www.carnage84.com/homepage/nancom.htm
7. Rediff, 'Prime Minister Apologises'.

   Seeking to assuage the sentiments of the Sikh community, Prime Minister Manmohan Singh on Thursday apologised for the 1984 anti-Sikh violence, saying he was not standing on any 'false prestige' and bowed his head in shame.

   Describing the assassination of the then prime minister Indira Gandhi as a 'great national tragedy', he said, 'what happened subsequently was equally shameful'.

   Intervening in a discussion on an opposition-sponsored motion in the Rajya Sabha on the Nanavati Commission's report, Dr Singh said he had seen statements by opposition leaders that he should seek forgiveness from the country.

   'I have no hesitation in apologising to the Sikh community. I apologise not only to the Sikh community, but to the whole Indian nation because what took place in 1984 is the negation of the concept of nationhood enshrined in our Constitution', he said.

   Dr Singh said, 'On behalf of our government, on behalf of the entire people of this country I bow my head in shame that such a thing took place'.

Due Process: Delhi

8. Grover, *Carnage 84*.
9. Ibid.
10. Ibid.
11. A. S. Gill's statement appears in 30 October 2015 in Bal, *The 1984 Massacre*.
12. Investigation personally carried out by Inderjit Singh Jaijee:

    In early 1990, Governor N. K. Mukarji attended a meeting of a human rights group in Mohali to learn about a recent fake encounter case. I knew that Mukarji was close to the Union Minister of Railways George Fernandes and conveyed to him that so far it had not been possible to find out how many Sikhs were killed in trains in October/November 1984. The government would give no figures. Mukarji gave us a letter of introduction to Fernandes. I met the minister at his office in Delhi and found him cordial but evasive. After some conversation, he asked me to come to his house in the evening. It sounded like he could not discuss the matter freely in his office. But at his house also, he never actually gave any specific figures. The evening ended with him asking me to meet him again in his office the next morning. Back in his office the next day, the embarrassed minister disclosed that the PMO had told him to disclose nothing. He assured me that he would keep probing the matter and see to it that next of kin were compensated. Later, he unofficially confided that the number of deaths was about 700.

13. The then Home Secretary of Delhi Administration R. K. Ahooja was asked to determine the total number of deaths in Delhi. According to the committee, which submitted its report in August 1987, 2,733 Sikhs were killed.
14. Grover, *Carnage 84*.
15. Times News Network, '1984 Anti-Sikh Riots'.
16. Sharma, 'No Justice 30 Years After'.
17. PTI, 'Over 400 People Convicted'.
18. Before appointment to the Commission, Justice Misra had been the Chief Justice of the Orissa High Court. In 1990, Justice Misra was elevated to Chief Justice of the Supreme Court. In 1993, he was appointed the Chairman of the newly established National Human Rights Commission, and, in 1998, after retirement, he became a Rajya Sabha MP on Congress ticket.
19. Badhwar, 'Justice Mishra Commission Report on 1984'.
20. Yadav, 'Judiciary must Share Equal Blame'.
21. Sharma, 'Sikh Riots'.

    On recommendations of the Jain-Aggarwal Committee, Delhi Police lodged 14 FIRs (arson, rioting, attempt to murder and dacoity) naming 49 BJP and RSS workers. Some of the prominent Delhi BJP and RSS workers against whom cases have been registered are Pritam Singh, Ram Kumar Jain, Ram Chander Gupta, Rattan Lal, Gian Lal Jain, Chander Sain, Pradeep Kumar Jain,

Hans Raj Gupta, Babu Lal, Ved Mahipal Sharma, Padam Kumar Jain and Suresh Chand Jain. The largest FIR, 446/93 dated August 1993, registered in connection with the 1984 riots in which 17 persons have been named. Most of the 14 FIRs lodged against the BJP and RSS workers have been registered at the Sriniwaspuri Police Station in South Delhi. The cases are from areas such as Hari Nagar, Ashram, Sunlight Colony and Bhagwan Nagar.

One of the accused, Ram Kumar Jain, named in FIR no 315/92 dated June 18 1992, was the election agent of the then Prime Minister Atal Bihari Vajpayee when he contested the Lok Sabha polls in 1980.

22. *First Post*, 'Modi Govt Offers Compensation'.
23. Bhatia, 'Evidence of Abominable Crime'.
24. Deswal, 'The Killings Spread'.
25. Sura, 'Hondh-Chillar Killings'.
26. Singh, 'RTI Reveals Sikhs were Killed'.
27. A personal recollection of Dona Suri.
28. Kulkarni, 'Assassination Plots and Other Rumors'.
29. Jaising, 'Who will Defend the Defenceless'.
30. Anyone who watches television news channels is struck by daily preponderance of the panel discussion.

Few television viewers realize that getting three or four highly vocal men or women with some sort of reputation into a studio works out much cheaper than sending a reporter and cameraman off to some place like Bastar, Wayanad or Meghalaya where something may actually be happening. Even train wrecks are given the panel discussion treatment. The economics of coverage goes a long way towards explaining why news reporting is so unsatisfactory.

*

4

If You Can't Be Good

Laws are set down in black and white; they are on the books, for better or worse. Administrators (including the police) not only work within the law but also apply and uphold the law. This assertion could be termed 'the ideal' or 'the theoretical' position. But, in Punjab of the 1980s and 1990s, officers of the government were faced with an immediate and dangerous problem—a politically created problem—and the theory did not help them. In response, they plunged into a world of 'anything goes'.

Everything went. Which is to say, the rule of law went. Back in 1985, the chief secretary, being a highly educated and refined gentleman, delicately described the smelly, scruffy reality of what was happening in Punjab as 'unofficial'.

> SS Dhanoa, who was chief secretary of Punjab at the time, has told me that the Governor's security advisor let the police know that all suspicious Sikhs could be eliminated without trial. The former chief secretary stressed that this was never the official policy.[1]

It is inaccurate to say that the practice of having an official policy and an unofficial policy started in Punjab in 1984. Neither is it true that India is the only country in the world to affect a lofty legal righteousness while resorting to means that are anarchic and criminal. However, the consequence of official/unofficial hypocrisy is a pervading cynicism that spreads throughout the entire population. Very soon, you have legislators, bureaucrats, police officers and the

The Legacy of Militancy in Punjab

general public all agreeing that the rule of law applies, but only when it is convenient.

During the era of militancy, the Punjab Police routinely acted outside the law. In the words of a former Punjab DGP:

> Except for a brief period when some ex-cadre police chiefs strove to resolutely deter such manifest misuse of power by police subordinates; encounters, abductions and disappearances would continue to be the preferred option in the state in the name of anti-terrorist operations throughout the decade of militancy and later.[2]

Instead of curbing lawlessness, the political masters and administrators of the state excused it. Or, as seen from the chief secretary's statement, encouraged it.

As the crackle of gunfire subsided in Punjab, the quiet murmur of graft took over. Chasing around from village to village eliminating 'all suspicious Sikhs' through extrajudicial executions can be, at best, a fleeting thrill. More lasting satisfaction comes through making money. Moreover, making money is a pursuit that is open to officers of all departments, not just the police. As Punjab entered the post-militancy years, concerns about legality had long since been tossed out the window and even the naturally timid officer was emboldened by the realization that 'everybody's doing it'.

Some of the cases related in Chapter 2—'Due Process: Punjab'—were shakedown cases: file a case against the victim, or threaten to file one, and then bleed him for all he's got.

Anti-terrorist operations did not necessarily connect directly to graft but it expanded the perception of what was possible. Between 1984 and 1995, the 'unofficial' power of government officers had been amply demonstrated, and this discouraged resistance from victims of misuse/abuse of official power and position. Wisdom lay in negotiating the best possible terms rather than 'taking a *panga*' (getting into a fight) with the police or some government officer.

The Law: Not so Majestic

As for the legal system, perception changed in two ways. On one side, public faith in obtaining the protection of the law through the courts weakened. People feared that if and when their case was finally upheld by the court, they might not be alive to benefit. When the average man strongly doubts the possibility of legal recourse, it means smooth sailing for all kinds of racketeers, especially those in positions of power. The second change was the perception that cases and courts were chiefly useful as instruments for neutralizing rivals.

Both perceptions bolstered the idea of 'all powerful' government and demonstrated the people's 50-year failure to transition from subject to citizen. Is that concept hazy? A subject owes allegiance to a sovereign and is governed by that sovereign's laws, whether reasonable or arbitrary. A citizen owes allegiance to the community: 'We the people'. In a democracy, the citizens 'give unto ourselves' a government (meaning authority vests in the people and the people are involved in making the law), and they are entitled to enjoy all the civil rights and protections or their government.

Looking back, and focusing just on the police, one can see how the fight against militancy itself offered scope for abuse of power, and, from there, scam-proficiency rapidly evolved and spread.

Worth More Dead than Alive

It started with bounty killings.

> The rush for claiming cash rewards is turning police into mercenaries.
>
> Besides the rewards for killing listed militants (annual outlay—official figure—for the purpose: ₹100 million) the department gives 'unannounced rewards' for killing unlisted militants. Every week the IGs of various ranges send their lists to Additional DG (Intelligence) AP Sharma. The amount can vary from ₹40,000 ($1,333) to ₹5 lakh

($16,666). The operation of the secret fund is only known to a handful of senior officers - the DGP, Additional DGs of intelligence and operations, and the IG (Crime). Even the home secretary is kept out of it. Whatever records are maintained are erased after a few weeks.[3]

The recipe was simple: secretly arrest a wanted man. Thereafter attribute murder after murder to him so as to raise the price on his head. When no further increase could be expected, stage an 'encounter' and shoot the prisoner. The daring and resourceful police officer in charge of the encounter party would claim the reward and often a promotion too. Subordinate cops would also receive their cut. (Unvarnished details of encounter deaths leaked out when the cut was disappointing or not forthcoming.)

Over time, a variation was introduced. Steps 1 and 2 remained the same but, in Step 3, the fake encounter was actually a *fake* fake encounter. Money and promotion were collected as before, but the 'dead' militant turned into a very much alive 'cat' who accompanied the police and identified other men as militants.

Some of these cats truly had nine or more lives and they eventually got away from the police. Occasionally they would make headlines when they turned up at the Punjab and Haryana High Court seeking protection. The best known of these cases concerned one Harpreet Singh 'Happy' son of Hazura Singh of village Burj Raike, district Amritsar.[4]

He was arrested from Amritsar on 18 November 1991 by SP (Operations) S. K. Singh and kept in illegal custody. On 22 November 1991, the police announced that he had been killed in an encounter along with another terrorist while two others escaped. They called him a dreaded terrorist and a lieutenant general of the Babbar Khalsa International, responsible for 150 killings. Those responsible for his demise collected a reward of ₹10 lakh.

Harpreet however related a different story: He told the court that the police continued to hold him in secret custody. In September

1992, he slipped away to Chennai. He returned to Punjab in July 1995, contacted his parents and sought the protection of the Punjab and Haryana High Court.

From *fake* fake encounters involving militants during the 1980s and 1990s, it was but a short step to faking a beneficial police 'martyrdom' in the post-militancy period.

The following story is about official chicanery but also illustrates the lengths to which a father will go for the sake of a child's education.[5]

20 August 2013. Staff at Baba Farid University of Health Sciences, in Punjab, said Sukhmani Hundal had been awarded a place to study medicine after she submitted a death certificate confirming her father, Senior Superintendent Rajjit Singh Hundal, had died in the line of duty.

Her place was offered under a quota scheme for the children of police officers killed in riots or terrorist attacks.

The apparent fraud was uncovered when university staff examined the certificate closely during a 'counselling session' ahead of the new academic year.

Further inquiries revealed that not only was her father not dead, but was going from strength to strength after he was awarded a coveted President's Police Medal award for 'meritorious service'. He is currently serving as Senior Superintendent of Police in Tarn Taran, in Punjab.

College officials said the certificate confirming his death had been issued on 25 June this year and that the registrar who issued it has since been suspended. SSP Hundal's 'death' has also been cancelled. But while his daughter has paid the price for the alleged fraud, SSP Hundal's own career will not be affected, his police chief told *The Telegraph*.

'He is a brilliant officer and has served the department for several decades. He was awarded a meritorious police officer's medal recently.

The Legacy of Militancy in Punjab

No investigation has been conducted into the allegations levelled against him. It has been considered as a private matter by the police department', said Deputy Inspector General S. Paramraj.

While a fake death certificate could confer some benefits, it didn't put big money in the bank. There was another aspect of anti-terror operations that pointed the way to real pay dirt.

Pay Dirt

Under TADA and POTA, the property and funds of an accused person could be attached during the course of trial and were forfeited in case of conviction. Normally, the power to confiscate lay with the court, but both these anti-terrorist laws granted confiscation powers to the police.[6]

Reporting for *India Today* during those days, journalist Kanwar Sandhu wrote:[7]

> The Punjab Police have now assumed the role of unofficial custodians of the militants' ill-gotten gains. Most of the houses that once belonged to militants are being used by the policemen for official or personal purposes.

Sandhu's report mentioned the property of four militants that had been occupied by the police. He quoted two senior police officers: one justified the practice on the grounds that it 'instilled confidence in people' and 'the public is not willing to buy these houses for fear', and another likened the situation to 'making cats keep vigil over a can of milk'. The properties were attractive assets, and they were to be had for the taking. Moreover, it seemed unlikely that any inquiries would be conducted into how they came into the possession of the police department or particular police officers.

By the end of the 1990s, militancy had been suppressed so this meant goodbye to spoils-of-war farms and houses. But as pious optimists like to say, 'God does not close one door without opening another'.

Real estate prices in Punjab had nosedived between 1984 and 1994. With the end of militancy, it was like a tightly coiled spring had been released. Land value spiralled upward in post-terrorism Punjab. An analysis of land price appreciation published in *The Tribune*, a 138-year-old English daily widely circulated in Punjab, spoke of an incredible 300 per cent hike.[8]

Easy Targets

With big bucks to be made, the real estate business was just too profitable to forego. Property owned by militants or their families (property which itself might have been illegally acquired or purchased through ill-gotten gains) was the target between 1984 and 1994, but thereafter eligibility for strong-arm takeover widened to include just any property. However, two kinds of property owners were soft targets: one was the owner whose property title was disputed and the other was the absentee owner. The latter were mainly Non-Resident Indians (NRIs). The NRI absentee owners were every bit as vulnerable as militants. By the time they found out what was going on, their land would be in someone else's possession with all the necessary records and documents 'fixed'.

During the days of militancy, reporting was strongly focused on the anti-terrorist actions of police or the occasional government policy statement. It was no time to snoop around uncovering the profitable connections between the actions of police and administrators and the interests of particular politicians. As militancy faded and fighting terrorism morphed into less heroic endeavours, journalistic curiosity turned in that direction. Reports started appearing. One reason for this is that there were many people involved. It was not possible to grab land without everybody doing their bit:

police providing the muscle-power, revenue department officials cooperating to suitably amend land ownership records, and politicians directing and protecting them all. Secrets do not keep well in crowded places.

Here's a typical headline from the period just after the decade of militancy. 'SHO's Involvement in Land Grab Case: DC Suspends Cop, DIG Asks Him to Stay'.[9] Senior bureaucrat and senior police officer working at cross-purposes: Whatever the story is, something like that *has* to come out.

Land grabbing could be done in several ways. The simplest involved only two operations. Step 1: Occupy the place, plough the land and change the locks. Step 2: Contact the owner and offer to buy the encroached property. Knowing that chances of reclaiming his property from the occupiers were slim, the NRI would accept whatever was offered. All involved in the successful grab got a cut. If the owner wanted to fight it out, where would he have to go? To the police. To the officer who maintained the land records.

When the Cops Say It

Police officers themselves admitted that policemen were involved.[10]

> 'We have come across a number of cases where organised gangs—comprising property dealers and maybe a few government revenue officials or police department personnel—may be involved…. They operate hand in glove with each other…' says Inspector General Gurpreet Deo, who is responsible for NRI (Non-Resident Indian) affairs in Punjab.

A policeman did not have to be an IPS to take a crack at the real estate game: Here's a story from Ludhiana:[11]

> *Ludhiana*. In a major development, the local police booked a former SHO (traffic), Pardeep Sandhu, in a land grabbing case here today

following a complaint filed by a nonresident Indian, Bhupinder Singh. The latter alleged Sandhu, an accomplished cyclist turned Punjab police cop had forcibly taken possession of his land measuring 1,200 square yards. The action follows an inquiry into the matter held by city police commissioner Ishwar Singh.

Land grabbing, and the involvement of government officers in it, became so rampant that even a chief minister of the state acknowledged it. Speaking of the vulnerability of NRI properties and the combined efforts of police and revenue officials to exploit them, Amarinder Singh put it diplomatically: 'We cannot have big investments unless the NRIs feel secure about their real estate assets'.[12]

Whether an NRI is involved or not, violent property disputes are the staple of news stories in Punjab. Police involvement is a common element in these reports. Here's a typical clipping:[13]

> *Amritsar, 7 Aug 2010.* A Tarn Taran family alleged on Friday that 75-year-old Subegh Singh has died at the PGIMER due to police torture and demanded action against the officials. Baldev Singh, son of the deceased, said that Tarn Taran police picked up his father from Patti Civil Hospital, where he was admitted after an attack over a land dispute, on June 26 and tortured him.
>
> Baldev alleged that Khemkaran SHO Surinder Singh, a relative of their rival Ajit Singh, had been forcing them to vacate 12 kanal 16 marla agricultural land at Bhura Karimpura village.
>
> 'When we resisted and said that we had been tilling the land for 33 years and were its lawful owners, the SHO warned us of adverse consequences', said Baldev. He said the SHO had the support of Akali MLA Virsa Singh Valtoha.
>
> The SHO denied the charge.

Crooked politicians and corrupt government officers are nothing new, but, from time to time, the level of audacity is eye-catching.

In the decade that immediately followed the militancy years, abuse and misuse of position for illegal gain went about naked and unashamed in broad daylight. Even the militants had the decency to strike under cover of darkness.

Feeding Frenzy

A Ludhiana case from 2012 is related in detail to show how property was usurped openly … with defiance, even. There were no hidden hands. Here's how the story broke in the *Indian Express*:[14]

In 2008, a neighbour informed Seattle resident Hardial Singh Hundal that Maninderpal Singh Johar, alias Sunny Goodwill, had occupied his ancestral house in downtown Ludhiana. It had been locked since 2005, the year that Hundal's father died. Johar was the President of the Youth Akali Dal and an aide of then Akali minister Bikramjit Singh Majithia.

Hundal's sister filed a case against Johar with the Ludhiana police. Nothing happened. Johar constructed a multi-storey restaurant where Hundal's house had stood.

In 2009, the Ludhiana Sub-divisional Magistrate examined Hundal's complaint and ruled in his favour and so did the Ludhiana Deputy Commission. Johar meanwhile filed cases against the Deputy Commissioner as well as Municipal Corporation officials and the SSP. The deputy commissioner changed his ruling.

Hundal's sister then filed a civil suit which went in her favour, but she was implicated in a false case and jailed for three months.

Through a relative, Hundal approached Bikramjit Singh Majithia, but the reply he got was 'Sunny has done many favours for the Badals. We will get you some relief but not the property'.[15] Majithia was then Minister for NRI Affairs in the Cabinet of SAD Chief Minister Parkash Singh Badal.

And Hundal got another message. This one from Johar who allegedly threatened, 'If I can spend lakhs to swallow your property, I can pay to get you killed'.[16]

By 2012, Johar's restaurant was flourishing. Among the customers on the night of 24 December 2012 was Punjab Police AIG S. S. Mand. The exact provocation is unclear, but Johar and his employees set upon Mand and beat him severely. Mand was taken to the hospital with a broken leg.

Now a word about Mand. Some 12 months prior to this incident, at the time of elections to the Punjab Assembly, former chief minister and Punjab Pradesh Congress Committee President Amarinder Singh complained to the Election Commission that Mand had personally delivered ₹25 lakh to a Congress rebel in Gurdaspur. The Election Commission responded by sending Mand to Uttaranchal (now Uttarakhand) for three months as an election observer.[17]

Why would an Akali Youth Wing president beat up a policeman with apparent Akali sympathies? One news item written long after the incident pointed to property business rivalry between Johar and Mand.[18]

The assault case went nowhere. Mand's name figured nowhere in the FIR and no charges were framed against Johar. No sooner had Mand's broken bone mended than he was promoted to SSP rank. With shiny new stars on each shoulder, S. S. Mand declared that he had broken his leg in a fall which occurred in his own home. At the restaurant, 'nothing happened'.[19]

Within about 18 months of the 'imaginary' run-in with Mand, Sunny Johar was dead at the age of 46. Sources said it was suicide; his family insisted 'natural causes'. It was a fact that on the last night of his life, Johar had travelled to Amritsar to attend a political rally, and, on the sidelines of this event, he had spoken with Bikramjit Singh Majithia.

Some sources close to the family said Johar had left a suicide note blaming several people, including an Akali Dal minister, but police denied knowledge of such a note.

In a statement, the Akali Dal vehemently repudiated reports that Johar was close to Majithia and declared that Johar had been shunted out of the party long ago.[20]

In February 2017, a Congress government was voted in and shortly thereafter Punjab's NRI Commission took up the case of Hardial Singh Hundal's stolen house. By August 2017, the commission complained that police had not delivered arrest warrants issued by a Ludhiana civil court against 19 persons, including government officials, who were named in the case. The commission also noted several other discrepancies in the investigation and alleged delaying tactics. Ordering an inquiry, the commission noted, 'There is a strong nexus between the police officials involved in the investigation and the accused'.[21]

No further developments have been reported since then.

Meanwhile, the Johar family continues to run the restaurant. The family's other businesses include real estate, hotels, transport and sand mining.

End of the Golden Age: Nayagaon

In those early millennial years, all an encroacher needed was a bold heart and solid political patronage. However, the golden age of grab could not last forever. While land grabbing has not ceased even today, around the year 2012, the entrepreneurial officers and their political backers discovered the wisdom of caution. It came about in a complicated and unintended way. This is the story of the Nayagaon land-grab scandal.

Perhaps the change was building up for quite some time, but one can also relate this change to a petition filed in the Punjab and Haryana High Court in 2007.

If You Can't Be Good

The petitioner, Kuldip Singh of Village Karoran (in Punjab but just outside the Chandigarh border) wanted security as well as registration of an FIR and a CBI probe into land dealings in his village. He told the court that Sanjeev Gupta, an ADGP of the Punjab Police wanted his land and was threatening him to force him to sell. He alleged that several influential officers of the Punjab government were pressurizing people to sell their land.[22]

Kuldip Singh said he was collecting evidence to show that a 15-acre farm was being developed, along with a palatial house, by an officer of the Punjab Police in Chandigarh's periphery near Forest Hill Golf Club at Nayagaon. He named Punjab Police IGP Sanjeev Gupta (IPS). The petitioner added that one Rana Iqbal Singh Jolly had purchased the land illegally.

Later, Kuldeep Singh had informed the bench that he was not willing to continue with the case. However, since the allegations were serious, the Bench decided not to drop the matter.

The Kuldip Singh petition was Development Number 2 of the Nayagaon Land Grab Case.

Development Number 1 had been slowly maturing since long. Nayagaon, a village on the northern edge of Chandigarh, had been attracting property dealers for many years. A Punjab Vigilance Bureau probe looked way back into the 1990s and found several moves to get village common land divided despite its status as protected forestland. Initially, all moves were thwarted but, in 1993, a division was wrongfully sanctioned by the then Patiala Division Commissioner, C. S. Srivastava. He ordered the mutation of land in favour of Rana Iqbal Singh Jolly (then a liquor distributor), an Amritsar-based property dealer Harbhajan Singh Kahlon and his family members, and a former Kharar tehsildar. (Kharar tehsil adjoins Chandigarh.) Remember these names; they turn up again, later in the story.[23]

Much of Nayagaon's land is locked under the Punjab Land Preservation Act, 1900, that forbids its use for any purpose other than forestry. But once parcels of common land had been sold, the new owners started encroaching the land along a seasonal stream, the Patiala ki Rao Choe.

Even before the state revenue department had transferred common land shares in the names of the new owners, the original residents of the village were objecting to the transfer.

In the 2007 case, Kuldip Singh painted an ugly picture of the man harassing him.[24] He said that the IGP Sanjeev Gupta had:

- Purchased tracts of land in nearby Siswan village.
- Invested in Rana Iqbal Singh Jolly's upcoming resort in Kasauli.
- Bought a house in Chandigarh's satellite town, Panchkula.
- Grabbed the house of NRI Pakhar Singh near Ganna farm in Jalandhar.
- Grabbed agricultural land near Jalandhar which he later transferred to local religious *dera*.
- Through abuse of his position, Gupta protected convicted gangster Sukhbir Singh Sandhu of Burj village, Amritsar (imprisoned since 2003) and Sandhu's family.
- In this connection, Gupta had bought a flat in Gurgaon (now Gurugram) where the convict's sister was residing.

The list of alleged misdeeds was remarkably specific. For a simple farmer, this Kuldip Singh knew a lot.

The Court Starts Digging

The court needed more information and asked the then Punjab ADGP (Law and Order) Shashi Kant to inquire and provide information on the illegal occupants of land.

Meanwhile, in October 2008, the Vigilance Bureau (then headed by Punjab Police IGP Sumedh Singh Saini) arrested Rana

Iqbal Singh Jolly (by this time, a Kasauli-based hotelier) on charges of forgery, fraud, conspiracy and corruption relating to mutation of 432 kanals of land at a nearby village, namely Nada.

The big surprise was that after arresting Jolly, the Vigilance Bureau did not ask for police remand on the grounds that it had nothing to recover from the hotelier. Eyebrows were raised. Jolly's proximity to Punjab Police IGP Sanjeev Gupta was well known and the fierce personal and professional rivalry between Gupta and Vigilance Bureau chief Sumedh Singh Saini (Gupta's 1982 batch mate) was no secret either.[25]

When the initial report came in, an angry judge blasted the state for producing a 'cover up' and failing to free government and forest land around Nayagaon from illegal possession.

The court ordered another inquiry and this time entrusted the work to a retired Punjab DGP, Chander Shekhar. This report came in within a year and named 49 big names—senior bureaucrats, police officers and politicians—who were benami owners of village land on the periphery of Chandigarh. It categorically mentioned that the properties detected during the probe did not tally with the revenue records.[26]

Chander Shekhar found that the land had been illegally purchased in benami deals by 49 powerful people. Among them were the following:

- Parkash Singh Badal, Akali MLA and chief minister
- Former Chief Secretary V. K. Khanna (IAS)
- Kewal Singh Dhillon, MLA
- S. S. Virk (IPS), former DGP
- Sumedh Singh Saini (IPS), then Director (Vigilance)
- Gurpreet Singh Bhullar (IPS), then Mohali SSP
- Surinder Singh Kairon, MP
- Late Captain Kanwaljit Singh, Akali MLA and minister, and his family members

Of special interest were 25 acres owned by retired SSP Gurcharan Singh Pherurai, 12 acres owned by J. S. Kesar Singh (IAS) and 5 acres acquired fraudulently by Inspector Gurmit Singh Pinky, then serving a life term on a murder charge. These were illegal possessions already under litigation in lower courts.

In his inquiry report submitted to the Punjab and Haryana High Court, Chander Shekhar, stated that his efforts to gain information had been baulked at every turn by the revenue department.

> The revenue department was supposed to possess the knowledge of ownership/possession of benami properties, but no information in this regard has been supplied by the department to this office so far. Keeping in view these circumstances, to unearth the truth and for hazard-free inquiry by an independent investigating agency out of the preview of influential authorities within the state and otherwise there being involvement of a nexus of land mafia with some politicians, bureaucrats, police officers etc., it will be appropriate to transfer this inquiry to the CBI to identify the culprits at various level so that a free, fair, unbiased and independent report could be submitted to the High Court.[27]

The judges handed over the report to the Punjab Chief Secretary who would be called to explain when the case resumed in April 2011.

The Real Dispute

In 2011, another petition landed before the court. This one filed by one Garja Singh of Nayagaon, brother of the first petitioner.[28] This petition was even more strongly worded, describing ADGP Sanjeev Gupta as

> [A] land shark in uniform [who] invests his black money/corruption money in immovable properties and is doing the business of property dealing while in service and is a colonizer and has acquired properties

including benami properties in the States of Punjab, Haryana, Delhi and Himachal Pradesh.[29]

It didn't take the judges long to figure out what was actually going on. When the ruling on this petition was handed down on 31 May 2016, it was scathing.[30] It noted that Gupta was the batch mate of Saini and went on to describe Garja Singh as a proxy for Saini. It noted that every time Gupta's promotion was due, a case would be filed against him. Garja Singh's petition was dismissed and the Court declared that it would not be turned into a battlefield in the war between the two officers nor would allow the judicial process to be misused to settle personal scores.

But the Gupta vs Saini tiff paled beside the revelations that were to come. In 2012, the High Court constituted a Special Tribunal headed by retired Supreme Court Chief Justice Kuldeep Singh to examine thousands of illegal land deals in the large villages on the periphery of Chandigarh.[31]

The Tribune, a prominent English daily published from Chandigarh, carried a 12-part series in November of 2013 which traced every twist and turn and named every single illegal purchaser and every record-fudging facilitator in the land grab process.[32]

Justice Kuldip Singh's report rocked the Punjab Assembly. Even people who were normally indifferent to the news couldn't help but notice the stink and where it was coming from. Something was rotten in the state of Punjab.

What could Punjab's Akali government do to deodorize the scandal?

The state came up with a two-pronged response. One was to get the Special Land Tribunal declared null and void by the Supreme Court. It forked over ₹1 crore to Supreme Court lawyers to get this done. The annulment move was undertaken in spite of the fact that the state government had submitted an affidavit to the

High Court that it would re-open the cases of fraudulent occupation of village common lands identified by the Justice Kuldip Singh Tribunal.[33] Despite the big payout, the effort in the Supreme Court backfired.

The other move was to 'blow up' the tribunal and this it did by telling Justice Kuldip Singh to expand his inquiry to cover every village in the state. At this point, citing his health, the 81-year-old retired Chief Justice threw in the towel.

A Natural Death

In any case, in mid-July 2013, to the immense relief of the government, the tenure of the tribunal lapsed and the Punjab and Haryana High Court did not give an extension. For that matter, the tribunal did not ask for an extension.[34]

Tribunal head Justice Kuldip Singh expressed his inability to continue on health grounds in July, while its two other members B. N. Gupta and P. N. Aggarwal received no communique either from the High Court or from the Punjab government whether to continue or not.

The Punjab government quietly shelved its affidavit submitted to the High Court in April 2013, promising to implement the tribunal's recommendations. Two ministerial committees were notified to probe illegal land deals but the move was purely cosmetic; the revenue department did nothing.[35]

Concrete Jungle

Today, the area north of Chandigarh, once mainly protected forestland, is now a different kind of forest if you can think of posh high-rise buildings as trees. It's called New Chandigarh, home to the elite of the city. Punjab's answer to the forest conservation law is an exclusive golf club.

When the scandal broke, the Akali government was not even half way through its term and the party was barely a year away from a General Election. When the results came out in May 2014, Akali strength in the Lok Sabha was held at 4 seats, Congress strength declined from 8 seats to 4, the BJP rose from 1 seat to 2 and first-time contestant, AAP, scored 4 seats. Although the Nayagaon land grab concerned only that tiny corner of Punjab adjacent to Chandigarh, politicians of both the Congress and the Akali Dal were involved in it. The results showed that voters throughout the state turned away from the Akalis and even more so from the Congress.

As for the police, politicians could not forget that the whole *gaphla* (fraud) burst into the open thanks to two *khakhi*-clad cats of Kilkenny hurling cases against each other. Everyone—politicians, bureaucrats and police—finally took the old adage to heart. If you can't be good, be careful.

What the land grab exposé did *not* mean was that land grabbing was a thing of the past. Even as the dirty details of Nayagaon hit the headlines day after day, the papers also carried reports of politicians, aided by police, strong-arming villagers to get their land.[36]

The Wind Starts to Change

Nevertheless, by 2012, the wind was definitely changing.

The Nayagaon case was not the only thing that encouraged government officers of all departments to think before pouncing on wealth that did not belong to them or blithely ignoring the law that they were sworn (and paid) to uphold.

In the two chapters on 'Due Process', we have already mentioned that back in 2001 and 2002 cases against the police (and, by extension, all government officers) were stayed by the Supreme

Court because the court wanted time to study the issue of sanction to prosecute a public servant.

In 2012, the year that revelations of blatant land grabbing were confirmed in minute detail, thanks to the Special Tribunal under Justice Kuldip Singh, the Punjab and Haryana High Court handed down another unsettling judgement.

The ruling by Justice Mehinder Singh Sullar pertained to 35 petitions filed by Atma Singh Bhullar and other police officers, Justice Sullar, ruled that sanction was not legally required to prosecute Punjab Police personnel who 'took law into their own hands' and eliminated 'helpless persons' after picking up and illegally detaining them. He did not mince words:

> Section 6 appears to afford adequate protection to public servant to ensure that they may not face the false prosecutions. Neither this section extends its protective cover to, nor to put a wall around, a guilty public servant, pertaining to every illegal acts and omissions.
>
> The petitioners-accused are neither entitled to the umbrella of protection under section 6 of the amended Act nor under section 197 of the CrPC. Thus, no sanction whatsoever is legally required to prosecute them for commission of the pointed heinous offences.
>
> To my mind, such barbaric acts complained of, cannot possibly be termed, by any stretch of imagination that, they have any remote nexus in performance of their official duties.[37]

Of course, the Punjab Police appealed the judgement in the Supreme Court and got another stay, but this one lasted a mere four years. By 2016, the justices of the apex court agreed with the Punjab and Haryana High Court and when they did, the umbrella of 'sanction to prosecute' under which the police had been sheltering for 20 years was finally snatched away. The Supreme Court said that sanction to prosecute a public servant is not required if the alleged offence was committed when he was not discharging official duty.[38]

'Sanction to prosecute' ... What did that actually mean?

Q. Who was to give such a sanction?

A. *The government*

Q. Who was the government?

A. *Ultimately, it was the minister in charge of the concerned department. In the case of the police, the home minister (a portfolio usually held by the chief minister)*

Q. Who was the minister?

A. *An elected politician*

In other words, no matter what the charge, a government officer was absolutely safe as long as he had the backing of a cabinet-rank politician or a politician capable of influencing the high-up politician. Without sanction to prosecute, no case went anywhere. Suppose the misdeeds of the accused officer were clear and could be proven but the politician nevertheless declined to sanction prosecution. What did that mean? Think for yourself.

Long Road to 'Normalcy'

The 'return of normalcy' to Punjab is frequently placed at around 1997, the first 'normal' election to the Punjab Assembly. Our argument is that normalcy stealthily peeked out of its hiding place only in 2012, and it wasn't until 2016 that the Supreme Court ruling finally told normalcy 'it's okay, you can come out now'.

This doesn't mean that all is clean and transparent in Punjab now.[39] Malfeasance hasn't stopped. Particularly when it comes to real estate, police, bureaucrats and politicians continue to team up with con men for mutual benefit. Recent years have brought some extremely complicated, positively filmi, stories of this nature into the media spotlight. They are all entertaining and worth telling. Alas, in the interest of keeping this chronicle trim and on track, they must be saved for another book!

Sooner or later, when the stories do come to light, usually the revelation is the old story of 'when thieves fall out'.

Year 1984 is now 35 years in the past. Has Punjab at last come to the point where 'official' respect for the law outweighs 'unofficial' contempt for it?

At least now, a government officer discovered in the middle of a scam faces the prospect of being tried, convicted and punished. An officer who knows he can be prosecuted is less likely to be an enthusiastic accomplice in the crimes of those higher up than himself, or even those who are at the very top of the government.

Notes

1. Tully, 'Wounds Heal'.
2. Dhillon, *Identity and Survival*.
3. Sandhu, 'Punjab Police Transgresses'.
4. Dogra, 'Dead or Alive?'; Vinayak, 'System of Inducting Terrorists'; High Court Correspondent, 'PIL Seeks Names'.
5. Nelson, 'Indian Policeman "Fakes His Own Death"'.
6. People's Union for Democratic Rights, 'Letter to Chairman, Review Committee on POTA', 22 September 2003. https://pudr.org/letter-chairman-review-committee-pota
7. Sandhu, 'Punjab Policemen Occupy Houses'.
8. Singh, 'From healing to dealing!

   Investigations by *The Tribune* revealed that none of business or industry has witnessed a boom comparable to real estate, which, has seen an average appreciation of over 300 per cent in a year's time. The multiplication of prices of prime properties situated along highways, main roads and the ones adjoining to big cities like Ludhiana, Jalandhar, Patiala, Bathinda, Hoshiarpur and Amritsar, was even more fast and touched the amazing mark of even 500 per cent during past one year. The hike in prices of agricultural properties, however, hovered between 20 and 30 per cent.

9. Singh, 'SHO's Involvement in Land Grab Case'.

   A piquant situation has arisen here over the issue of suspension of SHO, Koomkalan, Dogar Ram by the Deputy Commissioner, Mr Anurag Aggarwal, in the Bhupana landgrabbing case with the cop continuing in his official position even two days after his suspension was ordered.

   According to sources, SI Dogar Ram continues in his office because of an assurance by the Deputy Inspector General of Police, Mohd Mustafa, that the cop's case was being taken up with the Deputy Commissioner and till then he can continue functioning as the Station House Officer.

   Civil administration sources disclosed that an on the spot inquiry by the administration officials had found substantial evidence of irregularity of duty against the cop.

10. *BBC News*, 'India's Booming Land Values'.
11. *The Tribune*, 'Traffic SHO Booked'.
12. Vinayak, 'NRIs Duped of their Property'.
13. *Hindustan Times*, 7 August 2010.
14. Express News Service, 'NRI's House Forcibly Demolished'.
15. Ibid.
16. Ibid.
17. TNN, 'EC Transferred Mand'.
18. Singh, 'NRIs Properties'.
19. Singh, 'Mand Assault Case'.
20. Deogan, 'Former YAD Leader'.
21. Singh, 'Property Dispute'.
22. Malik, 'Nayagaon Land-Grab Case'.
23. Tribune News Service, 'Vigilance Mellows a Day after Arresting Hotelier'.
24. Malik, 'Nayagaon Land-Grab Case'.
25. Tribune News Service, 'Vigilance Mellows a Day after Arresting Hotelier'.
26. Ohri, 'Punjab Top-Shots Own Major Land'.
27. Express News Service, 'Ex-DGP Alleges Nexus'.
28. *Garja Singh vs State of Punjab and Ors: CRM-M-25269–2011 (O/M)*. https://indiankanoon.org/doc/123376624/; Tribune News Service, 'HC Issues Notice'.
29. Punjab-Haryana High Court, *Garja Singh vs State of Punjab and Ors* on 31 May 2016. https://indiankanoon.org/doc/123376624/
30. Garja Singh vs State Of Punjab And Ors: CRM-M-25269–2011 (O/M). https://indiankanoon.org/doc/123376624/
31. Tribune News Service, 'High Court Raps Punjab'.

32. Tribune News Service, 'Justice Kuldip Singh Special Tribunal Report' (parts I–XII).
33. Singh, 'Punjab Pays ₹1 cr'.
34. Ibid.
35. Singh, 'Murky Panchayat Land Deals'; Kaur, 'On HC Nudge'.
36. Tribune News Service, 'Beas Killing'.

Justice Mahesh Grover issued notices to former Akali ministers and an ex-legislator, besides some police officers. They have been asked to cause why proceedings under the Contempt of Court Act be not initiated against them for allegedly defying stay orders in a land matter.

The notice has been issued to former minister Sikandar Singh Malooka and his wife, ex-MLA Hari Singh Zira and his son Avtar Singh, besides Kharar DSP Raj Balwinder Singh Marar and ex-MLA Sukhdarshan Singh Marar.

In his petition, Khudda Ali Sher village resident Gurmail Singh had alleged the respondents had attempted with the help of musclemen and police to take possession of his land in Nayagaon-Karoran area of Chandigarh, despite the orders of the lower court against any interference in the present possession.

The petitioner also alleged recurrent attempts on the part of the respondents to implicate him and his family members in false cases.

The respondents, particularly those considered close to the present regime in Punjab, were also allegedly involved in grabbing lands around Chandigarh and operating like a land mafia, he alleged.

37. Malik, 'High Court Denies Relief'.
38. PTI, 'No Sanction Needed to Try Government Servants'; *Devinder Singh & Ors vs State of Punjab Through CBI* on 25 April 2016. https://indiankanoon.org/doc/71777130/
39. Randhawa, 'Punjab Police Top Brass'.

5

On the Cultural Front

Back in the 1960s, an age when radio was still the most important medium for pop songs, a tune called *Guantanamera* caught on among American youngsters. The lyrics were in Spanish so hardly anyone understood what the song was about, but it was cool and kids knew that it was somehow linked up with counter-culture politics. The better aware youngsters knew that it had a Cuba connection. Cuba was a no-no place as per the US government, so obviously Cuba was cool. This was also the time when the very first Che Guevarra t-shirts began to appear. Sales took off immediately. Few of the buyers could have named the face and even fewer could have said anything about the actual person whose image was depicted ... but so what? Kids liked the song and the t-shirt for the same reason: They were just cool, that's all.

The 1960s was not the last time goods of political provenance became money-spinners in the USA. Some 10–15 years ago, the Bedouin *keffiyeh* was a wardrobe 'must-have' for the teens-and-twenties crowd. Macy's sold them ... made in China. By now, of course, fashion has moved on.

What does this have to do with the post-militancy years in Punjab?

Radical Chic

For quite some time now, Sant Jarnail Singh Bhindranwale has been cool. The makers of t-shirts, coffee mugs, key-chains, car decals, framed photos and various other such items have struck gold in images of the Sant as well as Khalistan and Babbar Khalsa logos and just about anything written in Gurmukhi script.

When this development was first reported 4–5 years back, the sleuths of India's various state, central and military intelligence agencies were naturally thrilled as it gave them one more 'specter' to shout about. As of 2019, the shops are still doing brisk business, but the predicted disturbance has not materialized.

How logical is it to raise the alarm over militant memorabilia in first place? Ask yourself ... If *you* were preparing to loot an armory or blow up a police station, would you roam around flaunting a Babbar bumper sticker or a *kharkoo* t-shirt? As with the Guevarra t-shirts and *arabi rumals*, it is unlikely that many purchasers are preparing to overthrow the state.

Getting back to the t-shirts themselves ... the popularity of the Bhindranwale t-shirt comes with a heavy *tadka* (seasoning) of irony. (The irony being that strong evidence supports the contention that the Congress party bankrolled the Sant with the intention of cutting down the Akalis.) But irony is generally lost on shoppers. Cool quotient determines sales; cool is determined by image and image is determined by the angle of vision—in this case, the *shaheed* angle. It must be admitted that the Sant's image is perfect.

And the audio is perfect too. Aside from t-shirts, etc., recordings of the Sant's speeches do good business, which means that the emotional chord the Sant struck 40 years ago still resonates. Tape buyers want to be told that destiny calls them to freedom and honour if they will but purify themselves and return to the true faith.

Radical sentiments also find expression in music. For example, the *Straight Outta Khalistan* series of albums by Jagowala Jatha. Traditional *kavishar vaaran* has been updated to something that resembles Punjabi rap. Production values are highly sophisticated.[1]

If It's Cool in California

The Indian buyer's perception of cool is often imported. While it used to take at least a year for foreign trends to filter into the country; now, thanks to cyber speed, we get same-day delivery. Possibly, the fascination with confrontational merchandise reflects the tastes of a section of the vast Sikh diaspora.

But why would the fashion of defiance catch the fancy of Sikhs living abroad? Let's think about the USA. What persons there would a Sikh have to defy or face courageously? Armed and unhinged white men? Actually, armed and unhinged white men are a danger to everybody in America, but Sikhs might feel particularly at risk because mass murderers are just the type to suppose that turban plus beard equals jihadi.

What Sikhs do *not* have to stand up to is the government; the American government does not attack anyone on the basis of *any* religion. If a person expresses his faith by beating tom-toms and sacrificing black chickens in the middle of the night, that's not only okay, it's his constitutional right. The same situation obtains in Canada, Britain and European countries that are home to a large number of Sikhs.

Actually, fashion of assertion is a better term than fashion of defiance. Assertion implicitly involves the Self and the Other. It can mean the Self vis-à-vis a specific Other. Think of the red and black scarf of Manchester United versus the blue and white of Chelsea. It can assert the Self vis-à-vis '*all* Others'. Advertising copy often speaks of something as a 'fashion statement', in other words, wearable shorthand conveying a message. Spooky white robes with pointy hoods—instant message: violent intention toward *all* Others.

If Self is wearing a Khalistan/Babbar/Bhindranwala t-shirt then, logically, who would be the Other?

1. Government of India
2. Congress party
3. Moderate Akali party
4. Anyone not identifying as Sikh radical
5. All of the above

What we know of past events tells us that it has to be one or all of those answers, but the logic that nudges people to do a thing is not always on the surface. What's going on with Sikhs in multicultural USA, or Canada or Britain?

Hypothetically Speaking

But, forget Sikhs for the moment. Let's *invent* an ethnic group. Pecking out a random selection of alphabets on the keyboard produces a name with no semantic baggage: *Ngapuhi*. This imaginary group is distinct in language, culture, religion and appearance. If the number of *Ngapuhi* immigrants is very small and scattered geographically the choice before the individual would be (a) turn to the people he lives among for his social life or (b) remain isolated. But let's say that *Ngapuhi* numbers and concentration are sufficient to permit ghettos; sometimes ghettos within circumscribed location, but more often social ghettos. The workplace and public spaces are culturally mixed but social interactions are usually with other *Ngapuhi*.

In the *Ngapuhi*'s native land, a person had only to say his name and he was immediately placed in some social slot: He got automatic definition for better or worse. The *Ngapuhi*'s name means nothing in his new home, except to other *Ngapuhis*. They miss the satisfaction of being recognized in and by the wider society. So, what is the remedy?

The *Ngapuhi* observe other ethnic groups and see that some have projected themselves so successfully that, in certain fields, they are

On the Cultural Front

innovators that sway the rest of society. In the USA, Black people lead the way in projection of ethnicity, closely followed by Hispanics. Both are attractive markets because of their numbers, even though disposable income of individuals may be low. Incidentally, advertising aimed at ethnic groups serves to further project the group.

Meanwhile *Ngapuhi* families grow. The parents—first generation immigrants who showed utmost determination to get to America in the first place and then slogged to achieve security—worry that their children, Americans by birth, may become Americanized. Fortunately, kids are highly adaptable and quick to internalize a successful model. A bit of *Ngapuhi* cultural tweaking here and there, and before you can say *okifenoki!* along comes the first of many music videos featuring teenage *Ngapuhi* rappers wearing chunky chains and baggy knickers. They confront and oppose. It is not only the dominant culture that they confront, they are confronting their parent's generation too. And yet the idiom is so highly stylized, down to the smallest gesture, that the confrontation is clearly rhetorical and not literal. The *Ngapuhi* rapper acts out his identity as derived from parents but the idiom itself is derived, imitating the original Black rappers. What could be more American than rap?

Ethnic projection can pay off politically, but even if *Ngapuhi* do not dominate the voters list in some particular ward or constituency, the very fact that a group consciousness exists raises visibility and potential for influence. It is very good for visibility if the group is a victim of a historic wrong as well as some contemporary injustice. This gains sympathy and permission to simultaneously lash out and swell with righteousness. It provides a license for displays of intense feeling in a culture where impassioned expression is not the day-to-day norm. Or at least it wasn't the day-to-day norm until the advent of social media. *Ngapuhi* residing abroad may come to believe that it is their duty to espouse the cause of *Ngapuhi* back in the old country and provide political guidance to their third world cousins.

The World Laughs with You

One indicator that ethnic groups are projecting themselves successfully is the appearance of a kind of humour that is both self-deprecating and self-celebrating. This stage comes when the group at last feels comfortable and can subscribe to the adage: 'Laugh and the world laughs with you'. Before long, they are repeating the little jokes once associated with other ethnic groups. 'There are only two kinds of people: those who are *Ngapuhi* and those who want to be'. Not to forget the *Ngapuhi* t-shirts. What could be more American than a t-shirt?

We have mentioned political payoff, but the gain that is central is social in nature. It is the gratification that comes from rising above anonymity, spinning a bit of glamour, insisting on self-worth on one's own cultural terms (*Ngapuhi* pride) and keeping depersonalization at bay.

Substitute the name of any ethnic group for *Ngapuhi*; the process remains basically the same. The logic of this process is not a deliberate, calculated logic but more of an emotional logic. Central to the process of ethnic projection is the shaping of a group memory; very often it forms around the group's particular trail of tears.

All this is not to diminish or deny the memory that energizes and gives direction to a particular group but rather to say that the process is complex. Granted, the memory is historically real and merits an earnest response. We do not take away from its validity by recognizing that this memory also facilitates the group's creation of a place of its own in a multicultural world.

The Right to be Different

But what's the deal in India? Who is buying those Bhindranwale t-shirts and why?

The situation of Sikhs abroad is different from that of Sikhs in India. Abroad, the attitude to assimilation is positive; they are working out the terms of it on the belief that they have the power to create a good place for themselves. In 'the old country', assimilation is also the problem, but the attitude is defensive. By all means, ask Sikhs about the danger of being overwhelmed, decultured and disempowered. Then go ask the Meiteis and Bhils, prosperous Coorgis in Karnataka and entrepreneur Bhutias in Sikkim, ask De Silvas, De Souzas and Pereiras in Goa. Many population groups in India have a sense of nationhood that predates the Indian State and the British Empire. People don't want to be homogenized. Not in India. Not in Sri Lanka. Not in Scotland.

It was only recently that that Sikhs were engaged in a conflict that was both political and military; Sikh blood was literally flowing in Delhi, Punjab and other areas of North India. Retaining the memory of those years has profound value in the struggle to protect civil liberties and human rights; it has profound value in the assertion of Sikh identity. Memory can also prevent a real-life replay of the experience with a repetition of all the old mistakes. Thirty years down the road, t-shirts may be a good thing: a way to call to the heart without calling to the trigger-finger.

It is also worth noting that Bhindranwale t-shirts are not the only ones to be sold from the pavements of Indian cities. It is also possible to buy t-shirts emblazoned with the faces of Irom Sharmila, Burhan Wani and Kishenji.[2] This puts India in the same basket as the USA, Britain, Canada and European democracies at least as far as free t-shirt speech goes. How many Chechnya t-shirts are sold on the pavements of Moscow? How many Houthi t-shirts are sold on the pavements of Riyadh?

Hearts and Minds ... and the X-Box

Given the many ways that modern technology allows for commercial exploitation, it is fair to say the manufacturers and merchandizers can go much further. T-shirts, novelty items, audio tapes ... as commercialization goes, these are all low tech. What about video games? The makers are not quite there yet but maybe soon.

Already Sikh combatants figure are in a few video games, but these aren't well known in Punjab or India generally. The ones that have come out so far reach into previous centuries. In Sid Meier's Civilization V, players get the option of Sikh Empire, meaning empire of Maharaja Ranjit Singh. At one point, Meier uses Guru Nanak's verse: 'The merchants and the traders have come; their profits are preordained'. Empire Total War reaches an 18th-century India level. Get past the Mughals, go on to Maratha cavalry and face the Sikh cavalry with the option of allying with the Sikhs. One of the Assassins Creed Chronicles options places the player in the Anglo-Sikh wars. The closest any recent game has come close to painful 1984 reality is Hitman 2. This game presented a layout that very closely resembled the layout of the Golden Temple. Eidos has since removed the level; it is not known whether this was in response to an objection from someone or it was just no fun.[3]

This mention of video games is neither facetious nor far-fetched. On 1 March 2018, at a press conference in Beirut, Hezbollah, the Iran-backed Shiite army unveiled its latest video game, titled *Sacred Defence: Protecting the Homeland and Holy Sites*. This game is a spinoff of Hezbollah's 2016 bestseller, *Call of Duty*. Both are first-person shooter games glorifying the militia's battles in the Syrian conflict. A game that sells for about $5 (₹350).

The action starts with the player in plain clothes visiting one of the holiest in Shiite Islam, the Sayyidah Zeinab shrine on the outskirts of Damascus. Protection of the shrine has been a rallying cry for recruiting Shiite youth. The mausoleum is attacked and the player reappears as a Hezbollah fighter standing in front of a poster of Hezbollah leader Hassan Nasrallah.

The makers say that the aim is to make players understand 'what really happened and what the fighters who made sacrifices were doing. To finish one level and move to the next, the player will suffer ... He will see how difficult it is for the resistance fighters'.

If winning conflicts means winning hearts and minds, video games have tremendous potential. The persuaders—of whichever side—don't just talk to their audience, they 'recruit' them as participants. Video game players are young, they respond to the realism of the game which is set in contemporary or near contemporary context. They are also unlikely to realize the bias of the developers. As a medium, the game is a very powerful way to propagandize grievances as well as create an aura of glamour and glory around 'fighters and martyrs'. The game may reach thousands of players. Let us say that it is just a game for the majority of players, but for others it will be seen as a 'true and meaningful' game, and, for a small minority, it will lead into a real-life option. As a recruiting tool, what more do you want?[4]

Employees of the Indian government's intelligence agencies are serious people. Hanging out in video game arcades and game shops is below their dignity. This means that 'militant' video games with content designed to influence and possibly recruit could be keeping lakhs of youngsters happily engaged before any agency ever woke up to their existence.

Menace at the Movies

Punjabi cinema, has exploded in the last few years. The industry, which used to release barely six films a year until 2002, has cranked up to the point where it now churns out around 120. That's a new film every third day of the year. Profits are excellent: The budget for most Punjabi films comes in at around ₹4 crore, and, even if the film gets just average response, it will still tally up box office collection of ₹10 crore on average. An average Punjabi film has a shooting schedule of just 35–40 days.

In Punjab, Hindi films run a poor second to Punjabi films. A newspaper report quoted the manager of a cinema hall in Chandigarh who said, '*Aashiqui 2* (Hindi) and *Lucky di Unlucky Story* (Punjabi) released on the same day. While the Punjabi film got 22 shows, the Hindi one only got three shows'.[5]

In recent years, Canada has become a popular destination for shooting Punjabi films and is the second largest market of Punjabi cinema. About 50 per cent of the revenue for all successful Punjabi films is generated from the overseas markets, including Australia, Canada, Malaysia, New Zealand, United Kingdom and United States. A number of Punjabi films have also surpassed the gross collections of Bollywood films in the overseas markets.[6]

Punjabi moviegoers flock to see romcoms laced with a heavy dose of slapstick. Devotional films are also bankable. Social dramas involving impoverished people in tragic circumstances? Not so much. Occasionally an action thriller comes along but film-makers themselves prefer romcoms because they are cheap to make as compared to action films where you have to engage stuntmen, blow up sets and burn a lot of stuff. One thing a film-maker cannot skimp on is music; many films ride to success on the strength of their music alone. Another *sine qua non* is a saleable title. If possible, the name of the film should incorporate the word *Jatta* in some way.

70mm History

Do Punjabi film-makers find economically viable space for 'historical' films that portrays serious and relatively recent events?

Cinema audiences don't expect 'historical' films to be historical. If the movie poster reads 'based on a true story' that automatically means some dry archival crust smothered under a mountain of celluloid whipped cream. Film-makers are entertainers, and like film-makers all over the world, they know that they are not constrained by a demand for accuracy. While they may turn to history in search of a story, they are at liberty to twist the story to fit the requirements of the box office. If we think of Hollywood rather than Pollywood, this gives us *Battle of Stirling* won by Mel Gibson, *Battle of Stalingrad* won by Jude Law, *Battle of Gettysburg* won by Jeff Daniels, *Battle of Jerusalem* won by Orlando Bloom, and many more.

With a theme of armed resistance, triumphant or doomed, the action film potential is clearly present, but what does the film-maker do with the hero in the last reel? The options are grim.

Cine-goers in general, and certainly Punjabi cine-goers, may not mind plunking down good money to see a historical film in which the hero wins and gets the girl. But if the hero dies, no matter how gloriously, who wants to see that?

Have there been any films about Punjab's era of militancy that are exceptions to this rule?

Several Punjabi films and a couple of Hindi films have been made in recent years with Punjab and/or Delhi riots as their backdrop. The peak years for such films were 2013–2015. The number of films in those years was enough to put the wind up the IB which in May 2015, warned the Union Home Ministry of the dangerous development.[7]

The IB fretted that films were being made about Bluestar, the 1984 riots in Delhi and illegal police actions; they took strong exception to films portraying militants as saviours of the Sikh community and favoured clamping down firmly and immediately lest the films produce an unsettling effect on the minds of young and impressionable cine-goers.

The Legacy of Militancy in Punjab

View from the Box Office

'Film industry' is an accepted term and an accurate one: Like any other business, making a film requires substantial investment which has to be recouped at the box office. Rather than get into the artistic merits of films with the theme of Punjab/Delhi of the 1980s and 1990s, let's see how those dangerous and alarming films fared commercially. Our list starts from top box office collection and goes to lowest. By way of comparison, you should remember that the highest grossing Punjabi film of 2018 was *Carry on Jatta* which brought in ₹57 crore worldwide.[8]

2014, *Punjab 1984* (Punjabi). Directed by Diljit Dosanjh, produced by Gunbir Singh Sidhu and Manmord Sidhu. Pathos and bathos: Mother searches for son gone missing during 1984 Delhi riots. From the point of view of the Censor Board, this was not a controversial movie. If the film hit resistance anywhere, it was in Punjab where many viewers thought that it was soft on the central government. Worldwide box office collection came to an impressive ₹34 crore.

2013, *Saada Haq* (Punjabi). Directed by Mandeep Benipal, produced by Kuljinder Sidhu who was also the lead actor. Twist of fate turns one-time star hockey player Kartar Singh into militant. Soon he is an imprisoned militant. Female lead is Canadian Sikh graduate student visiting India to research thesis on minorities at war. She discovers and interviews him. The story unfolds through her research.

Originally, the film was to be released in December 2009, but Censor Board disapproval kept it in the can. The ban was lifted in 2013 on directions of Supreme Court after some cuts, and, on 5 April 2013, the film was released for worldwide distribution. But the road to cinema halls in Punjab, Chandigarh, Haryana, Delhi and Jammu and Kashmir was blocked by state government bans on the grounds that it glorified Khalistan. The film was never released in India but earned well in the international market: Worldwide box office collection came to ₹19 crore.

2017, *Toofan Singh* (Punjabi). Directed by Baghal Singh, produced by Dilbag Singh. Central Board banned the movie in 2016 and a subsequent revising committee refused certification that same year on the grounds that it glorified Khalistan. The film performed well in the overseas market. *Toofan Singh* was released in Australia, the United Kingdom and New Zealand and, by 17 August 2017, it had earned about ₹11 crore. It is yet to be released in India.

2014, *Quom De Heere* (Punjabi). Directed by Ravinder Ravi and produced by Pardeep Bansal, Sandeep Bhalla and Raman Aggarwal. Based on the lives Beant Singh and Satwant Singh, the bodyguards who assassinated Indira Gandhi to avenge the attack on the Golden Temple. The film was praised for addressing the Bluestar issue in depth. Controversy not only swirled around the content of this film but also around the involvement of Censor Board CEO Rakesh Kumar. Kumar was arrested for accepting a bribe to release it. Both the Congress party and the BJP demanded that the film be banned. In February 2014, the Censor Board refused to clear it but after cuts were made the film got its certificate and was released in India in August that year. All the controversy should have brought in a good audience, but the worldwide box office collection shows that the film did not gain substantially: The total came to just ₹8.14 crore.

1996, *Maachis*. This Hindi language film was the first ever movie made about terrorism in Punjab. The hero is a simple youngster devastated by the torture of an innocent man who is also his childhood friend. Thus primed, he is easily recruited to a militant group. The shadowy handler of this group is the villain and the only one of the main characters still alive at the end. The ingredients: Love, angst, idealism, disillusionment and cynicism with soft focus on gunfire and explosions. At the time of its release, BJP's K. R. Malkani and the

CPM's Biplab Dasgupta objected that it didn't unequivocally portray militants as evil, but the Censor Board cleared it anyway with a few cuts. The film's big-name director, Gulzar, might have felt some personal affinity with the topic. Until he landed in Mumbai as a teenager in the early 1950s, he was Sampooran Singh Kalra, originally from Dina (West Punjab). It was shot on a budget of ₹2.5 crore and the box office collection worldwide came to about ₹7 crore. (This take doesn't sound like much now, but given the value of the rupee at that time, *Maachis* was a commercial success.)

2003, *Hawayein* (Hindi and Punjabi). Directed by Ammtoje Mann and produced by Nippy Dhanoa. Following the Delhi riots, the life of a Delhi music student is turned upside down. He and his grandmother return to Punjab where more trouble awaits. Many twists and turns until finally the hero dies in a hail of bullets. The Censor Board passed the film, but it was banned by the governments of Delhi, Punjab and Jammu and Kashmir. These bans were eventually rescinded. Box office collection worldwide came to a just-okay ₹5.2 crore.

2015, *Insaaf Di Udeek: Dilli 1984* (Punjabi). Directed by Ashok Gupta, and produced by Subhash Gupta. It depicts the 1984 Delhi riots through the story of a victim who is an elderly woman who came to the city at the time of Partition. It shows despicable role of Congress leaders. Initially banned by the Censor Board but cleared after cuts. Total worldwide box office collection came to about ₹4.5 crore

2015, *Patta Singhan Da Vairi* (Punjabi). Directed by Naresh Garg, produced by Punjabi folk singer Raj Kakra, who also made *Quom De Heere*. The movie revolves around fake encounters, crimes of police, cowardice and opportunism of political leaders. Censor Board passed it, reviewers panned it, and the audience stayed home. Worldwide box office collection was just average ... about ₹3.8 crore.

2015, *The Mastermind Jinda Sukha* (Punjabi). Directed by Sukhjinder Singh Shera and produced by Sukhchain Singh. The movie is based on the lives of Harjinder Singh Jinda and Sukhdev Singh Sukha of KCF. These two murdered former Army Chief General A. S. Vaidya about two years after Operation Bluestar. Vaidya was the head of Armed Forces when Operation Bluestar was carried out. Although initially cleared by the Censor Board, permission was withdrawn in September 2015 after the Union Ministry of Home Affairs directed the Board to re-examine the film. The film was released abroad shortly after the ban in India was announced. Production costs came to ₹2.5 crore while box office collection from theatres abroad was a disappointing ₹3 crore.

2015, *Chauthi Koot* (Punjabi). Directed by Gurvinder Singh and produced by Kartikeya Narayan Singh. The film weaves together two short stories. One is about a village family's dilemma over what to do about their beloved pet following a militant ban on barky dogs, and the other is about a family who lose their way travelling on backroads at night. They fear to knock on the door of a house to ask directions and the occupant of the house is just as afraid to open the door. These stories are exchanged among passengers who force their way onto a freight train, having missed the last passenger train. The film won National Film Award for Best Feature Film in Punjabi and was highly praised at international film festivals but found no audience in Punjab. The box office collection worldwide came to about ₹2.5 crore.

2015, *Blood Street* (Punjabi). Directed by Darshan Darvesh, produced by Canada-based Jasbir Singh Boparai. The movie depicts suffering of Sikh families during Delhi riots and police atrocities. The film-makers went into loss: Box office collection worldwide came to ₹1.2 crore.

2015, *Kaun Kare Insaaf* (Punjabi). Directed by Baljit Singh and produced by Avtar Singh Gill and Salinder Singh Salindra. This film was set in Delhi during the 1984 riots. It earned a meagre ₹40 lakh at the box office.

When we work out the average box office collections of these 11 militant-themed films, it comes to ₹9 crore. Examining the figures more closely reveals that three films earned between ₹34 crore and ₹11 crore; three earned between about ₹8 crore and ₹5 crore; three earned between ₹4.5 crore and ₹3 crore; and three earned less than ₹3 crore going down to a dismal ₹40 lakh. Year 2018's highest earning Punjabi film, a comedy, brought in ₹57 crore.

This tells us that Punjabi movie goers did not break down the cinema hall doors, desperate for a dose of religiopolitical radicalization. To be honest, Punjabi moviegoers did not like serious films before the militancy era, and they do not like them now. It is doubtful that they will ever like them.

The actual box office figures also show us how easy it is to spook the IB and the Censor Board too.

Arrested and Booked

A decade as jolting as 1984–1994 was bound to wake up many different kinds of storytellers.

The memoirists, biographers and auto-biographers got down to work immediately. Among the first books to come out were non-fiction accounts by retired Army commanders involved in Operation Bluestar. Their books focused on what happened immediately before, during and after the first week of June 1984. These books had a double message: the Indian Army as invincible and irresistible and the Indian Army as restrained and even pious.

Right behind the military men were the editors and reporters. Their output was more non-fiction. With boxes full of already published material to draw on, slapping together a book was a quick job for them. The only care needed was to weed out pieces that time had proved to be embarrassing misjudgements.

Officers of the government were also quick off the block. Retire on Monday and start dictating anecdotes from the corridors of power on Tuesday. Some very interesting beans spilled out of these books. The revelations reminded readers that truth can be stranger than fiction. The ones that come to mind are *Time Present and Time Past: Memoirs of a Top Cop* by the late DGP Kirpal Dhillon, *Bullet for Bullet: My Life as a Police Officer* by DGP Julio Ribeiro and *Open Secrets: India's Intelligence Unveiled* by IB Joint Director (retd) Maloy Krishna Dhar.

Political machinations and the shock of violence in Punjab and Delhi cast shadows in the autobiographies of Khushwant Singh (*Truth, Love and a Little Malice*) and Patwant Singh (*Of Dreams and Demons: A Memoir of Modern India*).

Only one memoir/autobiography/biography has emerged from a person in the Khalistan camp. It is *The Stolen Years*, an account of Simranjit Singh Mann's years in prison, written by his daughter Pavit Kaur. While Mann strongly opposed the Indian government, at the same time, he belongs to the Punjab's generation-to-generation elite. Simranjit Singh's extremism could be very extreme, but it was verbal; he never physically harmed anyone.

Readers are still waiting for a Punjabi equivalent of Visier Meyasetsu Sanyü, a man whose childhood and teenage years were spent dodging the Indian Army, and who, amazingly, emerged from the jungles of Nagaland to write a gripping autobiography. Maybe one day some survivor, some released convict, some escapee settled abroad, will open his notebook and write *Maiñ uhanā de naal si ...* (I was with them.)

Slow March of Fiction

Literature is history with no need for footnotes. This means that producing fiction ought to be easier and quicker than producing non-fiction, but it's not. Long gaps punctuate the publication of writers depicting the militancy period through fiction.

A collection of reviews, book after book after book, doesn't belong in an overview like this, but it may be helpful to do some categorizing. This has been done with a very broad brush at the risk of losing the finer points of each book, and we make no guarantee that all novels or short stories on Punjab/Delhi 1984 and thereafter are mentioned here.

Here are our categories.

Caught in the storm. Shock as it happens. Stories of this nature may sweep over the vast extent of catastrophe or portray it in microcosm. Ajeet Cour's *Wail of the Black Breeze* and *Delhi 84* by Roopinder Singh are of this type. Another good example is a short story, *Nihatha Nahin Haan Main* in Jaswant Deed's collection titled *Dharti Hor Pare*. Likewise, *Nadarshah di Wapsi* by Ajit Rahi. The Delhi riots have been depicted by a well-known Tamil novelist. This is *Mounappuyal* (*maun* = silent, *puyal* = storm) by Vaasanthi. (Should a Tamil-language novel of the Delhi riots be astonishing? If a Punjabi wrote a novel on death and devastation in coastal Tamil Nadu after the 2004 tsunami would *that* be astonishing?)

On the edge of the storm. Individuals trying to remain functional in dysfunctional catastrophic circumstances. *The Assassinations*, a novel of 1984 by Vikram Kapoor fits here.

Post-catastrophe 1. Struggle to fit long-held belief onto contrary reality or to fit reason, logical thought onto an 'insane' milieu. *Mainu Hanera Kyun Nahin Lagda* by Kuldip Nayar and Ninder Gill's *Deshat de Dinan Wich* belongs here. The Nayar book was unexpected. The writer was one of the doyens of Indian journalism, had never written fiction, had always written in English and four years before he died (in 2018) at age 90, he came out with a novel in Punjabi.

Post-catastrophe 2. Struggle through catastrophe to create/find a workable identity or repair a damaged one. *Roll of Honour* by

Amandeep Sandhu is an identity story. Identity is the nub of Tejinder Singh Gagan's *Wah Mera Chehra* (Hindi). He did not belong to Punjab or Delhi; home was not *phoren* but *videsh*,[9] specifically, the Indian state of Chhattisgarh where he spent his life. In 1984, suspicion fell on all Sikhs and targeting Sikhs in other states was even easier than targeting them in Punjab. His writing offers an angle that rarely surfaces when the turmoil of the period is discussed.

Justification 1. Portrays victimization, suffering, persistence in the face of persecution. *Na Maro* by Ajeet Cour is a strong example and so are Boota Singh Shaad's *Tera Keea Meetha Lage*, Darshan Singh's *Gallery Shaheedan* and Simarjit Kaur's *Saffron Salvation*.

Justification 2. The protagonist, as a stand-in for his group or generation, confronts terrible deeds or shame of silence and inaction. Two examples: Jaspreet Singh's *Helium* and Kanjit Deol's *Year of the Hawks*.

For those who want some of everything, try *1984: In Memory and Imagination* edited by Vikram Kapoor. This book dishes up both fiction and essays. Seven good choices in each category.

The literature that has come out of the era of militancy offers nothing for those in search of uplifting feel-good stories, but that is exactly why they are beneficial. The writers remind us that everything didn't turn out okay back in those days. Carrying the message forward, it's clear that a future spasm, as bad or worse, can't be ruled out. In fact, if we look around the country, we can see plenty of ongoing spasms that have been in progress for quite some time now.

All of India is waiting for the writer who will distil the whole sorry miasma into a self-help book for apprehensive citizens; suggested title: *The Power of Negative Thinking*. The writer would harp on a single lesson: 'Take nothing for granted. Keep a sharp eye on parliament, legislation, parties, politicians, the government, the courts, fanatics, useful idiots, thugs, spin doctors and rabble-rousing opportunists. The only one responsible for your safety is YOU'.

Summing Up

On the scales of cultural expression, with remembering in one pan and forgetting in the other, it is literature that has lent the most weight to the side of remembering. After all, storytellers *have* to be people who remember. Even a childish and stumbling writer reinforces the memory of his readers while the perceptive and skilled one goes further and helps his readers make sense of the past. Cinema has not done so well. A few film-makers have tried to look back but got little encouragement from cine-goers. As for the area of commerce, howsoever much intellectual types look down on the bazaar, the fact is that, for complex reasons, buyers are ready to spend on the goods of memory.

Notes

1. Jagowala Jatha: The Background. https://soundcloud.com/jagowalajatha&hl=en&gl=in&strip=1&vwsrc=0
2. Irom Chanu Sharmila, a civil rights activist, political activist and poet from the Indian state of Manipur. On 5 November 2000, she began a hunger strike which she ended on 9 August 2016, after 16 years of fasting.
    Burhan Muzaffar Wani was a commander of Kashmiri militant group Hizbul Mujahideen. He gained popularity through his social media presence, which modernized the image of militancy in Kashmir, spoke to Kashmiri youth.
    Mallojula Koteshwar Rao alias Kishenji, a CPI(M) politburo member, seen as the face of Maoist movement in India and a key face of Lalgarh movement. He was killed on 24 November 2011 in an encounter in jungles of Burishole, West Bengal.
3. http://searchguide.level3.com/search/?q=http%3A//https:/www.reddit.com/r/Sikh/comments/31l0zj/video_games_%2520with%2520_sikh_content/%2520%23thing_t1_cq2n5bu&r=&bc=
4. *France 24*, 'New Hezbollah Video Game'.
5. Sharma, 'Jatt *di* Film'.
6. Mehta, 'New Age Filmmakers Bring Hope'.
7. Mail Today Bureau, 'Intelligence Bureau Alerts Home Ministry'.
8. Box office figures are from https://www.the-numbers.com/box-office and https://www.facebook.com/officialpunjabicinemaboxoffice/

9. If you live in *phoren*, meaning some country outside the borders of India, as in *foreign*, then you have got it made. Within India, you may live in Punjab (otherwise known as *desh*—your country) or you may live in Delhi. Any state within India where a Punjabi will have difficulty understanding the local lingo is *videsh*. *Videsh* means *foreign*, but an unenviable sort of foreign. A song in Tamil is *videshi gana*. *Pardes* and *pardesi* also mean foreign and foreigner, but the nuance is exotic and romantic. Numerous Punjabi songs refer to *pardesi*, that is, some fascinating stranger.

6

Khalistan Redux

As the 1990s drew to a close, violence dwindled to near zero. The men who assassinated Punjab Chief Minister Beant Singh in August 1995 had been arrested that very year, but the trial dragged on for nearly 12 years.[1]

Ramrajya Meets Sher-e-Punjab

The 1997 Assembly election in Punjab was conducted without boycotts or threats. The BJP, which had fared poorly in the 1996 General Election, saw the need for partners, which meant that it had to soften its Hindutva line. The SAD, knowing it was unlikely to pull in more than 30 per cent of the vote, saw clear benefit in joining hands with a Hindu party. Their manifesto proclaimed 'Ramrajya and governance as in the days of Maharaja Ranjit Singh' and, on the campaign trail, their candidates belaboured the incumbent Congress regime for corruption.[2]

It was a time when one expected to hear just one song: *Kharkoo haar gaye, Super Cop jeet gaya, jai ho!* The paean was often sung by the state's strutting, tache twirling DGP K. P. S. Gill himself. But in the Assembly campaign, when Congress candidates might have had campaigned on their party's role in quelling militancy, they did not. Like the non-barking dog in the Sherlock Holmes story, the curious incident of the 1997 election was the silence on militancy.

155

Turnout was a respectable 68.7 per cent and when the votes were counted, Parkash Singh Badal had led the SAD to a 75-seat victory: It's the largest tally ever and an absolute majority. The voters of Punjab prayed for better days.

Peaceful election, stable government ... Human rights activists felt encouraged and thought that the time was right to try resurrecting the rule of law. A People's Commission on human rights violations in Punjab was set up to examine allegations of abduction, torture, extrajudicial execution and illegal mass cremations.[3]

The government panicked; the People's Commission had to be stopped. On 11 June 1998, Chandigarh Police said they had foiled a conspiracy to blast open the gates of Chandigarh's Burail Jail and spirit away the Beant Singh assassins. One Satnam Singh had tried to smuggle plastic explosives disguised as sweets into the jail but they caught him. This alleged conspiracy provided a pretext to implicate and arrest many human rights workers and lawyers. Those that were not arrested were harassed. Most of those implicated in the Burail Jail-break conspiracy case were charge-sheeted, and in consequence, denied bail. Ultimately, they were acquitted,[4] but the purpose was served: They languished in judicial custody until the trial was completed and were further dissuaded from future human rights work through torture and threats. The People's Commission was effectively crippled.

Both the state and central governments were nervous and they remained nervous for a long, long time.[5] As shown in the two chapters—'Due Process: Punjab' and 'Due Process: Delhi'—in many cases, more than 20 years elapsed between the time a heinous crime was committed and the judgement day when someone was either acquitted or found guilty in a court. Why such a long, long wait for justice? Was it just a matter of a particular judge finally coming along and lifting a stay on prosecution? Maybe. The fact is that the courts gave both the state and central governments ample time to calm down and pull themselves together. They also gave the cases themselves a long, long time to fade from media attention and public recollection.

Millennium Fiascos

The events of the next several years teach us that nothing is simple. War, peace, things far away and things up close, events appear to be unrelated; they appear to be moving independently and moving in separate ways, but, sooner or later, they turn out to be tangled together.

Peace. In February 1999, a smiling Prime Minister Atal Bihari Vajpayee was trading Urdu couplets with President Nawaz Sharif in Lahore; it looked like peace might break out. All the while Pakistani generals were stealthily airlifting heavy artillery to the top of Tololing, a high ridge overlooking the highway connecting the Kashmir valley and Leh. Pakistan was infiltrating troops across the border and high up in the mountains.

War. The shooting in the mountains above Kargil and Dras started in May 1999. The gobsmacked India Army, at great cost, barely managed to beat back Pakistan and hang on to the high passes. It wasn't just the incursion ... India felt duped, stabbed in the back.

Events far away. The analysts in the Ministry of External Affairs and Ministry of Defence sized up the future and it did not look good. In 1998, the USA had placed India and Pakistan under sanctions after both countries conducted nuclear tests.[6] But Afghanistan was hotting up. Taliban hijackers, backed by the well-equipped Al Qaeda, had seized an Air India plane and flown to Kandahar to compel India to release three of their men. In 1999–2000, it already seemed likely that the USA would wade into Afghanistan, and, when it did, Pakistan's cooperation would be vital. Pakistan would cooperate on the condition that the USA lifted sanctions and forked over

The Legacy of Militancy in Punjab

big bucks. India's job was to woo the Americans and convince Clinton that Pakistan had long since gone over to the really really dark side.

American President Bill Clinton accepted India's invitation to visit—the first American president to do so in 22 years—and his five-day tour started on 20 March 2000.

Events close to home. On the night of 20 March, 36 Sikh men, generation-to-generation residents of village Chittisinghpura, in Kashmir's Anantnag district, were rousted out of their homes and shot in cold blood. Union Minister of Home Affairs L. K. Advani thundered that the guilty would pay. So on 25 March, men of the 7 Rashtriya Rifles carried out an operation to take down five 'foreign militants' in the forests of Pathribal in Kashmir's Anantnag district.[7] The army claimed that the slain men were responsible for the Chittisinghpura massacre.

Local people knew that the five men (all labourers and shepherds) were in fact residents of villages around Pathribal, who had been taken away by the army a couple of days before the encounter. When civilians came out on the streets to protest the extrajudicial killings, another eight people in Brakpora were shot dead by the CRPF. In all, 49 civilians were killed in a matter of 15 days.

Clinton was horrified. Kashmir was incensed. The soldiers who carried out the Pathribal killings were identified, indicted for murder in a CBI investigation and 14 years later let off by the Army. The matter is pending before the Supreme Court since 2017, and it looks like it's going to pend forever.

Peace. Punjab was quiet in 2000. Nevertheless, many Sikhs were knocking on Denmark's door asking for asylum. The Danish Immigration Service wanted to know how much stock they should put in the stories of these people, so they sent a team to Punjab to scope out how things were on the ground.[8] The Danes spent two weeks talking to people ranging from political officers of foreign diplomatic missions to senior officers of the union home ministry, Punjab government officers, Punjab Police officers, leaders of political parties, political dissidents, lawyers and judges, journalists and activists of human rights organizations.

Their report quoted informants as saying that they saw no support for militant groups in Punjab and no recruitment was taking place. There was general agreement that the conflict in Punjab had ended in 1991 and that there had been no security problems since then. At the same time, many of their informants mentioned that both the police and political parties had a vested interest in keeping the fear of militancy alive—the police for the sake of claiming more resources and the political parties for the sake of finding anything to distract public attention from economic stagnation and continuing human rights abuses.

Post-Traumatic Shock

Meanwhile in Delhi, the Government of India was still shaking. Critics were shouting about just how closely the country had come to defeat in Kargil in 1999; the Army and the intelligence agencies had been caught napping. The government's response was to set up a Group of Ministers (GoM) panel to review threats to the country and recommend improvements. Heads had to roll. The GoM 2001 report, *Reforming the National Security System*,[9] was strongly focused on the threat from fundamentalist terrorism. Muslims were Danger Number 1:

> Funded by Saudi and Gulf sources, many new madrassas have come up all over the country in recent years, especially in large numbers in the coastal areas of the west and in the border areas of West Bengal and Northeast. Reports of systematic indoctrination of Muslims in the border areas in fundamentalist ideology is detrimental to the country's communal harmony.

The report warned that secessionist movements in Jammu and Kashmir and elsewhere in the country were being transformed into a pan-Islamic movement against India.

> The Taliban success in Afghanistan has brought about a qualitative change in the security environment of the region. It has also given rise to groups of jihadi forces. These forces are unlikely to stop in Afghanistan and Pakistan. These bands of religious fanatics are indulging in subversive activities and have expansionist designs. They will work relentlessly for the break up of the Indian union.

The GoM also saw the possibility of more Khalistan trouble and wanted the situation in Punjab kept under close watch.

> Many pro-Khalistan militants continue to enjoy shelter in Pakistan and there are reports of plans to revive terrorism in Punjab. Subversive propaganda is being aired from Pakistani Punjab. The appointment of a former head of the ISI as chairman (a Muslim) of the Sikh Gurdwara Prabandhak Committee in Pakistan is an indicator of Pakistan's malafide intentions.

Sikhophobia

Considering the world situation (bad then and worse now) fear of terrorist strikes was justified; no country in the world was safe. Doubting the long-term viability of the Indian Union harked back to British Raj sentiments.[10] As for fear of a resurgence of Khalistan trouble ... a word may have to be invented here—Sikhophobia.

Unless you were aware of Congress versus Akali political calculations in the early 1980s, the Khalistan threat was a puzzle even back in 1984. Supposing every single Sikh in the entire country was solidly in favour of seceding from India, numerically, what kind of threat did that come to? In 1981, Sikhs—*all* Sikhs in every state of India—constituted only 1.92 per cent of country's total population of 684 million. In numbers, that comes to about 13 crore. In Punjab,

Khalistan Redux

where Sikhs were concentrated and constituted 60.75 per cent of total population, their absolute numbers in 1981 were still only about 1.02 crore. In 2000, India's population crossed the 1 billion mark; eight hundred million of those people were Hindus. When the numbers of a group come to eight hundred million, individuals belonging to that group ought to feel fairly secure.

At the beginning of the millennium, vague talk of a Khalistan comeback made no sense. And yet political leaders, military and police officers and even free-floating op-ed writers swore that they could hear the ominous buzz of the Babbar bees. Khalistan warnings continue to this day.

In fact, from around 2001 onwards, dire warnings about Khalistan came along at frequent intervals: The headlines spoke of attempts to revive Khalistan, foreign-based Khalistan terrorists, Khalistan terrorists funded by Sikhs living abroad, Pakistan ISI-sponsored Khalistan terrorists, Sikhs as a major pillar of Pakistan's anti-India designs.

But where was pro-Khalistan sentiment in Punjab? Even the idea of a Pakistani ISI plan to harm India by using the Sikhs seemed far-fetched to people who actually lived in Punjab. Particularly the part about some wing of the Pakistan military dreaming it up. What kind of Sikhs would a Pakistani general see when he put his head on the pillow and floated off to dreamland? Maybe a vision of General Rajinder Singh Sparrow rolling over Zoji La or taking out 67 Patton tanks at Phillora? How about General Harbakhsh Singh crossing the Ravi River and driving straight for Sialkot? Or General Gurbaksh Singh flooding the cane fields at Asal Uttar and picking off the Pakistani tanks as their tracks spun in the mud?

20-Year Comeback Trail

People who lived in Punjab observed that Khalistan was finished by 1991 or 1992.[11]

The Legacy of Militancy in Punjab

No militancy problem arose during the Punjab Assembly election of 1997 or the General Elections of 1998 and 1999. But if we look at newspaper reports since 2000, do we get anything about Khalistan? Indeed, we do and here we have listed a few chronologically:

2000	Gaurav Vivek Bhatnagar. 'Concern Over Revival of Terrorism'. *The Hindu*, 21 October 2000. https://www.thehindu.com/thehindu/2000/10/21/stories/14212188.htm
2001	K. P. Nayar. 'Pak Man in Khalistan Funds Net'. *The Telegraph*, 21 December 2001. https://www.telegraphindia.com/india/pak-man-in-khalistan-funds-net/cid/747486
2002	The Hindu Correspondent. 'Terrorists' Plan Foiled'. *The Hindu*, 8 April 2002. https://www.thehindu.com/thehindu/2002/04/08/
2003	The Hindu Correspondent. 'Bid to Revive Khalistan Movement: Gill'. *The Hindu*, 9 June 2003. https://www.thehindu.com/thehindu/2003/06/09/stories/2003060901750300.htm
2004	Staff Reporter. 'Two Khalistan Militants Gunned Down in Encounter'. *The Hindu*, 30 April 2004. https://www.thehindu.com/2004/04/30/stories/2004043006490300.htm
2005	Rajesh Deol. 'Cry for Khalistan Again'. *Deccan Herald*, 5 January 2005. http://www.sikhtimes.com/news_011805b.html
2006	PTI. 'Police Say KZF Behind Jalandhar Blasts'. *Indian Express*, 19 June 2006. http://archive.indianexpress.com/news/-kzf-behind-jalandhar-blasts-/6802/
2007	Ajai Sahni. 'Terror in The Wings'. Outlook, 25 June 2007. https://www.outlookindia.com/website/story/terror-in-the-wings/234926
2008	PTI. 'Attempts on to Revive Terrorism in Punjab: Cops'. Rediff.com, 6 June 2008. https://www.rediff.com/news/2008/jun/06sikh.htm
	Dinesh K. Sharma. 'Punjab Police Sniff Out Major KCF Plan to Kill Dera Chief'. *Times of India*, 9 November 2008. https://timesofindia.indiatimes.com/india/Punjab-police-sniff-out-major-KCF-plan-to-kill-Dera-chief/articleshow/3690452.cms

2009	Nishit Dholabhai. 'Delhi Vigilant on Khalistan'. *The Telegraph*, 12 June 2009. https://www.telegraphindia.com/india/delhi-vigilant-on-khalistan/cid/617367
2010	Jangveer Singh. 'Sikh Ultras May Target Delhi Games'. *The Tribune*, 24 July 2010. https://www.tribuneindia.com/2010/20100724/main6.htm
2011	Asit Jolly. 'Pakistan's Plan for Khalistan'. *India Today*, 14 November 2011. https://smedia2.intoday.in/indiatoday/cover-story-punjab-militancy-pakistan-plan-for-khalistan.pdf
2012	PTI. 'Massive Fund Raising Campaign in West by Separatist Sikh Organisations'. BusinessLine, 7 October 2012. https://www.thehindubusinessline.com/news/Massive-fund-raising-campaign-in-West-by-separatist-Sikh-organisations/article20511552.ece
2013	IANS. 'Ominous Signs of Revival of Sikh Militancy: Security Agencies on Alert'. *IANS*, 4 September 2013. https://www.newsbharati.com/Encyc/2013/9/4/Ominous-signs-of-revival-of-Sikh-militancy-Security-agencies-on-alert.amp.html
2014	*City Air News*. 'Joint Terrorist Module of Khalistan Zindabad Force and Khalistan Liberation Force Busted'. *City Air News*, 4 August 2014. https://cityairnews.com/content/joint-terrorist-module-khalistan-zindabad-force-kzf-khalistan-liberation-force-klf-busted
2015	Seema Mustafa. 'Governments Cower as Bhindranwale Re-emerges'. *The Citizen*, 7 June 2015. https://www.thecitizen.in/index.php/en/NewsDetail/index/1/3914/GOVERNMENTS-COWER-AS-BHINDRANWALE-RE-EMERGES
	Express News Service. 'Congress is Anti-national, Derecognise It, Says Sukhbir Badal'. *The Indian Express*, 22 November 2015. https://indianexpress.com/article/india/india-news-india/congress-anti-national-party-should-be-derecognised-for-encouraging-secessionists-sukhbir-badal/

(continued)

(continued)

	Rajendra Khatry. 'Is Sikh Radicalism Riding on Politics to Make a Comeback in Punjab?' *First Post*, 24 November 2015. https://www.firstpost.com/politics/is-sikh-radicalism-riding-on-politics-to-make-a-comeback-in-punjab-2519590.html
2016	Rohan Dua. 'Former CBI Chief Warns Against Growing Pro-Khalistan Support'. *Times of India*, 24 August 2016. http://timesofindia.indiatimes.com/india/Khalistan-terror-camp-in-Canadaplotting-attacks-in-Punjab-India-to-Trudeau-govt/articleshow/52495693.cms
	Rohan Dua. 'Khalistan Terror Camp in Canada Plotting Attacks in Punjab: India to Trudeau Govt'. *Times of India*, 30 May 2016. http://timesofindia.indiatimes.com/india/Khalistan-terror-camp-in-Canadaplotting-attacks-in-Punjab-India-to-Trudeau-govt/articleshow/52495693.cms
	Sandipan Sharma. 'Ahead of Punjab Elections, Pro-Khalistan Elements Make Desperate Bid to Stay Relevant'. *First Post*, 6 June 2016. https://www.firstpost.com/politics/ahead-of-punjab-elections-pro-khalistan-elements-make-desperate-bid-to-stay-relevant-2819004.html
2017	ANI. 'Punjab Police Bust Terror Module under "Khalistan Zindabad" banner'. *Outlook*, 30 May 2017. https://www.outlookindia.com/newsscroll/punjab-police-bust-terror-module-under-khalistan-zindabad-banner/1063786
	Asit Jolly. 'How Punjab is Threatened by Revival of Khalistan Movement, Considered Defeated in 1990s'. *India Today*, 26 June 2017. https://www.indiatoday.in/magazine/nation/story/20170626-khalistan-punjab-terrorism-extremist-sikh-outfits-986585-2017-06-19&hl=en&gl=in&strip=1&vwsrc=0
	PTI. 'ISI Trying to Revive Khalistan Movement: Govt'. *Outlook*, 27 December 2017. https://www.outlookindia.com/newsscroll/isi-trying-to-revive-khalistan-movement-govt/1218062

2018	Namrata Biji Ahuja. 'Red Alert or Red Herring: How Real is the Threat of Sikh Militancy?' *The Week*, 22 March 2018. https://www.theweek.in/news/india/2018/03/22/sikh-militancy-threat-isi-pakistan-khalistan-punjab.html
	Ruchika M. Khanna. 'Centre Alerts State on Efforts to Revive Khalistan Movement'. *The Tribune*, 3 September 2018. https://www.tribuneindia.com/news/punjab/centre-alerts-state-on-efforts-to-revive-khalistan-movement/646871.html
	Anju Agnihotri Chaba. 'Jalandhar Blast: Pro-Khalistan Group Claims Responsibility for Explosions'. *Indian Express*, 16 September 2018. https://indianexpress.com/article/india/jalandhar-blast-pro-khalistan-group-claims-responsibility-for-explosions-5358492/
	Tribune News Service. 'Police: Pro-Khalistan Modules "Active" in UP'. *The Tribune*, 18 October 2018. https://www.tribuneindia.com/news/punjab/police-pro-khalistan-modules-active-in-up/669870.html
	PTI. 'Bid to Revive Insurgency in Punjab Through "External linkages": Army Chief Bipin Rawat'. *Hindustan Times*, 3 November 2018. https://www.hindustantimes.com/india-news/bid-to-revive-insurgency-in-punjab-through-external-linkages-army-chief-bipin-rawat/story-i5kCpBubcNJJZqJrUuoGBK.html
	FP Staff. 'Amritsar Grenade Attack: Theories Abound About Possible Hand of Pakistan's ISI, Khalistan Hardliners'. *First Post*, 19 November 2018. https://www.firstpost.com/india/amritsar-grenade-attack-theories-abound-about-possible-hand-of-pakistans-isi-khalistan-hardliners-5576021.html
	Rachna Khaira. 'For Punjab Govt, Amritsar Blast is Proof that Demand for Khalistan Never Died'. *Huffington Post*, 22 November 2018. https://www.huffingtonpost.in/2018/11/22/for-punjab-govt-amritsar-blast-is-proof-that-demand-for-khalistan-never-died_a_23596614/

(continued)

(continued)

	ANI. 'Pakistan's Plot to Back Khalistan Movement Exposed', *Business Standard*, 18 December 2018. https://www.businessstandard.com/article/news-ani/pakistan-s-plot-to-back-khalistan-movement-exposed-118121800593_1.html
	PTI. 'Govt Bans Khalistan Liberation Force'. *The Economic Times*, 27 December 2018. https://economictimes.indiatimes.com/news/politics-and-nation/govt-bans-khalistan-liberation-force/articleshow/67275538.cms
	Manjeet Sehgal. 'US-Based Pro-Khalistan Group Seeks Pakistan's Support for Anti-India Campaign'. *India Today*, 18 December 2018. https://www.indiatoday.in/india/story/us-based-pro-khalistani-group-seeks-pakistan-s-support-for-anti-india-campaign-1412215-2018-12-18&hl=en&gl=in&strip=1&vwsrc=0
2019	Staff News. 'Centre Says It Cracked Down on 18 Khalistani Terror Modules, Arrested 95 Suspects Over Two Years'. *Scroll.in*, 2 January 2019. https://scroll.in/latest/907935/centre-says-it-cracked-down-on-18-khalistani-terror-modules-arrested-95-suspects-over-two-years
	PTI. 'Efforts to Revive Khalistan-Linked Terrorism in Punjab'. *The Economic Times*, 12 February 2019. https://economictimes.indiatimes.com/news/defence/efforts-to-revive-khalistan-linked-terrorism-in-punjab/articleshow/67958238.cms?from=mdr
	ANI. 'India Slams "Referendum 2020", Says It Tantamount to Separatism. *ANI News*, 16 March 2019. https://www.aninews.in/news/world/asia/india-slams-referendum-2020-says-it-tantamounts-to-separatism20190316170557/

It turns out that we can search any year from 2000 to the present and turn up Khalistan stories. On the Internet world, newer stuff eventually pushes older stuff off the web which may partly account for why Khalistan stories become more numerous as the year specification moves closer to the present. Year 2018 brought a bumper crop of Khalistan warnings—well in time for pre-election bogey-raising.

These stories have seven basic themes:

- 'Khalistanis arrested/shot dead'
- 'Khalistanis behind attack'
- 'Khalistani plot foiled'
- 'Pakistan/ISI reviving Khalistan'
- 'Khalistanis join hands with Hizb-/Lashkar-/Tehrik-/Harkat-/ etc.'
- 'Intelligence agencies/army chief/minister warns'
- 'Diaspora Sikhs arming/funding Khalistanis, or otherwise making trouble'

What to Believe?

Except for pleasant little fibs such as 'Oh! You've lost weight!' people do not like to be lied to. Remember the lesson we preached in our imaginary self-help book? That line about 'the only one responsible for your safety is *you*.' The same applies when you are trying to assess all the information beamed at you, some of it true, some of it false, much of it with an ulterior motive. Here's the next lesson: 'The only one responsible for sifting out reliable information is *you*'.

There was a time when people believed that if they read a thing in the newspaper then it was true. Today, newspapers are relics of a quaint and simple age. People who know the meaning of 'newspaper' might also know the meaning of 'doily', 'floppy disc', 'watch-stem' and 'carrom board'. Faith in the disinterested credibility of news published through any medium has been greatly weakened over the past 20 years. The two sentence headlines provided by smart phone apps or even the two paragraph stories available on the Internet don't carry the same sense of 'certification' and in-depth detail that stories on newsprint had. Believe it or not, some of those old print stories could be up to a thousand words long. Today, readers/viewers know they are targets for fake news, disinformation and spin, and they have even learned useful foreign words such as *kompromat*.

Let's go back to the list of stories taken from the Internet. Say that you read only the stories in which some named person has been arrested. That would be a story with a definite who-what-where-when-why-and-how; it should be pretty credible, right? Except that there is *never* a follow-up story, meaning a story whose headline would say something like 'Alleged terrorist remanded ... /charged with ... /brought to trial ... /found guilty ... /sentenced ...'. Such follow-up stories would be backed up by court records which are public documents. If anyone doubted the news as published (and wanted to take the trouble), he could verify it from court records. The story may be true, but when we don't find out what happened after the arrest, some doubt is sure to linger.

A journalist is not a tiny insect that can creep unseen into the private space of someone-who-knows-something and get information by stealthily watching and listening. When a story is based on information from someone-who-knows-something, it means that either that someone gave a press conference or issued a press note, or the journalist has requested an interview from that person, or that the person has himself summoned the journalist and handed out the specific information that he wanted people to get.

In our list of categories, six of them depend entirely on quoting people: SSP says, DGP says, chief minister says, union minister says, IB chief says, Army chief says. If the reader/viewer thinks the person/s quoted do in fact know what they are talking about, that they are credible and do not lie or mischievously omit or twist, then, and *only* then, are the stories credible.

Slant also affects credibility. Journalism courses don't teach students how to slant a story, but, on the job, every journalist learns how to do it. The information in the story is true to the best of the journalist's knowledge, but it is presented with a particular angle. Headlines, which are the work of editors, can be slanted. 'Thousands attend peaceful protest' versus 'Agitation brings city to standstill'; same story, different slant.

Credibility of sources and slant are not only things to consider; a reader has also to ask 'why is this coming out *now*?' A story may look absolutely straight and solid: 'Bollywood director accused of sexual assault'. Same story appearing 10 days before Filmfare Awards night? *Hmmm...*

Not even the simplest story should be swallowed uncritically, but when a story is primarily assertion and/or speculation, then it needs to be read through a high-powered lens of scepticism. Assertion/speculation stories are very likely to be planted stories. Someone wants the public to believe some particular thing or internalize some particular attitude. Double the power of your scepticism lens when the someone quoted is not identified and instead all you get is sources. Every single member of the sources tribe is a fishy character and that includes *official sources, intelligence sources, party sources* and that out and out scoundrel, *reliable sources*.

Looking over all the dire warning stories, it is a safe bet that some of them express sincere and legitimate concerns. It is not difficult to believe that Pakistan would be gratified to see trouble in India and would try to make trouble if it didn't already exist. Pakistan faces trouble in Balochistan. How does India feel about that? Would India go so far as to encourage trouble?

Some of the stories display the jagged edge of paranoia, although the underlying insecurity may be reasonable and genuine. To quote Joseph Heller, 'Just because you're paranoid doesn't mean they aren't after you'.

Some of the stories arouse the suspicion of pretended paranoia with an axe to grind. Be on guard when you come across that type.

The Legacy of Militancy in Punjab

Real or pretend, for 20 years, the warnings have kept wafting down from on high: 'The Khalistanis are trying to come back'.

Ballot-Proof

Khalistanis are trying to come back? Fine. Let them come. All they have to do is win 59 seats in Punjab's 117 seat Assembly. Punjab would then have a Khalistani government.

Punjab has several Sikh 'hardliner' organizations; among them are Dal Khalsa, United Akali Dal, Akhand Kirtani Jatha, Akali Dal 1920. These groups advocate neither secession nor violence, so they are perfectly legal and are as free as anybody else to put up candidates in an election. But since they don't, let us not refer to them as political parties. Only one hardliner group regularly contests elections and that is the Shiromani Akali Dal (Amritsar) led by Simranjit Singh Mann.[12]

But what does the record look like there? Does public sentiment favour a Khalistani government?

The radical high point was 1989 when Simranjit Mann's Akali Dal Amritsar won eight seats in the Lok Sabha. In 2007 Assembly Polls, all the 37 candidates fielded by Mann, including himself and son Emaan, forfeited their security deposits. In the 2009 General Election, wherever SAD Amritsar candidates stood, the voters rejected them and in the 2012 Assembly Elections, Mann, contesting from Fatehgarh Sahib, got slightly more 3,000 votes and lost his deposit. In the 2014 Lok Sabha Elections, Mann again lost his deposit, getting only 14,000 votes and that too standing from erstwhile militancy hot-spot Khadoor Sahib. That time around, he polled exactly 13,999 votes: 1.34 per cent of the total. In 2017, votes polled by 54 candidates fielded by Mann's SAD (Amritsar) failed to cross even the total number of times NOTA (none of the above) option was used by the electorate.[13]

The electoral record suggests that the time is not yet ripe for a Khalistan revival.

Still, look at that long list of *Khalistan danger* stories listed earlier. Ever since 2000, lots of people have been worried. Even General Bipin Rawat sounded a warning as recently as November 2018. If the man who commands the world's second largest standing army has got Khalistan jitters, how are the rest of us supposed to feel?

On the other hand, if that list represents 20 years of scaremongering, then who has benefited? Or tried to benefit?

Budget Cravings

Punjab Police budgets rose rapidly until about 1994, but for 16 years thereafter annual budget increases were paltry. *The Tribune* of 21 January 2001, reported that year's annual Punjab Police budget to be about ₹900 crore. By 2002, as reported in the *Times of India*, 16 February, the annual budget of Punjab Police of that year rose to ₹909 crore. The figure for 2017, dredged up from the *Deccan Herald* of 6 July 2017, is ₹919.3 crore for Punjab Police annual budget of 2015–2016.[14] When you factor in inflation, an increase of ₹19 crore over a 15 year period isn't much.

More figures are available for sanctioned strength of the police. Sanctioned strength figures from 2010 onwards have been taken from the Bureau of Police Research & Development.[15] Figures from years before 2010 have been found in articles/reports carried in newspapers and magazines.

Punjab Police	
Year	Sanctioned Strength
2017	87,672
2016	78,967
2015	78,455
2014	80,064
2013	79,478
2012	79,446
2011	79,565
2010	71,888
1994	70,228
1993	65,658
1989	51,833
1986	34,000
1984	32,855
1980	29,000

These figures show a period of very rapid expansion between 1986 and 1994, then a long levelling-off followed by a jump in from 2010 to 2011 and another jump from 2016 to 2017.

In 2005, touting a newly launched scheme for community policing, IGP Sanjeev Gupta, then head of the Community Affairs Division of the Punjab Police, explained that the idea was to make the vast infrastructure created to deal with terrorism relevant to present needs. He said that six separate police districts carved out during the times of terrorism continued to function through 259 police stations and 110 police posts. It was feared that the force, whose numbers grew from nearly 29,000 in 1980 to more than 71,000 in 2001, would remain underutilized in the post-terrorism phase.[16]

When even the police acknowledged overstaffing, it is likely that the state Finance Department would have taken the same view and declined to allocate more money to an already bloated department. Another possibility is that the state government planners feared that a bigger budget would only mean more money to swindle (e.g., the 2006 Punjab Police wireless scam[17]).

Even the Danish Immigration Service report had mentioned Khalistan danger as a pretext of seeking a higher budget for the police department.

Turf Cravings?

Federalism, which is what the Anandpur Sahib Resolution[18] was all about, brought the Akalis into conflict with Mrs Gandhi back in the early 1980s. Throughout the terrible 1980s and 1990s, the party did not forget about it and when the issue came up again in 2012, then Punjab Chief Minister Parkash Singh Badal was ready. The provocation was the National Counter Terrorism Centre (NCTC).

Khalistan Redux

First some background. The near-disaster of Kargil was blamed on intelligence failure and so was the November 2008 attack on Mumbai. The Government of India's answer was the same both times. Set up another intelligence agency—an agency to streamline all the other agencies. The new NCTC was to have sweeping powers to collect, collate and disseminate data, maintain a database on terrorist and their associates including their families, have power to conduct searches and arrests in any part of India, formulate a response to terror threats and carry out counter-terror operations. The government planned to place the NCTC within the IB, which meant that it would not be accountable to Parliament.

The central government argued that it needed an ultra-powered agency to counter ultras and bring down on them the full weight of the UAPA wherever they were found, the minute they were found... Tamil Tigers, Bodo Tigers, Mizo Tigers, Tripura Tigers, Khalistan Tigers, Liberation Army of [fill in the blank], People's [fill in the blank]. India was in *danger* and only a heavy-duty agency could save her.

The problem was the Constitution. The Seventh Schedule of the Constitution set outs Central List, State List and Concurrent List. 'Public Order' and 'Police' are in the State List. This means that a state exercises full and exclusive power over its police force: It takes no direction from the Centre. In a natural catastrophe or some serious emergency, a state may take the help of Central forces but these Central forces cannot go in until asked.

To the states with non-Congress governments,[19] the proposed NCTC looked like the Centre's big, intrusive foot pushing through their door—just one more instance of the Centre encroaching on state turf. Since the NCTC was initially proposed by the Congress-led UPA government, states with non-Congress governments blocked the plan. The SAD was ruling in Punjab. Aside from the natural antipathy towards any proposal from a Congress government, Badal represented

The Legacy of Militancy in Punjab

a state that had been subjected to more than 10 years of President's Rule. It was not liked by either the Akalis specifically or Punjab generally. Speaking at the chief minister's conference in New Delhi on 5 May 2012, Punjab Chief Minister Parkash Singh Badal, normally given to diplomatic language in dealings with the Centre, thumped out a speech that was federalist hot gospel.[20]

For a change, central retaliation did not come in the form of baleful references to the steps that would be taken to thwart a revival of Khalistan. By August that year, the monsoon had failed all across North India. The Centre gave generous drought relief to Rajasthan, Gujarat, Maharashtra, Haryana, and Karnataka. Can you spot the missing state?[21]

Power Cravings?

Democracy is a game of money, lots of money. Obviously, it is the rich who fund parties and leaders. (The average person can barely fund himself.) The government is in the hands of a ruling party and that party is ruling largely thanks to the backing of wealthy individuals and corporations. He who pays the piper calls the tune.

It is now futile to tell a poor man, even an *illiterate* poor man, that he is poor because God wills it so. A factory is set up; politicians take credit for it and congratulate themselves on their wise policies and dynamic leadership. The very ordinary man sees this and concludes, 'Ah-hah, that factory shows that the government *can* do something!' And then he looks at himself, unemployed, no jobs to be had, no security for himself or his family and he concludes, 'The government *can* do something but it *does nothing*. I have less this year than I had the year before'.

Election after election, the parties trade places in the driver's seat; year after year the gap between the top economic layer and the bottom layer widens. More and more wealth floats to the top for fewer and fewer people. The number of peoples at the bottom layer grow even as their resources are siphoned away.[22] Frustration grows.

Is this the situation in Punjab only? Or in India only? By no means. The income gap is rapidly widening in the USA: An American business magazine reports: 'The incomes of the top 1 per cent grew faster than the bottom 99 per cent in 43 states between 2009 and 2015. In nine states in the U.S., the top 1 per cent represents more than half of all income growth'.[23]

But democracy is also a game of numbers. The poor vote vastly exceeds the rich vote. This means that every politician, every party, faces the same challenge: How to attract or retain support from the vast majority of hand-to-mouth voters whose expectations from the leader, the party, the government, have been belied every single time?

Is this the situation in Punjab only? Or in India only? By no means.

America has a leader who gained the presidency by demonizing immigrants and making white Middle American voters very, very afraid. Britain is currently wrestling with the consequences of its Brexit decision. One reason Brexit was favoured is that it closes the door on all the *anians*—Romanians, Albanians, Slovenians, Bohemians, Lithuanians, Ukrainians, etc. The far-right in Europe—Alternative für Deutschland, Rassemblement National, Hungary's Fidesz—they all beat the same drum: Keep out people who are not *real* Britons, or *real* French or *real* whoever.

For Real Indians

In India, as of this writing, people are choosing their representatives in 17th Lok Sabha. The incumbent prime minister who is hoping for re-election with an absolute majority has time and again declared that India should be ruled by *real* Indians. US President Donald

Trump can close the door on *unreal* would-be Americans, but that is not possible in India. The *unreal* Indians here have not come from somewhere else. They and all their forebears were born here. Voters, who have by now stopped scanning the horizon to catch the first glimpse of oncoming *achhe din*, will soon know how much agreement there is on the definition of *real* Indian.

How to get votes from people to whom you have given nothing in the past and to whom the nature of your campaign financing dictates that you can give nothing in future? Build up the enemy, paint vivid images of threat, keep the message simple. Harp on invasion, unfairness, conspiracy, exacerbate divisions and foster tension. Tell voters that you stand for *real* Indians and will protect them from *unreal* Indians. Make the voters afraid.

This strategy works for a while. Over the past 20 years, Punjab has become a good example. The Congress chief '*exposes*' the violent, anti-national separatist Khalistani tendencies of the Akali chief. The Akali chief lobs the same charge right back where it came from. Then both Congress and Akali leaders denounce the Khalistan romance of the AAP chief who replies that his opponents have resorted to 'photo-shopping'.[24]

Eventually, Us versus Them will show diminishing returns. Parties and leaders have traded the 'Khalistan sympathizer' smear so frequently that people are weary of it. A slur that should be sharp and piercing is now broader than a horse's back and twice as dull.

On the List and Off the List

Wikipedia provides a list of organizations that the Government of India has found to be violent, lawless and in defiance of the Government and Constitution of India; accordingly, these groups have been proscribed by under the UAPA.[25] All the usual suspects are there: Urdu-name groups active in Kashmir, mainly English-name groups active in Assam, Nagaland, Manipur, Mizoram and Tripura, English-name outfits all lumped together as Left Wing Extremism active in the tribal areas of central India and three or four Punjab-focused groups having either Khalistan or Bhindranwala in their names.

What's missing from this Government of India list are Hindi/Sanskrit-name groups. It's not that intimidating Hindi/Sanskrit-name groups don't exist in India. Offhand one recalls Bajrang Dal, Abhinav Bharat, Bharat Gau Raksha Dal, Sanatan Sanstha, Hindu Janajagruti Samiti, Akhil Bharatiya Vidyarthi Parishad, Hindu Jagran Manch, Shri Ram Sena, Shiv Sena, Samadhan Sena, Dharmashakti Sena, Guru Kripa Pratisthan, Vishwa Hindu Parishad. Sometimes these are all referred to under the umbrella term of Sangh Parivar. When these groups figure in media reports, it is not because their members are highly talented bhajan singers. They too have got their hands bloody on many occasions,[26] and they defy the law of the land. But they haven't made the terrorist list of the Government of India. Why?

By all means, go after terrorist groups. Go after *all* of them.

The terrorist organizations we read about are real; they threaten the lives and livelihoods of people wherever they operate. Granted. No dispute. And from a politician's point of view, thank God they exist; if they didn't, then they would need to be created. In the case of Khalistan, there is strong evidence of creation: Extremism in Punjab was a drama initially scripted by the ruling party at the Centre to cripple its rival.[27] That drama spun into a decade of disruption followed by two decades of frustration with political institutions (including the courts), administrative corruption and economic stagnation.

Nobody who is even moderately informed needs any special reminder of Punjab's painful history because it is still the present reality. Frustration, corruption and stagnation hang over the state.

In Punjab, combating terrorism provided an iron-clad excuse for a wide range of wrong-doing. It excused police raj with the attendant abduction, extrajudicial killing and extortion. Abuses did not stop when the decade of militancy wound down. Police raj morphed into goonda raj which was indispensable for grabbing property or otherwise acquiring wealth by illegal means. Combating terrorism justified draconian laws that violated the rights of the individual, and it justified attempts to establish secretive central agencies in contravention of state's rights.

As a subject for speeches, campaigning and party manoeuvring, terror, foreign and domestic, is a staple. This is particularly so at national level. Meanwhile, at the grassroots level, the citizen, irrespective of region or religion, is concerned about employment and job security, running the home on a tight budget, paying school fees, praying that none of their family will require medical treatment and seething with anger over the bribes they must pay to get even simple jobs done. There is simply no connect between these two levels.

Addressing corruption, lack of employment,[28] the ever-widening wealth gap, agricultural prices, or *any* of the issues that impinge on people's lives would give the impression that the leader or party is prepared to actually do something. Fulminating about terrorists, in Punjab or elsewhere, is a much better option: It requires no great political will or political courage to vow war on terror. From time to time, it may be necessary to spin statements, articles or even arrest dramas to keep the appearance of imminent danger alive, but that is cheaply and easily managed.

Here's an interesting world record: A man in Britain, John Prestwich, died at the age of 67, after a Guinness Book certified 50 years on artificial respiration.[29] One wouldn't be surprised if Khalistan surpasses that record.

Notes

1. Punjab and Haryana High Court advocate Rajwinder Singh Bains, points out that even this trial was problematic. In a personal communication to the authors, Bains observed: 'Such was the bias of the court during 12 years until the final arguments that no court examined the record or trusted the CBI. In the case of one of the accused, Navjote Singh, for 12 years, we had told the court that there was no evidence against him yet he remained behind bars the whole time and his bail applications were repeatedly dismissed. In 2007 the court finally had to acquit him. He received no compensation whatsoever for 12 years unjust imprisonment'.
2. Chandhoke and Priyadarshi, 'Electoral Politics in Post-Conflict States'.
3. On 26 April 1998, the Committee for Coordination on Disappearances in Punjab announced formation of a panel of three judges (retired Supreme Court judge and former chairman of the Law Commission, K. J. Reddy, former Chief Justice of the Calcutta High Court, D. S. Tewatia, and retired Bombay High Court judge, H. Suresh). Over the spring and summer of 1998, volunteers carried out the difficult and often dangerous documentation work. The Commission's first sitting took place on 8–10 August 1998. During these three days, the Commission received about 3,200 complaints and issued about 90 notices or requests to appear to various officials, including senior police.
4. TNN, 'RDX in "Pinnis"'.
5. 'Thrice is he armed that hath his quarrel just; And he but naked, though locked up in steel, whose conscience with injustice is corrupted' (William Shakespeare, *Henry VI*, 3.2.240–243).
6. The 1998 post-nuclear test sanction cost India $51.3 million in US aid. In the case of Pakistan, sanctions had already been imposed (through the 1985 Pressler Amendment). Pakistan received only a small amount described as humanitarian aid (Morrow and Carriere, 'The Economic Impacts of the 1998').
7. Kaur, 'Pathribal: A Timeline'. The Jammu and Kashmir Government handed over the Pathribal encounter case to CBI in January 2003. Three years later, on 9 May 2006, the CBI submitted its charge sheet, establishing that the encounter was stage-managed and the five men who had been killed were innocent civilians. The CBI called it a 'cold-blooded' plot by Army officers that involved fraud, forgery and coercion of witnesses. The Supreme Court told the Army to try the accused by court martial. But on 20 January 2014, without even convening a court martial, the Army let off the accused for 'lack of evidence'. Family members of the Pathribal victims petitioned the Jammu and Kashmir High Court against the acquittal, and, when the High Court rejected the case, they went to the Supreme Court. In August 2017, the Supreme Court agreed to examine a plea issued and directed the case to be

listed for disposal after six weeks. More than a two years later, the Supreme Court has yet to hear the case.
8. Danish Immigration Service, *Report on Fact-Finding Mission.*
9. GoM, *Report of the Group of Ministers.*
10. 'The first and most essential thing to learn about India is that there is not, and never was an India or even any country of India, no Indian nation, no "people of India" of which we hear so much. That men of the Punjab, Bengal, the North-West Provinces and Madras, should ever feel that they belong to one great Indian nation is impossible'. Sir John Strachey, Finance Minister under Viceroy Robert Lytton, speech at Cambridge 1880.
11. Danish Immigration Service, *Report on Fact-Finding Mission.*
12. Simranjit Singh Mann (born 20 May 1945) hails from a political family. His father, Lt Col Joginder Singh Mann, was a speaker of the Punjab Vidhan Sabha. He is the brother-in-law of the current Congress Chief Minister of Punjab Capt. Amarinder Singh. Mann joined Indian Police Services in 1967, but resigned on 18 June 1984 to protest the attack on the Golden Temple. He was imprisoned for five years and arrested or detained some 30 times but never convicted. He is the President of the Shiromani Akali Dal (Amritsar) and a two-time Member of Parliament, winning from Tarn Taran in 1989 and Sangrur in 1999 (https://en.wikipedia.org/wiki/Simranjit_Singh_Mann).
13. HT Correspondent, 'Punjab Election Results'.
14. Singh, 'Punjab Police'.

The present strength of the Punjab police, including its India Reserve Battalions and Commando Battalions, is about 79,000 men and officers. Nearly 90 per cent of the ₹900 cr annual budget of the state police goes towards disbursement of salaries and perks to its men and officers.

Agnihotri, '9,336 SPOs Go Without Wages in Punjab'. 'Total budget of ₹909 crore for the Punjab police'.

Dhaliwal, 'Police Dept Gets ₹3203.99 cr'. Finance Minister P. S. Dhindsa during his Budget speech informed, 'For the current fiscal year, a provision of ₹3203.99 crore has been made in the Budget for the police. ... The annual interest payment in terms of percentage of revenue ... The number went up to 769 in 2008, 853 in 2009 and 907 in 2010'.

Joy, 'States Spend Paltry 3%'. The total police annual budget for 2015–2016 is 5.8 per cent of Punjab's total annual budget. The annual budget that year was ₹158,493 crore. Therefore, Punjab Police annual budget in 2015–2016 equals ₹919.3 crore.
15. http://bprd.nic.in/
16. Pandher, 'A Pioneering Effort'.
17. Rakesh and Siwach, 'Top Cops Named in Wireless Scam'.

Police officers in connivance with wireless suppliers had embezzled ₹5.25-crore scam over a period of three years between 2000 and 2003. DGP- cum-commandant (Punjab homeguards) K. K. Attri and ADGP (vigilance) Izhar Alam were charged with cheating and forgery, and also under Prevention of Corruption Act....

Other senior officers named in the FIR included IG (crime) G D Pandey, DIG (intelligence) R P Singh and SP (Lokpal) Malvinder Singh Sidhu besides former ADGP D R Bhatti, former ADGP S C Jain and IG R C Prasad, now dead.

18. This resolution characterized India as a nation of different linguistic and cultural sections, religious minorities. It wanted the Constitution recast so as to implement real and meaningful federal principles. It said that India's millions of people would be better represented by giving greater autonomy to the states and this would obviate the possibility of any danger to the unity and integrity of the country. If the states were able to exercise their powers in a meaningful way, they would achieve progress and prosperity for people in their respective areas. In November 1982, SAD President Harchand Singh Longowal announced that his party would agitate in New Delhi to focus world attention on the 'persecution of Sikhs in India' and to press the Centre to accede to demands set forth in the Anandpur Sahib Resolution.
19. Bihar, Chhattisgarh, Gujarat, Himachal, Karnataka, Madhya Pradesh, Maharashtra, Odisha, Punjab, Uttarakhand, Tamil Nadu, Tripura and West Bengal.
20. *5 Dariya News*, 'Badal for Setting up a New Constituent Assembly'.
21. Singh and Koshy, '₹2,000 Crore Drought Relief'.
22. As per IANS, 'India Second Most "Unequal" Country', as of November 2016, India is the second most unequal country in the world after Russia. Livemint, 'The Richest 1% of Indians'. The richest 1 per cent of Indians own 58.4 per cent of wealth. The richest 10 per cent of Indians own 80.7 per cent of the wealth, with the wealth gap widening year by year.
23. Paul, 'America's 1% hasn't Controlled'.
24. TNN, 'Sukhbir Badal'.

The sharp Akali attack comes in the wake of widespread disturbances in Punjab over alleged incidents of desecration of the Sikh holy book and the Sarbat Khalsa that appointed Khalistani terrorist Jagtar Singh Hawara, convicted for assassination of late Congress leader Beant Singh, as chief priest of the Akal Takht.

Vasudeva, 'Punjab Congress Accuses AAP'; Sharma, 'In Bathinda, Amarinder Blames Badal'.

Addressing a gathering in support of Congress candidate from Bathinda Rural constituency, Harvinder Singh Laddi, at Kotshamir, Captain Amarinder said Badal was responsible for thousands of innocent people killed by the terrorists. He referred to the CIA report, as reported in Hindustan Times, to point out that Badal had always been working 'to promote his personal agenda by colluding with the Sikh extremists'.

Rediff, '"Fascist" AAP will Turn Punjab'.

'The rise of communal forces under the Badals, and now the extremist threat posed by Kejriwal to Punjab need to be countered before it can destroy the secular fabric of the state', the former chief minister cautioned that the nexus between the Naxals and the Khalistanis in the AAP will bring back the dark the days of terrorism in Punjab, which lost more than 35,000 lives to extremist violence.

PTI, 'Kejriwal doesn't Care'.

Accusing AAP leader Arvind Kejriwal of promoting extremist forces like Khalistan Commando Force in Punjab, Congress state chief Amarinder Singh today said the bomb blast in Maur Mandi of Bathinda showed that the terror cells of the Khalistanis were again getting active. Kejriwal, who had allegedly stayed at a KCF extremist's house in Punjab, was fanning terror forces through his actions, led by the dangerous mix of the AAP extreme left and extreme right ideologies, he said

Kamal, 'Amarinder Singh's Harsh Words'.

Q. AAP and Congress claim SAD is behind desecration incidents?

A. Everybody knows who's behind the acts of sacrilege. AAP is behind the desecration and is conniving with extremist elements.

IANS, 'Amarinder Government has Surrendered'.

SAD president Sukhbir Singh Badal, flanked by former chief minister Parkash Singh Badal, told media in Bathinda on Friday that the Amarinder Singh government was colluding with radical elements to vitiate the atmosphere in Punjab to serve the Congress' political interest.

Babushahi Bureau, 'Badal writes to Rajnath Singh'.

Political support and cover encouraging enemies of peace in Punjab…

Former Chief Minister Parkash Singh Badal today cautioned the Union Government that the Congress government in Punjab was 'actively and openly in cahoots with the dangerous elements who threaten peace and communal harmony in the state'.

25. https://en.wikipedia.org/wiki/List_of_organisations_banned_by_the_Government_of_India
26. Griswold, 'The Violent Toll of Hindu'. 'A populist Prime Minister has legitimized India's more militant groups, and targeted attacks against religious minorities are on the rise'.
27. Mukherjee, *A Centenary History*.
28. Singh, 'Unemployment, the Elephant'. Data from the National Sample Survey Office that came out in February 2019 showed that more than half of India's Labour Force Participation Rate (the proportion of a country's working-age population that engages actively in the labour market) stood at 49.8 per cent in 2017–2018, falling sharply from 55.9 per cent n 2011–2012.
29. Villazon, 'How Long Can You be Kept'.

Epilogue

Think of democracy as revolution every five years … an orderly, bloodless revolution in which citizens decide whether the incumbent government should remain or whether they should remove it and install another. By voting the citizens give power to candidates who (as far as they can guess) offer the best chance of benefit or the least chance of harm, while denying power to those in whom they have no confidence or who have failed them in the past.

In a perfect world, a well-functioning democracy would be one in which the voters have complete and accurate information on which to base decisions. The likely consequences of what various candidates and parties propose would be clear, and the voter would remember what has been done in the past—who did what and how and why and what it meant for the citizens and the state generally. The voter would be able to enforce accountability on those whom he entrusts with the power to legislate and oversee the functioning of the state.

Real-world voters have varying levels of experience to guide their choice of candidate. According to the latest available data, there are 20,475,053 registered voters in Punjab.[1] At the time of the 2019 Lok Sabha Elections, voters aged 60 and above numbered about 43 lakh. Only those voters who are today on the wrong side of 50 years would be able to personally remember the events of the 1980 and 1990s that have shaped present day Punjab

In the age group of 18–39, the number is 10,851,778; this is 52 per cent of the total.[2] A voter at the senior-most end of the 18–39 years group would have been born in 1980, so s/he would have been a year too young to vote in Punjab's first tension-free election in 1997. But that voter could have voted subsequently in five Lok Sabha and four Assembly elections. A nine-election veteran has quite a lot of experience on which to base his voting decision. The juniormost in the group are of course novices with one election or none at all to look back on.

From 1997 to the present, Punjab's government has changed hands five times. Thrice the SAD–BJP combine formed the government (1997, 2007 and 2012) and twice the voters gave power to the Congress (2002 and 2017).

Triumph of Hope

Humourist Will Rogers noted that 'the short memory of the American voters is what keeps our politicians in office', and that little nugget comes from the 1930s, before people were benumbed with late breaking alerts on a 24-hour basis. Rogers' remark applies to Punjab too. Come election time and each party paints rosy pictures of their previous stints at the helm and declares that the state has been ruined by the rampant corruption, nepotism and wrong policies of the other party. In election campaigns, candidate X accuses candidate Y of being simultaneously a parasite, a pirate and a pimp, and candidate Y accuses candidate X of being simultaneously a liar, a looter and a laughingstock.[3]

Both parties know what they're talking about; nevertheless, voters go right ahead and elect candidate X, then, in the next poll, they turn around and elect candidate Y.

Do the voters know no better? Is it that they have bad memories or are too young to possess the experience that would enable them to make better decisions? Is it dearth of political choice? In the 2014 Lok Sabha Election, and again in the 2017 Assembly Election, the two long-established parties were challenged by a newcomer, AAP,

Epilogue

but it had very limited success at the ballot box and those AAP candidates who were elected to the Vidhan Sabha soon fell out. Punjab voters are now disenchanted with AAP and show little inclination to give it another chance.[4]

Dismal Reckoning

Rather than making their choices on the basis of what political leaders claim, people might be wiser to make up their minds after studying the economic data. Economics is called the 'dismal science', and it lives up to its name where Punjab is concerned.

A couple of quick Internet searches yielded this information:

In terms of per capita income, Punjab ranked at number four in 2000, but in 2015–2016, it slid to number 16 among the states and UTs. Punjab GDSP growth in 2014–2015 was ranked 28 among Indian states.[5]

In the early 1980s, Punjab's per capita output was the highest in India. By 2012, six states—Maharashtra, Haryana, Gujarat, Himachal Pradesh, Kerala and Tamil Nadu—had overtaken Punjab.

The reason for this is found in investment-to-GDP ratios in Punjab and in the rest of India. In 1980, the ratio in nearly all states was 15 per cent. By 2010, it was 38 per cent in India but still 15 per cent in Punjab.[6]

In Punjab, the unemployment rate among youth—the proportion of the labour force between 18–29 years that is unemployed—is 16.6 per cent while the Indian average is 10.2 per cent. Punjab also has India's eighth highest rural youth unemployment rate.

As many as 18,770 factories closed between 2007 and 2014, when the SAD was in power, the *Hindustan Times* reported on 3 February 2014, quoting Right to Information data obtained by the Punjab Pradesh Congress Samiti (Punjab State Congress Committee).[7]

Statistics are one way to show the state of Punjab's economy. Another is to listen to what businessmen have to say.

For example, back in December 2018, the President of the Federation of Punjab Small Industries Association wrote to the chief minister to tell him what small-scale entrepreneurs were going through when they tried to get their VAT refunds released by the state's Excise and Taxation Department. The association president Badish Jindal complained,

> Assessees are forced to pay 5 to 10 per cent for getting their refunds released. Our members informed that they have paid from ₹5 lakh to ₹20 lakh per unit. They are forced to pay because in case of denial to pay the bribe, the officers illegally delay their refunds for years and even try to deduct the amounts on account of various minor reasons.[8]

He claimed that corrupt officers were collecting refund payments on bogus units, and, even after the intervention of the High Court, the department took no action against such officers.

Jindal went on to outline several other corrupt practices, but the few mentioned here suffice to give one solid reason why industry is struggling in Punjab.[9]

Legitimacy Deficit

Likewise, the citizen's lack of confidence in the government as a guarantor of his security and civil rights is apparent from another small piece of information.

Epilogue

In 2018, Common Cause, a well-known Indian non-governmental organization dedicated to public causes and redress for problems of the people, in cooperation with the Centre for the Study of Developing Societies, Lokniti Programme for Comparative Democracy and Tata Trust, conducted an all-India survey of people's attitudes toward and perception of the police in their states.

In the introduction to this report, the authors wrote,

> The police are the most visible face of the state. A sovereign government is called a 'failed state' if it is unable to control law-and-order, but when it uses repression as the instrument of control, it is condemned as a 'police state.' There is a 'legitimacy deficit' in both situations.[10]

In other words, public attitudes towards the police also reflect the public's confidence in the state in the matter of the state itself abiding by the rule of law, ensuring justice and protecting the legal rights of the citizen. The report notes that in Punjab, people's attitude towards the police is highly negative and highly fearful. Punjab ranked at the top of the list when it came to people's fear of the police. The authors note, 'A possible connection to the particular history of Punjab in the last four decades'.[11]

We have been talking about Punjab in the years after the era of militancy and what kind of political choices people are making 40 years after the shooting stopped. But are elections the only indicator of people's political choices?

Maybe not. It may not actually matter whether a person can pass a history test on the deeds and misdeeds of the past 40 years. It may not matter whether s/he has a political scientist's insight into the competing claims of political parties. It may not matter whether s/he's any good at economics or has a clear picture of the growth indicators and statistics. It may not even matter if s/he participates in elections.

Voting with Their Feet

People also vote with their feet. Travel through towns in Punjab, even small towns far from the main urban centres. As you pass through, signs for two types of business will catch your eye: one will say IELTS Coaching[12] and the other will say Immigration Consultant. Parents scrape together everything they've got to send their children abroad, and the kids are ready to risk their very lives if need be to get out.

A story in the *Indian Express* of 6 May 2019 reported that while Punjab enrolled the highest ever number of voters in the age group of 18–19 years ahead of the 2019 Lok Sabha Election, 58 per cent of the voters of this age group are missing from the voter list.[13]

Voters Aged 18–19 Years in the Final List of Registered Voters Released on 29 April 2019				
18–19-yr olds total population	18–19-yr olds registered to vote	18–19-yr old registered voters % of total	18–19-yr olds missing from voters list	Missing 18–19-yr old voters % of total
947,900	394,780	41.6	553,120	58.6

The reporter quoted a district electoral officer who estimated that every year more than one lakh students from Punjab go abroad to study.

The DEOs estimation may be on the low side. Figures cited in a story in the *Vancouver Sun* of 18 September 2018[14] put the number of Indian students in Canada (mostly from Punjab) at 130,000. It estimated the number at 20,000 in Britain and at 70,000 in Australia. The report said that the number of Indian students in Canada, mostly from the Punjab, has increased about five-fold in the past few years, since the federal government began to favour international students as future permanent residents.

The data from the 2009 report of the United Nations Office on Drugs and Crime (UNODC)[15] may be a little out of date by now, but it couldn't be more official. The UNODC investigators reported, 'Analysis of the data and the information available, suggests that irregular migration from Punjab is substantial. Every year more than 20,000 youths from Punjab attempt irregular migration'.

Twenty thousand was the average number of youths from Punjab who were *apprehended* every year between 2000 and 2004. The annual number succeeding in their attempt at irregular migration might have been more than 20,000.

The report went on:

> Option of legal migration for most of the potential migrants was ruled out. Because of limited opportunities for unskilled migrants, they resort to irregular migration.... Why certain districts report large number of cases of irregular migration ... may be due to the past migration history, social network, high unemployment rate, failed agriculture, rural debt, proactive role of agents etc. Of all these reasons, those which are significantly important are the high unemployment rate and the general attitude of young men that migration abroad is perhaps the best alternative. The social structure in the village which was traditionally based on caste, landholding, family background and educational achievements has now changed and distinguishes between those families which have members in other countries and those families which do not.[16]

The *Economic Times* reported that the number of Indians in Italy has now crossed 200,000, making it the largest Indian diaspora in continental Europe. Another 30,000 have migrated to Spain.[17] They are nearly all Punjabis.

Even National Geographic picked up on the Punjab migration story.

> If you are young, if you are ambitious, the temptation to take drugs—to dull your disappointment, to escape your boredom, to retreat deep inside yourself while not moving—is powerful. Or you might choose instead to run away. Exile can be another kind of narcotic.[18]

Noting the ever-present advertisements of IELTS coaching and agents 'guaranteeing' migration to Canada, New Zealand, Australia, the United Kingdom, the United Arab Emirates, or, rarely, South Africa, the writers observed:

> It is as if the Punjab, India's fabled breadbasket and one of its richest states, whose people are renowned go-getters, hustlers, hard workers, were experiencing a mass evacuation of its youngest and brightest. 'There is no future in farming here', says Harpreet Singh, a middle-aged potato grower in a village called Dhindsa. 'Mostly you just lose year by year. I've lost my investment for two years in a row. At best you break even'…
>
> Faridkot has a battered three-star hotel called the Trump Plaza and 96 private English language schools. 'If they could afford it, probably 100 percent of our kids would leave', says Gulabi Singh, the director of one of the schools, which prepare aspiring migrants for their English exams. 'Even driving a cab in Vancouver is better than staying here'.[19]

So much has been reported on the flight of young people from Punjab.[20]

Experience Trumps Argument

The average man, particularly the average young man, or woman, may have trouble articulating their situation, but they know what they are experiencing: stagnant economy, deep trouble in agriculture, symptomized by an appalling number of rural suicides every year,[21] collapse of industry, no jobs and no hope of jobs, a state government that in fact has no money and falls deeper into debt with every passing year. The report by Common Cause points towards an ingrained distrust of the police and by extension, the government. Some people may be able to identify a year or a period when this distrust took root; for others, it is just a 'given' that they grew up with.

Militancy itself was a symptom of a long-standing sense of alienation. The state's response drove that alienation deeper. Ruthless measures employed to crush it perverted administrative culture, particularly police culture. The courts were paralyzed for 20 years. Industry was always denied to Punjab on the pretext that the state was vulnerable to attack, and, in recent years, tax-holiday packages granted to neighbouring states have drained away industry and jobs. Traditionally, Punjab has been an agricultural state; but, if any hope remained in agriculture, then farmers and farm labourers would not be committing suicide.

Successive state governments have come in on big talk but, either because of indifference or inability, all the indicators show the state on a downward path. Parties woo the voters with solemn oaths to provide corruption-free and efficient governance; they promise to rescue agriculture and revive the villages; they commit to attracting industry and creating jobs.

If the claims were believed, would lakhs of young people and their parents make such heroic effort to get out of Punjab, get out of India? It must also be pointed out that the politicians of Punjab send their own children abroad, which strongly suggests that they do not believe what they say either.

'It Can't be Worse There'

The motivations of those desperate to leave Punjab are largely economic, but not *only* economic. Another thing that drives them to risk everything to get out of Punjab is the belief that there is absolutely nothing that they can do to change a corrupt administration, a rapacious police force, and a selfish, static, unresponsive political culture.

A story in *Indian Express* of 3 March 2018,[22] quotes a youngster from a village in Gurdaspur district:

> He has studied up to Class 10 and wants to 'get out of here'. 'I don't believe Greece can be worse than Punjab. The agent has told me that there is always work for those who are willing to work hard. I am. At least I can go out and see the world', he says.

Within decade or two, most of the generation that witnessed events of the 1980s and 1990s will be gone. Some of that generation were sufficiently alienated from the government to get into a war with it. They were not alienated from home and faith so fighting still seemed worthwhile. Very few of their children and grandchildren have much awareness of, or interest in, the traumas suffered by the preceding generation. They see so little hope in their homeland that fighting does not seem worthwhile; they simply leave. If militancy was a symptom of alienation, then the present generation is even more alienated than their elders were. Legacies do not always have to be recognized or articulated to endure.

Notes

1. https://www.news18.com/lok-sabha-elections-2019/punjab/
2. Kumar, 'It's Anybody's Game'.
3. Invective in English does not rise to the level of invective in Punjabi either in colour or in creativity, but we have done our best to reproduce the spirit of such exchanges.
4. Phukan, 'Capital Contest.'
5. Singh, 'How Punjab Economy'.
6. https://www.brookings.edu/blog/future-development/2017/03/03/whats-in-store-for-indias-punjab/
7. IndiaSpend Team, 'Punjab: Slow Growth, High Unemployment'.

8. This is from the KNN-India website https://knnindia.co.in/news/newsdetails/state/fopsia-president-writes-letter-to-punjab-cm-alleging-of-huge-corruption-in-sgst-department 2018 December 28 | KNN-India *FOPSIA* President writes letter to Punjab CM alleging of huge corruption in SGST department.
9. KNN, 'FOPSIA President Writes Letter to Punjab CM'.
10. This is from http://commoncause.in/pdf/SPIR2018.pdf *Status of Policing in India Report 2018,* Common Cause The quoted matter is from the Introduction, page 11.
11. Common Cause et al., *Status of Policing in India Report 2018.*

    The statewise distribution shows the high incidence of this fear in Punjab (Table 5.2). Given that a majority of the Sikh responses are coming from this state, it is the high fear levels in Punjab which are contributing to the high figures. When further disaggregated, the likelihood of poor Sikhs being scared is higher, a trend which is repeated across all other groups. But in comparison to the response of upper classes from other religions, the Sikh upper class is much more likely to be scared (42%) as against upper class Hindus (14%) or upper class Muslims (9%) (a trend that can have a possible connection to the particular history of Punjab in the last four decades).

12. International English Language Testing System (IELTS). It is a globally accepted test of proficiency in English. To qualify for a student or permanent resident visa in Canada, Australia, New Zealand or the UK, the applicant is required to get a certain minimum IELTS score.
13. Chaba, '58.6% Population Aged 18–19 yrs'.
14. Todd, 'Popular Canadian Student Visas'.
15. UNODC, *Smuggling of Migrants from India to Europe.*
16. Ibid.
17. Tumbe, 'How the Recent Punjabi Migration'.
18. Salopek, 'Walking Through a Youthful Exodus in India'.
19. Ibid.
20. Nanda, 'Unsettling Migration's'; Gopal, 'Foreign "attraction"'; Patel, '"Foreign Dreams"'.
21. Chaba, 'Farmer Suicides'. '16,000 farmers, rural labourers committed suicide in 15 years in Punjab'.
22. Brar, 'Fewer Jobs, but Many Still Risk'.

Bibliography

'Conference Report: After 1984? A workshop held at the University of California, Berkeley'. *Sikh Formations* 5, no. 2 (2009): 115–141.

'Who are the Guilty? Causes and Impact of the Delhi Riots, People's Union for Civil Liberties (PUCL) and People's Union for Democratic Rights (PUDR)'. *Economic & Political Weekly* 49, no. 41 (2014): 1979–1985. https://www.epw.in/journal/2014/41/glimpses-past-web-exclusives/who-are-guilty.html

5 Dariya News. 'Badal for Setting up a New Constituent Assembly to Restructure the Indian Constitution'. *5 Dariya News*, 5 May 2012. http://www.5dariyanews.com/news/548-Badal-For-Setting-Up-A-New-Constituent-Assembly-To-Restructure-The-Indian-Constitution

Agnihotri, Amit. '9,336 SPOs Go Without Wages in Punjab'. *The Times of India*, 16 February 2002. https://timesofindia.indiatimes.com/9336-SPOs-go-without-wages-in-Punjab/articleshow/1105290.cms

Amnesty International. *Human Rights Violations in Punjab: Use and Abuse of the Law*. Author, 1991. https://www.amnesty.org/download/Documents/196000/asa200111991ar.pdf

———. *India: Break the Cycle of Impunity and Torture in Punjab*. (AI Index: ASA 20/002/2003) Author, 2003. https://www.amnesty.org/download/Documents/104000/asa200022003en.pdf

Anderson, John Ward. 'Punjab's Cycle of Violence'. *Washington Post*, 2 September 1992. https://www.washingtonpost.com/archive/politics/1992/09/02/punjabs-cycle-of-violence/53c9bd31-c8a4-407f-9035-413ccfb46cf8/?noredirect=on&utm_term=.4a5ffdc08692

Babbar, Gurcharan Singh. *Government Organised Carnage*. Babbar Publications, 1998.

Babushahi Bureau. 'Babushahi: Badal Writes to Rajnath Singh: "Cong Govt Using Radicals to Distract Attention from Own Failures"'. *Babushahi.com*, 21 November 2018. http://www.babushahi.com/full-news.php?id=81351&headline=Badal-writes-to-Rajnath-Singh:-%E2%80%98Cong-govt-using-radicals-to-distract-attention-from-own-failures%E2%80%98

Badhwar, Inderjit. 'Justice Mishra Commission Report on 1984 Anti-Sikhs Riots May Find Few Takers'. *India Today*, 30 April 1986. https://www.indiatoday.in/magazine/indiascope/story/19860430-justice-mishra-commission-report-on-1984-anti-sikhs-riots-may-find-few-takers-800825-1986-04-30

Bal, Hartosh Singh. 'The 1984 Massacre: How Senior Leaders from the Congress Sanctioned Organised Violence'. *The Caravan*, 30 October 2015. https://caravanmagazine.in/vantage/1984-massacre-how-senior-leaders-congress-sanctioned-organised-violence-indira-gandhi-death

BBC News. 'India's Booming Land Values Spark Family Feuds'. *BBC News*, 28 January 2013. https://www.bbc.com/news/world-asia-21171262

Bhatia, Ramaninder K. 'Evidence of Abominable Crime Against Sikhs'. *The Times of India*, 23 February 2011. https://timesofindia.indiatimes.com/india/Evidence-of-abominable-crime-against-Sikhs/articleshow/7552776.cms?referral=PM

Brar, Jasmail Singh. *Communist Party in Punjab: The Politics of Survival*. New Delhi: National Book Organisation, 1989.

Brar, Kamaldeep Singh. 'Fewer Jobs, but Many Still Risk It All to Reach Greece'. *The Indian Express*, 4 November 2018. https://indianexpress.com/article/india/fewer-jobs-but-many-still-risk-it-all-to-reach-greece-5433059/

Brass, Paul, ed. *Riots and Pogroms*. London: Macmillan Press, 1996.

Butalia, Urvashi, and Uma Chakravarti. 'Mita Bose's Account of 1984'. In Olivia Benett, Jo Bexely, and Kitty Warnock, ed., *Arms to Fight Arms to Protect: Women Speak Out About Conflict*. London: Panos, 1995.

Chaba, Anju Agnihotri. '58.6% Population Aged 18–19 yrs Missing from Punjab Voter List'. *The Indian Express*, 6 May 2019. https://indianexpress.com/elections/58-6-population-aged-18-19-yrs-missing-from-punjab-voter-list-5711811/

———. 'Farmer Suicides: Armed with Data from Three Varsity Studies, Unions to Argue Case in HC'. *The Indian Express*, 11 January 2018. https://indianexpress.com/article/india/farmer-suicides-armed-with-data-from-three-varsity-studies-farmer-unions-to-argue-case-in-hc-punjab-5019960/

Chakravarthi, Uma, and Nandita Haksar. *The Delhi Riots: Three Days in the Life of a Nation*. South Asia Books, 1987.

Chandhoke, Neera, and Praveen Priyadarshi. 'Electoral Politics in Post-Conflict States: The Case of Punjab'. *Ace Project*. http://aceproject.org/ero-en/regions/asia/IN/chandhoke.pdf

Chopra, Radhika. 'Commemorating Hurt: Memorializing Operation Bluestar'. *Sikh Formations* 6, no. 2 (2010): 119–152.

Citizen's Commission. *Report of the Citizen's Commission 1984*. Delhi: Tata Press, 1984.

Common Cause, CSDS, Lokniti, Tata Trust, and Lal Family foundation. *Status of Policing in India Report 2018: A Study of Performance and Perceptions*. Centre for the Study of Developing Societies, New Delhi, 2018. http://commoncause.in/pdf/SPIR2018.pdf

Crossette, Barbara. 'Killings by Police Stir Punjab's Fury'. *The New York Times*, 16 December 1989. https://www.nytimes.com/1989/12/16/world/killings-by-police-stir-punjab-s-fury.html

Bibliography

Dalrymple, William. *City of Djinns*. London: Penguin Books, 1994.

Danish Immigration Service. *Report on Fact-Finding Mission to Punjab, India: 21 March to 5 April 2000*. Author, 2000. https://www.nyidanmark.dk/NR/rdonlyres/14E13983-B03D-4EC8-9D65-194DAB45DED7/0/FactfindingmissiontoPunjabIndia2000.pdf

Das, Veena. *Life and Words: Violence and the Descent into the Ordinary*. University of California Press, 2006.

———. *Mirrors of Violence: Communities, Riots and Survivors in South Asia*. New Delhi: Oxford University Press, 1990.

Deogan, Tarsem Singh. 'Former YAD Leader Sunny Johar Dies'. *Hindustan Times*, 27 April 2014. https://www.hindustantimes.com/punjab/former-yad-leader-sunny-johar-dies/story-q436STcvDsPQnUujyewzGP.html

Deol, Harnik. *Religion and Nationalism in India: The Case of the Punjab*. London: Routledge, 2000.

Deswal, Deepender. 'The Killings Spread to Haryana Too'. *The Tribune*, 23 December 2018. https://www.tribuneindia.com/news/sunday-special/people/the-killings-spread-to-haryana-too/702667.html

Dhaliwal, Sarbjit. 'Police Dept Gets ₹3203.99 cr: More Than That to Health & Family Welfare'. *The Tribune*, 20 June 2012. https://www.tribuneindia.com/2012/20120621/punjab.htm

Dhillon, Kirpal. *Identity and Survival: Sikh Militancy in India 1978–1993*. London: Penguin UK, 2006.

Dogra, Chander Suta. 'Dead or Alive? Many "Dead" Punjab Terrorists are Still Living. But Most of Them Prefer to Stay "Killed"'. *Outlook*, 13 March 2006. https://www.outlookindia.com/magazine/story/dead-or-alive/230550

Ensaaf. *Punjab Police: Fabricating Terrorism through Illegal Detention and Torture*. October 2005. https://ensaaf.org/publications/reports/fabricating-terrorism/

———. *The Punjab Mass Cremations Case, India burning the Rule of Law*. January 2007. https://ensaaf.org/programs/legal-advocacy/punjab-mass-cremations-case/

ET Bureau. 'US Court Summons Congress for Sikh "Genocide" in 1984'. *Economic Times*, 3 March 2011. https://m.economictimes.com/news/politics-and-nation/us-court-summons-congress-for-sikh-genocide-in-1984/articleshow/7616384.cms

Express News Service. 'Ex-DGP Alleges Nexus Between Land Mafia and Politicians, Cops, Babus; Seeks CBI Probe'. *The Indian Express*, 18 December 2010. http://archive.indianexpress.com/news/exdgp-alleges-nexus-between-land-mafia-and-politicians-cops-babus–seeks-cbi-probe/726318/0

———. 'Kid Murder Case: Moga SSP Among 7 Acquitted'. *The Indian Express*, 11 May 2012. http://archive.indianexpress.com/news/kid-murder-case-moga-ssp-among-7-acquitted/948046/

Express News Service. 'NRI's House Forcibly Demolished to Open Restobar, Alleges Kin'. *The Indian Express*, 5 January 2013. http://archive.indianexpress.com/news/nri-s-house-forcibly-demolished-to-open-restobar-alleges-kin/1054918/0

———. 'SC Upholds Life Term for Five Cops in Khalra Murder'. *The Indian Express*, 5 November 2011. http://archive.indianexpress.com/news/sc-upholds-life-term-for-five-cops-in-khalra-murder/870940/0

First Post. 'Modi Govt Offers Compensation of ₹5 Lakh to Kin of Each 1984 Riot Victims'. *First Post*, 30 October 2014. https://www.firstpost.com/politics/modi-govt-offers-compensation-of-rs-5-lakh-to-kin-of-each-1984-riot-victims-1780265.html

France 24. 'New Hezbollah Video Game Lets Players Annihilate IS Fighters in Syria'. *France 24*, 1 March 2018. https://www.france24.com/en/20180301-hezbollah-video-game-syria-lebanon

GoM. *Report of the Group of Ministers on National Security, 2001*. Vivekananda International Foundation, 2001. https://www.vifindia.org/sites/default/files/GoM%20Report%20on%20National%20Security.pdf

Gopal, Navjeevan. 'Foreign "Attraction": Migration Abroad has Become Status Symbol'. *The Indian Express*, 20 January 2016. https://indianexpress.com/article/cities/chandigarh/foreign-attraction-migration-abroad-has-become-status-symbol/

Grewal, Jyoti. *Betrayed by the State, the Anti-Sikh Pogrom of 1984*. New Delhi: Penguin Books India, 2007.

Griswold, Eliza. 'The Violent Toll of Hindu Nationalism in India'. *The New Yorker*, 5 March 2019. https://www.newyorker.com/news/on-religion/the-violent-toll-of-hindu-nationalism-in-india

Grover, Vrinda. *Carnage 84: Massacre of 4,000 Sikhs in Delhi*. https://www.carnage84.com/judge/analysis.htm

High Court Correspondent. 'PIL Seeks Names of Persons Declared Dead'. *The Tribune*, 23 February 2006. https://www.tribuneindia.com/2006/20060223/punjab1.htm

Hobbes, Thomas. *Leviathan: Or, The Matter, Forme, & Power of a Common-Wealth Ecclesiasticall and Civill*. London, 1651.

HT Correspondence. 'Ropar Fake Encounter: Three Cops Found Guilty, One Gets Life Term for Killing Two'. *Hindustan Times*, 28 February 2019. https://www.hindustantimes.com/chandigarh/1993-ropar-fake-encounter-three-cops-found-guilty-one-gets-life-term-for-killing-two/story-evVLmlH3u7Xe0TM0npflBL.html

———. 'Fake Encounters: HC Dismisses PIL for CBI Probe'. *Hindustan Times*, 9 July 2013. https://m.hindustantimes.com/chandigarh/fake-encounters-hc-dismisses-pil-for-cbi-probe/story-AFafyqIJyeOME8laZlFOKL_amp.html

Bibliography

HT Correspondence. 'Punjab Election Results: Simranjit Mann, Jagmeet Fail to Make any Difference'. *Hindustan Times*, 12 March 2017. https://www.hindustantimes.com/assembly-elections/punjab-election-results-simranjit-mann-jagmeet-fail-to-make-any-difference/story-AXfocwxza2Cn6FCJfkxDNN.html

IANS. 'Amarinder Government has Surrendered to Radical Forces: Akali Dal'. *Business Standard*, 4 September 2018. https://www.business-standard.com/article/news-ians/amarinder-government-has-surrendered-to-radical-forces-akali-dal-118091401225_1.html

———. 'India Second Most "Unequal" Country After Russia: Report'. *The Pioneer*, 4 September 2016. https://www.dailypioneer.com/2016/business-and-finance/india-second-most-unequal-country-after-russia-report.html

India Today. 'I.K. Gujral Writes Off Outstanding ₹8,500 Crore Debt Punjab Accumulated Since 1984. *India Today*, 4 August 1997. https://www.indiatoday.in/magazine/indiascope/story/19970804-i.k.-gujral-writes-off-outstanding-rs-8500-crore-debt-punjab-accumulated-since-1984-831853-1997-08-04

IndiaSpend Team. 'Punjab: Slow Growth, High Unemployment Big Challenges for New Government'. *IndiaSpend*, 15 March 2017. https://archive.indiaspend.com/cover-story/punjab-slow-growth-high-unemployment-big-challenges-for-new-government-39427

Indira Jaising. 'Who will defend the defenceless when the human rights activists and lawyers are already in jail?' *The Leaflet*, 28 August 2018. http://theleaflet.in/when-human-rights-lawyers-activists-are-arrested-who-will-remain-to-defend-the-defenceless/#

Joy, Shemin. 'States Spend Paltry 3% of Budget on Police: Study'. *Deccan Herald*, 6 July 2017. https://www.deccanherald.com/content/621213/states-spend-paltry-3-budget.html

Judge, Paramjit Singh. *Insurrection to Agitations: The Naxalite Movement in Punjab*. New Delhi: Popular Prakashan, 1992.

Kamal, Neel. 'Amarinder Singh's Harsh Words Make Us Stronger: Parkash Singh Badal'. *Economic Times*, 3 February 2017. https://economictimes.indiatimes.com/news/politics-and-nation/amarinder-singhs-harsh-words-make-us-stronger-parkash-singh-badal/articleshow/56949805.cms?from=mdr

Kant, Shashi. 'Ex-DGP: "Dead" Cop Living in Canada'. *The Tribune*, 11 December 2015. https://www.tribuneindia.com/news/punjab/ex-dgp-dead-cop-living-in-canada/169365.html

Kaur, Jaskaran, and Barbara Crossette. *Twenty Years of Impunity: The November 1984 Pogroms of Sikhs in India, 2nd ed*. New York: Ensaaf, 2004.

Kaur, Jaskaran, and Dhami Sukhman. *Protecting the Killers: A Policy of Impunity in Punjab, India*. New York: Human Rights Watch, 2007.

Kaur, Pavit. *Stolen Years* (Memoir). New Delhi: Random House, 2014.

Kaur, Sukhdeep. 'On HC Nudge, Punjab Govt Forms Panel to Free Land Grabbed by "High and Mighty"'. *Hindustan Times*, 5 May 2018. https://www.hindustantimes.com/punjab/on-hc-nudge-punjab-govt-forms-panel-to-free-land-grabbed-by-high-and-mighty/story-6KHSj0ZY69uRIUSKzWY0OK.html

Kaur, Surangya. 'Pathribal: A Timeline of 18 Years of Injustice'. *Newsclick*, 26 March 2018. https://www.newsclick.in/pathribal-timeline-18-years-injustice

Khanna, Ruchika M. 'CBI Exposes Cops' Extortion Racket'. *The Tribune*, 17 August 2001. https://www.tribuneindia.com/2001/20010817/punjab1.htm

KNN. 'FOPSIA President Writes Letter to Punjab CM Alleging of Huge Corruption in SGST Department'. *KNN-India*, 28 December 2018. https://knnindia.co.in/news/newsdetails/state/fopsia-president-writes-letter-to-punjab-cm-alleging-of-huge-corruption-in-sgst-department

Kothari, Smitu, and Harsh Sethi, eds. *Voices from a Scarred City: The Delhi Carnage in Perspective*. New Delhi: Lokayan, 1985.

Kulkarni, Pavan. 'Assassination Plots and Other Rumors: The Story of How Left-Wing Activists were Hounded in India'. *Peoples Dispatch*, 1 September 2018. https://peoplesdispatch.org/2018/09/01/assassination-plots-and-other-rumors-the-story-of-how-left-wing-activists-were-hounded-in-india/

Kumar, Ashutosh. 'It's Anybody's Game in Punjab'. *Live Mint*, 31 January 2017. https://www.livemint.com/Opinion/J9WkH82vJwoweFSOuiJQoO/Its-anybodys-game-in-Punjab.html

Kumar, Ram Narayan, Amrik Singh, Ashok Agrwaal, and Jaskaran Kaur. *Reduced to Ashes: The Insurgency and Human Rights in Punjab*. South Asia Forum for Human Rights, 2003.

Livemint. 'The Richest 1% of Indians Now Own 58.4% of Wealth'. *Live Mint*, 24 November 2016. https://www.livemint.com/Multimedia/rqjHrs2zDQN6w66kVKd9dN/The-richest-1-of-Indians-now-own-584-of-wealth.html

Mahmood, Cynthia Keppley. *Fighting for Faith and Nation, Dialogues with Sikh Militants*. University of Pennsylvania Press, 2010.

Mail Today Bureau. 'Intelligence Bureau Alerts Home Ministry over Films on Sikh Militancy'. *India Today*, 5 May 2015. https://www.indiatoday.in/mail-today/story/sikh-militancy-ib-alert-blue-star-films-251591-2015-05-06

Malik, Saurabh. 'Cop Acquitted in Fake Encounter Death'. *The Tribune*, 8 April 2009. https://www.tribuneindia.com/2009/20090408/punjab.htm#17

———. 'High Court Denies Relief to Accused Cops: Says Sanction Not Legally Required to Prosecute Those Who "Took Law into Their Own Hands"'. *The Tribune*, 16 May 2012. https://www.tribuneindia.com/2012/20120515/punjab.htm#4

———. 'Nayagaon Land-Grab Case: IGP Shielding Convict's Family'. *The Tribune*, 17 November 2007. https://www.tribuneindia.com/2007/20071117/punjab1.htm#5

Bibliography

Mehta, Parvinder. 'Repressive Silences and Shadows of 1984: Erasures, Omissions and Narrative Crisis'. *Sikh Formations* 6, no. 2 (2010): 153–175.

Mehta, Sunanda. 'New Age Filmmakers Bring Hope to Punjabi Cinema'. *The Indian Express*, 13 February 2019. https://indianexpress.com/article/entertainment/play/beyond-balle-balle/99/

Mitta, Manoj, and H. S. Phoolka. *When a Tree Shook Delhi*. New Delhi: Roli Books, 2007.

Morrow, Daniel and Michael Carriere. 'The Economic Impacts of the 1998 Sanctions on India and Pakistan'. *The Nonproliferation Review* 6, no. 4 (1999): 1–16. https://www.nonproliferation.org/wp-content/uploads/npr/morrow64.pdf

Mukherjee, Aditya, ed. *A Centenary History of the Indian National Congress, Vol V*. New Delhi: Academic Foundation, 2012.

Nanda, Aswini Kumar. 'Unsettling Migration's Underbelly'. *The Tribune*, 3 March 2018. https://www.tribuneindia.com/news/sunday-special/people/unsettling-migration-s-underbelly/737217.html

Nelson, Dean. 'Indian Policeman "Fakes His Own Death" So Daughter Can Get Free Education'. *The Telegraph*, 16 August 2013. https://www.telegraph.co.uk/news/worldnews/asia/india/10247482/Indian-policeman-fakes-his-own-death-so-daughter-can-get-free-education.html

Ohri, Raghav. 'Punjab Top-Shots Own Major Land Chunks in City Periphery'. *The Indian Express*, 18 December 2010. http://archive.indianexpress.com/news/punjab-topshots-own-major-land-chunks-in-city-periphery/726306/

Pandher, Sarabjit. 'A Pioneering Effort'. *Frontline*, 12–25 March 2005. https://frontline.thehindu.com/static/html/fl2208/stories/20050422002612000.htm

Patel, Anand Kumar. '"Foreign Dreams": Rural Punjab Way Ahead of Urban Population'. *NDTV*, 5 December 2015. https://www.ndtv.com/india-news/foreign-dreams-rural-punjab-way-ahead-of-urban-population-1251199+&cd=12&hl=en&ct=clnk&gl=in

Paul, Kari. 'America's 1% hasn't Controlled this much Wealth since before the Great Depression'. *Market Watch*, 5 August 2018. https://www.marketwatch.com/story/wealth-inequality-in-the-us-is-almost-as-bad-as-it-was-right-before-the-great-depression-2018-07-19

People's Union for Democratic Rights and People's Union for Civil Liberties. *Who are the Guilty? Report of a Joint Inquiry into the Causes and Impact of the Riots in Delhi from 31 October to 10 November, 1984*. New Delhi: PUDR & PUCL, 1984.

People's Union of Democratic Rights. *Justice Denied: A Critique of the N Misra Commission Report on the Riots in November 1984*. New Delhi: PUDR, 1987.

Pettigrew, Joyce. *The Sikhs of the Punjab: Unheard Voices of State and Guerrilla Violence*. Zed Books Ltd, 1995.

Phukan, Sandeep. 'Capital Contest: AAP Slides; BJP, Congress Fancy Chances'. *The Hindu*, 7 May 2019. https://www.thehindu.com/news/national/other-states/capital-contest-aap-slides-bjp-congress-fancy-chances/article27061316.ece

Preet, Jatinder. 'Centre Rejects Punjab Plea for 69,000 cr Debt Waiver'. *The Sunday Guardian*, 17 April 2011. http://www.sunday-guardian.com/news/centre-rejects-punjab-plea-for-69000-cr-debt-waiver

PTI. 'Kejriwal doesn't Care Who "Lives or Dies", AAP Must be Kept Out of Punjab: Captain Amarinder Singh'. *DNA-India*, 1 February 2017. https://www.dnaindia.com/india/report-punjab-elections-2017-captain-amarinder-accuses-kejriwal-of-promoting-extremist-forces-2306160

———. 'No Sanction Needed to Try Government Servants for Illegal Acts: Supreme Court'. *Economic Times*, 8 July 2016. https://economictimes.indiatimes.com/news/politics-and-nation/no-sanction-needed-to-try-government-servants-for-illegal-acts-supreme-court/articleshow/53117427.cms

———. 'Over 400 People Convicted for 1984 Anti-Sikh Riots in Delhi: Govt. *The Quint*, 23 December 2015. https://www.thequint.com/news/india/over-400-people-convicted-for-1984-anti-sikh-riots-in-delhi-govt

PUDR. *1984 Carnage in Delhi: A Report on the Aftermath*. New Delhi: PUDR, 1992.

———. *Jain Banerji Panel: Murder of a Corpse*. New Delhi: PUDR, 1989.

———. *Remembering the Victims of 1984 Riots: In Sorrow and in Anguish*. New Delhi: PUDR, n.d.

Puri, Harish, and P. S. Judge. *Terrorism in Punjab, Understanding Grassroots Reality*. New Delhi: Har Anand Publications, 2007.

Rakesh, Kumar, and Sukhbir Siwach. 'Top Cops Named in Wireless Scam'. *The Times of India*, 3 September 2006. https://timesofindia.indiatimes.com/india/Top-cops-named-in-wireless-scam/articleshow/1951329.cms&hl=en&gl=in&strip=1&vwsrc=0

Ram, Ronki. 'Third Alternative in Punjab: What Went Wrong with the Third Alternative? Exploring the Rise and Demise of the Aam Aadmi Party in Punjab'. *International Journal of Punjab Studies* 25 no. 1 (2018): 3–36. https://www.researchgate.net/publication/324220335_What_Went_Wrong_With_the_Third_Alternative_Exploring_the_Rise_and_Demise_of_the_Aam_Aadmi_Party_in_Punjab

Rambani, Vishal, and Navrajdeep Singh. 'Former VB SSP, Others Indicted for Frame-Up'. *Hindustan Times*, 15 May 2012. https://www.hindustantimes.com/chandigarh/former-vb-ssp-others-indicted-for-frame-up/story-Qb9d6gnC2xSiZiLs48hOiI.html

Randhawa, Manpreet. 'Punjab Police Top Brass No Stranger to Murky Deals'. *Hindustan Times*, 5 September 2014. https://www.hindustantimes.com/chandigarh/punjab-police-top-brass-no-stranger-to-murky-deals/story-yGmnMyOqWD9wRtxzgbMhLM.html

Rao, Amiya, and Aurobindo Ghose, N. D. Pancholi. *Truth about Delhi Violence, Report to the Nation*. New Delhi: Citizens for Democracy, 1985.

Rediff. '"Fascist" AAP will Turn Punjab into Kashmir: Amarinder'. *Rediff*, 31 January 2017. https://www.rediff.com/news/report/fascist-aap-will-turn-punjab-into-kashmir-amarinder/20170131.htm

———. 'Prime Minister Apologises for 1984 anti-Sikh Riots'. *Rediff*, 11 August 2005. https://www.rediff.com/news/2005/aug/11pm.htm

Salopek, Paul. 'Walking Through a Youthful Exodus in India: On Foot Across the Punjab, Where Roads Lead to Escape. *National Geographic*, 12 July 2018. https://www.nationalgeographic.org/projects/out-of-eden-walk/articles/2018-07-walking-through-youthful-exodus-india/

Sandhu, Kanwar. 'Punjab Police Transgresses Limits of Law Fighting Terrorism'. *India Today*, 15 October 1992. https://www.indiatoday.in/magazine/special-report/story/19921015-punjab-police-transgresses-limits-of-law-fighting-terrorism-767008-2012-12-26

———. 'Punjab Policemen Occupy Houses Belonging to Militants'. *India Today*, 31 December 1992. https://www.indiatoday.in/magazine/investigation/story/19921031-houses-belonged-to-militants-being-used-by-punjab-police-for-official-or-personal-purposes-767049-2012-12-31

Shan, Harnam Singh. *An Indian Torture Chamber: The Full Story of Ladha Kothy*. Punjab Human Rights Organisation, 1990

Shani, Giorgio. 'The Memorialization of Ghallughara: Trauma, Nation and Diaspora'. *Sikh Formations* 6, no. 2 (2010): 177–192.

Sharma, Aabhas. 'Jatt *di* Film'. *Business Standard*, 21 June 2013. https://www.business-standard.com/article/beyond-business/jatt-di-film-113062101038_1.html

Sharma, Betwa. 'No Justice 30 Years after Sikh Slaughter'. *Al Jazeera*, 31 October 2014. https://www.aljazeera.com/indepth/features/2014/10/india-justice-30-years-congress-sikh-goldentemple-20141030142222751433.html

Sharma, Pawan. 'SC Stays Further Trial Against Accused Cops'. *Hindustan Times*, 14 July 2012. https://www.hindustantimes.com/chandigarh/sc-stays-further-trial-against-accused-cops/story-iMlNBc7buUNGxYb6207VpO.html

Sharma, Rajnish. 'Sikh Riots: BJP Names Figure in Records'. *Hindustan Times*, 2 February 2002.

Sharma, Sachin. 'In Bathinda, Amarinder Blames Badal for Terrorism, Operation Bluestar'. *Hindustan Times*, 25 January 2017. https://www.hindustantimes.com/assembly-elections/in-bathinda-captain-amarinder-blames-badal-for-terrorism-operation-bluestar/story-1fW78PZj8rWhQwHDtsdrUM.html

Silva, Romesh, Jasmine Marwaha, and Jeff Klingner. *Violent Deaths and Enforced Disappearances During the Counterinsurgency in Punjab, India: A Preliminary Quantitative Analysis*. Palo Alto: Ensaaf and the Benetech Human Rights Data Analysis Group—HRDAG, 2009.

Singh, Annapurna. 'Unemployment, the Elephant in the Room'. *Deccan Herald*, 17 April 2019. https://www.deccanherald.com/opinion/comment/unemployment-the-elephant-in-the-room-729181.html

Singh, Anurag. *Giani Kirpal Singh's Eye-Witness Account of Operation Bluestar: Mighty Murderous Army Attack on the Golden Temple Complex*. B. Chattar Singh Jiwan Singh, 1999.

Singh, Attar, and Ravi Dhaliwal. 'Fake Encounters: HC to Find Out If Cases were Fixed in Registry'. *The Tribune*, 13 May 2008. https://www.tribuneindia.com/2008/20080513/punjab1.htm

Singh, Chanchal Manohar. 'NRIs Properties: Beware Land Mafia Supported by Powerful Politicians Active in Punjab to Grab Them'. *Punjab Khabar*, 3 August 2014. http://www.punjabkhabar.com/news/print.aspx?ac=431

Singh, Gajinder. 'Govt Term for Terror Loan Waiver'. *The Telegraph*, 2002 December 25. https://www.telegraphindia.com/india/govt-term-for-terror-loan-waiver/cid/849240

Singh, Gurharpal. *Communism in Punjab: A Study of the Movement Up to 1967*. Ajanta Publications, 1994.

Singh, I. P. 'RTI Reveals Sikhs were Killed at the Spots in Gurugram Where Police were Present in Nov 1984'. *The Times of India*, 18 December 2018. https://timesofindia.indiatimes.com/city/ludhiana/rti-reveals-sikhs-were-killed-at-the-spots-in-gurugram-where-police-were-present-in-nov-1984/articleshow/67737495.cms

Singh, Inderjit. *Bahujan Samaj Party in Punjab: Origin, Support Base and Performance* (PhD thesis). Faculty of Social Sciences, Punjabi University, Patiala, 2011.

Singh, Iqbal. *Punjab Under Siege: A Critical Analysis*. New York: Allen McMillan and Enderson, 1986.

Singh, Jarnail. *I Accuse: The Anti-Sikh Violence of '84*. New Delhi: Penguin Books India, 2009.

Singh, Joginder. 'How Punjab Economy can be Revived'. *The Tribune*, 31 August 2018. https://www.tribuneindia.com/news/comment/how-punjab-economy-can-be-revived/645211.html

Singh, Jupinderjit. 'Property Dispute: NRI Panel Orders VB Probe'. *The Tribune*, 4 August 2017. https://www.tribuneindia.com/news/punjab/property-dispute-nri-panel-orders-vb-probe/446906.html

———. 'Punjab DGP for Relief to Cops in Militancy Cases'. *The Tribune*, 3 September 2018. https://www.tribuneindia.com/news/punjab/punjab-dgp-for-relief-to-cops-in-militancy-cases/646979.html

———. 'SHO's Involvement in Land Grab Case: DC Suspends Cop, DIG Asks Him to Stay'. *The Tribune*, 23 November 2002. https://www.tribuneindia.com/2002/20021124/ldh1.htm#2

———. 'Witnessed 50 Fake Encounters: Police 'Cat' Pinky'. *The Tribune*, 6 December 2015. https://www.tribuneindia.com/news/punjab/witnessed-50-fake-encounters-police-cat-pinky/167204.html

Bibliography

Singh, Khushwant. *Tragedy of Punjab: Operation Bluestar & After*. New Delhi: Vision Books, 1984.

Singh, Navrajdeep. 'Punjab Vigilance Bureau Books Ex-SSP Grewal in Assets Case'. *Hindustan Times*, 27 December 2017. https://www.hindustantimes.com/punjab/punjab-vigilance-bureau-books-ex-ssp-grewal-in-assets-case/story-hYspVzRGEvlTrzxATN1GnK.html

Singh, Prabhjit. 'Mand Assault Case: Elevated, SSP Mand Says He Just "Fell Down"'. *Hindustan Times*, 26 November 2013. https://www.hindustantimes.com/chandigarh/mand-assault-case-elevated-ssp-mand-says-he-just-fell-down/story-I1URuIoXlMLYrWuKqtasEM.html

———. 'Murky Panchayat Land Deals: SC Says No to Annul Tribunal; Issue Back in High Court'. *Hindustan Times*, 9 April 2015. https://www.hindustantimes.com/chandigarh/murky-panchayat-land-deals-sc-says-no-to-annul-tribunal-issue-back-in-high-court/story-S6G6q8kzs5f0XcXA8fWRML.html

———. 'Punjab Pays ₹1 cr to Legal Experts Seeking Annulment of Kuldip Tribunal in SC'. *Hindustan Times*, 29 November 2013. https://www.hindustantimes.com/chandigarh/punjab-pays-rs-1-cr-to-legal-experts-seeking-annulment-of-kuldip-tribunal-in-sc/story-wrRDuJM5qyuXMl8tneMgLN.html

Singh, Prabhjot. 'Punjab Police to Raise 2 More IRBs'. *The Tribune*, 21 January 2001. https://www.tribuneindia.com/2001/20010121/punjab1.htm

Singh, Ruchira, and Koshy, Jacob P. '₹2,000 Crore Drought Relief for Five States'. *Live Mint*, 1 August 2012. https://www.livemint.com/Politics/zkecLJ0aIuqvOhh5RWT1VJ/Rs-2000-crore-drought-relief-for-five-states.html

Singh, Sabarmeet. 'Kin of Former, Serving MLAs, Ministers Debut with Victory'. *Hindustan Times*, 24 September 2018.

Singh, Varinder. 'From Healing to Dealing!' *The Tribune*, 20 May 2006. https://www.tribuneindia.com/2006/20060520/real.htm#3

Sirhindi, Manish. 'Supreme Court Rejects Interim Bail of Former SSP in Corruption Case'. *The Times of India*, 14 April 2018. https://timesofindia.indiatimes.com/city/chandigarh/sc-rejects-interim-bail-of-former-ssp-in-corruption-case/articleshow/63754141.cms

Sodhi, S. S. *The Other Side of Justice*. Delhi: Hay House, 2007.

Stevens, William K. 'Indian Army Goes Into 9 Cities as Anti-Sikh Battling Flares: Throngs File by Gandhi's Bier'. *The New York Times*, 2 November 1984. https://www.nytimes.com/1984/11/02/world/indian-army-goes-into-9-cities-anti-sikh-battling-flares-throngs-file-gandhi-s.html

———. 'With Punjab the Prize, Militants Spread Terror' *The New York Times*, 3 April 1984. https://www.nytimes.com/1984/04/03/world/with-punjab-the-prize-sikh-militants-spread-terror.html

Sura, Ajay. 'Centre Agrees to Pay Those Detained After Operation Bluestar'. *The Times of India*, 2 July 2018. https://timesofindia.indiatimes.com/india/centre-agrees-to-pay-those-detained-after-operation-blue-star/articleshow/64831908.cms

Sura, Ajay. 'Hondh-Chillar Killings: No Action Against Haryana Cops Yet'. *The Times of India*, 18 December 2018. https://timesofindia.indiatimes.com/city/chandigarh/hondh-chillar-killings-no-action-against-haryana-cops-yet/articleshow/67140532.cms

———. 'No High Court Reprieve for 12 Punjab Cops in 1992 Disappearance of Six of Family'. *The Times of India*, 25 March 2019. https://timesofindia.indiatimes.com/city/chandigarh/no-high-court-reprieve-for-12-punjab-cops-in-1992-disappearance-of-six-of-family/articleshow/68555640.cms

Tandon, Aditi. 'Punjab Mass Cremations-1: How a Habeas Corpus & a Press Note Nailed Culprits'. *The Tribune*, 6 April 2012. https://www.tribuneindia.com/2012/20120406/main6.htm

———. 'Punjab Mass Cremations-2: How Centre, Punjab challenged Supreme Court's Probe Move'. *The Tribune*, 6 April 2012. https://www.tribuneindia.com/2012/20120407/nation.htm#5

Tatla, Darshan Singh. *The Sikh Diaspora: Search for Statehood*. University of Washington Press, 1999.

The Tribune. 'Cops Killed Eleven for Awards'. *The Tribune*, 10 November 1994. https://www.govinfo.gov/content/pkg/CREC-1994-11-30/html/CREC-1994-11-30-pt1-PgE35.htm

———. 'HC "raps" Ex-Judge for Order on Punjab Fake Encounters'. *The Tribune*, 27 November 2013.

———. 'Key Witness in Khalra Murder Case Dies'. *The Tribune*, 28 October 2011. https://www.tribuneindia.com/2011/20111028/punjab.htm

———. 'Killed Once, Twice'. *The Tribune*, 1 November 1993.

———. 'Traffic SHO Booked for Grabbing NRI's Land'. *The Tribune*, 6 February 2011. https://www.tribuneindia.com/2011/20110207/ldh.htm

Thukral, Gobind. 'Punjab Borrows to Service Debts'. *The Tribune*, 30 May 2000. https://www.tribuneindia.com/2000/20000531/punjab.htm#1

Times News Network. '1984 Anti-Sikh Riots: Government recommends SIT to LG'. *The Times of India*, 7 February 2014. https://timesofindia.indiatimes.com/city/delhi/1984-anti-Sikh-riots-Government-recommends-SIT-to-LG/articleshow/29964783.cms

———. 'EC Transferred Mand for Supporting Akalis'. *The Times of India*, 27 December 2012. https://timesofindia.indiatimes.com/city/chandigarh/EC-transferred-Mand-for-supporting-Akalis/articleshow/17774948.cms&hl=en&gl=in&strip=1&vwsrc=0

———. 'RDX in "Pinnis": None Convicted'. *The Times of India*, 15 January 2003. https://timesofindia.indiatimes.com/RDX-in-pinnis-None-convicted/articleshow/34353707.cms

———. 'Sukhbir Badal: Congress Stoking Khalistan Flame Again'. *The Times of India*, 22 November 2015. https://timesofindia.indiatimes.com/india/Sukhbir-Badal-Congress-stoking-Khalistan-flame-again/articleshow/49877072.cms

Bibliography

Todd, Douglas. 'Popular Canadian Student Visas Leading to Exploitation'. *Vancouver Sun*, 18 September 2018. https://vancouversun.com/news/local-news/douglas-todd-popular-canadian-student-visas-leading-to-exploitation

Tribune News Service. '26 Yrs On, 2 Ex-Cops Get Life Term in Fake Encounter Case, 15-Year-Old Boy was Picked Up from House and Later Shown Killed'. *The Tribune*, 27 September 2018. https://www.tribuneindia.com/news/punjab/26-yrs-on-2-ex-cops-get-life-term-in-fake-encounter-case/659410.html

———. 'Beas Killing: Accused Denied Bail'. *The Tribune*, 13 February 2009. https://www.tribuneindia.com/2009/20090214/punjab.htm

———. 'HC Issues Notice to ADGP Gupta: Petitioner Says Officer a Land Shark, Wants CBI Probe'. *The Tribune*, 2 December 2011. https://www.tribuneindia.com/2011/20111202/punjab.htm#3

———. 'High Court Raps Punjab on Encroachments Tells State to Submit List of Illegal Occupants in Nayagaon'. *The Tribune*, 2 March 2012. https://www.tribuneindia.com/2012/20120302/punjab.htm#16

———. 'Justice Kuldip Singh Special Tribunal Report Part-I: How High & Mighty Grabbed Public Land in Punjab Villages Near Chandigarh. *The Tribune*, 9 November 2013. https://www.tribuneindia.com/2013/20131110/main6.htm

———. 'Justice Kuldip Singh Special Tribunal Report Part-II: Illegal Orders, Mutations of Kansal Public Land Enriched Buyers'. *The Tribune*, 10 November 2013. https://www.tribuneindia.com/2013/20131111/main6.htm

———. 'Justice Kuldip Singh Special Tribunal Report Part-III: Self before Service in Bartana Village Deals. *The Tribune*, 11 November 2013. https://www.tribuneindia.com/2013/20131112/main7.htm

———. 'Justice Kuldip Singh Special Tribunal Report Part-IV: In Mirzapur Village, the Civil Court Itself Violated Law'. *The Tribune*, 12 November 2013. https://www.tribuneindia.com/2013/20131113/main8.htm

———. 'Justice Kuldip Singh Special Tribunal Report Part-V: Fraudulent Civil Decree Enabled Illegal Sales'. *The Tribune*, 13 November 2013. https://www.tribuneindia.com/2013/20131114/main6.htm

———. 'Justice Kuldip Singh Special Tribunal Report Part-VI: Amarinder Singh & Family Figure in Majrian Illegal Deals'. *The Tribune*, 14 November 2013. https://www.tribuneindia.com/2013/20131115/main7.htm

———. 'Justice Kuldip Singh Special Tribunal Report Part-VII: Special Courts Mooted to Resolve 30-Year Disputes in Mullanpur'. *The Tribune*, 15 November 2013. https://www.tribuneindia.com/2013/20131116/main6.htm

———. 'Justice Kuldip Singh Special Tribunal Report Part-VIII: Well-Planned Land Grab Scandal Around Chandigarh'. *The Tribune*, 16 November 2013. https://www.tribuneindia.com/2013/20131117/main4.htm

———. 'Justice Kuldip Singh Special Tribunal Report Part-IX: Sales Based on Illegal Mutations, Connivance of Revenue Officials'. *The Tribune*, 17 November 2013. https://www.tribuneindia.com/2013/20131118/main4.htm

Tribune News Service. 'Justice Kuldip Singh Special Tribunal Report Part-X: Scandal Right under the Nose of State Govt'. *The Tribune*, 18 November 2013. https://www.tribuneindia.com/2013/20131119/main4.htm
———. 'Justice Kuldip Singh Special Tribunal Report Part-XI: GMADA Compensated Illegal Occupants'. *The Tribune*, 19 November 2013. https://www.tribuneindia.com/2013/20131120/main5.htm
———. 'Justice Kuldip Singh Special Tribunal Report Part-XII: Tribunal Advocates Special High Court Bench, CBI Probe'. *The Tribune*, 20 November 2013. https://www.tribuneindia.com/2013/20131121/main7.htm
———. 'Vigilance Mellows a Day after Arresting Hotelier: Refuses to Seek Police Remand'. *The Tribune*, 16 October 2008. https://www.tribuneindia.com/2008/20081016/cth1.htm#8
Tripathi, Manoj. 'Punjab's Slowing Economy'. *Business World*, 3 February 2017.
Tully, Mark, and Satish Jacob. *Mrs Gandhi's Last Battle*. New Delhi: Rupa, 2006.
———. 'Wounds Heal but Another Timebomb Ticks Away. *The Times of India*, 3 June 2014. https://timesofindia.indiatimes.com/home/sunday-times/deep-focus/Wounds-heal-but-another-time-bomb-ticks-away/articleshow/35871055.cms
Tumbe, Chinmay. 'How the Recent Punjabi Migration to Spain & Italy is a Departure for the Diaspora'. *Economic Times*, 29 July 2018. https://economictimes.indiatimes.com/magazines/panache/how-the-recent-punjabi-migration-to-spain-and-italy-is-a-departure-for-the-diaspora/articleshow/65180012.cms
UNODC. *Smuggling of Migrants from India to Europe and in Particular to UK, 2009*. UNODC, New Delhi, 2009. https://www.unodc.org/documents/human-trafficking/Smuggling_of_Migrants_from_India_to_Europe_-_Punjab_Haryana.pdf
Vasishth, Saroj. *Kala November: The Carnage of 1984*. New Delhi: Rupa, 1995.
Vasudeva, Vikas. 'Punjab Congress Accuses AAP of Adopting Anti-National Agenda; Kejriwal Denies. *The Hindu*, 12 February 2016. https://www.thehindu.com/news/national/other-states/Punjab-Congress-accuses-AAP-of-adopting-anti-national-agenda-Kejriwal-denies/article15618244.ece
Villazon, Luis. 'How Long Can You be Kept on a Life-Support Machine?' *Science Focus*. https://www.sciencefocus.com/the-human-body/how-long-can-you-be-kept-on-a-life-support-machine/
Vinayak, Ramesh. 'Narasimha Rao's Punjab Visit Comes as a Morale Booster for CM Beant Singh'. *India Today*, 20 April 1995. https://www.indiatoday.in/magazine/indiascope/story/19950515-narasimha-raos-punjab-visit-comes-as-a-morale-booster-for-cm-beant-singh-807256-1995-05-15
———. 'NRIs Duped of Their Property in Punjab, Government Moves to Ease Their Legal Woes'. *India Today*, 30 January 2013. https://www.indiatoday.in/magazine/states/story/20030120-nris-duped-of-their-property-in-punjab-government-moves-to-ease-their-legal-woes-793524-2003-01-20

Bibliography

Vinayak, Ramesh. 'System of Inducting Terrorists as Double Agents Leaves them at Mercy of Police in Punjab'. *India Today*, 15 December 2015. https://www.indiatoday.in/magazine/special-report/story/19951215-system-of-inducting-terrorists-as-double-agents-leaves-them-at-mercy-of-police-in-punjab-808078-1995-12-15

Walia, Arunjeev Singh, and Tejinder Singh Sudan. *Genesis of State Terrorism in Punjab*. Chandigarh: Lawyers for Human Rights International, 2001. http://lfhri.org/genesis-of-state-terrorism-in-punjab/

———. 'Dark Clouds of State Repression: Police Excesses have Broken Punjab'. *Asian Human Rights Commission*, 2002. http://www.humanrights.asia/resources/journals-magazines/article2/0103/dark-clouds-of-state-repression-police-excesses-have-broken-punjab/

Walia, Varinder. 'Warrants Issued Against DSP, 6 Others'. *The Tribune*, 19 September 2001. https://www.tribuneindia.com/2001/20010919/punjab1.htm

Yadav, Puneet Nicholas. 'Judiciary Must Share Equal Blame for Lapses In 1984 Riots Cases: SIT Head Justice Dhingra'. *India Legal*, 16 January 2019. http://www.indialegallive.com/interview/il-interview/judiciary-must-share-equal-blame-lapses-1984-riots-cases-sit-head-justice-retd-dhingra-59484

Zaidi, Hussein. *Black Friday: The True Story of the Bombay Bomb Blasts*. New Delhi, Penguin Books, 2002.

About the Authors

Inderjit Singh Jaijee is well known in Punjab for his work to ensure education for rural children whose fathers have committed suicide as well as for his advocacy of civil rights and human rights. In the course of this work, he has been arrested 17 times and imprisoned five times. He remains active in this cause. The organizations with which he is associated—the Baba Nanak Educational Society and the Movement Against State Repression—are both scrupulously apolitical and non-sectarian.

Until 1983, he was a marketing executive for Dunlop India Ltd. In that year, as the situation in Punjab deteriorated, he took voluntary retirement and returned to Punjab. He was elected to the Punjab Vidhan Sabha on the Akali ticket in 1985, but he resigned in 1986 in a protest against government actions at the Golden Temple.

Dona Suri came to India at the age of 22 and has remained here ever since. She looks back on 35 years as an editor, starting her career with *India Today* and subsequently working for *The Tribune, The Indian Express* and *Hindustan Times*. She retired as associate editor from *Hindustan Times*. She provided editorial and research assistance in Inderjit Singh Jaijee's previous two books and has written two books of science history for young readers (*The Story of Iron* and *The Story of Copper*).

Let this book be your companion and guide as you try to make sense of the forthcoming tumultuous events in Indian politics.

Lord Meghnad Desai
Economist, Author and Politician

A political tale of India through the first-person narratives of political leaders

For special offers on this and other books from SAGE, write to marketing@sagepub.in

Explore our range at
www.sagepub.in

Paperback
978-93-532-8298-1